DO NOT REMOVE
CARDS FROM POCKET

ALLEN COUNTY PUBLIC LIBRARY

FORT WAYNE, INDIANA 46802

You may return this book to any agency, branch,
or bookmobile of the Allen County Public Library.

DEMCO

MY PERSONAL COMPUTER

AND

OTHER FAMILY CRISES

MY PERSONAL COMPUTER
AND
OTHER FAMILY CRISES

or,

Ahab and Alice in Microland

Ben Ross Schneider, Jr.

"Madness: To be enraged with a dumb thing, Captain Ahab."
Starbuck

"The Question is, which is to be master, that's all."
Humpty Dumpty

MACMILLAN PUBLISHING COMPANY
A Division of Macmillan, Inc.
NEW YORK

COLLIER MACMILLAN PUBLISHERS
LONDON

Copyright ©1984 by Macmillan Publishing Company
a division of Macmillan, Inc.

Macmillan Publishing Company
866 Third Avenue, New York, NY 10022

Collier Macmillan Canada, Inc.

Printed in the United States of America

printing number
1   2   3   4   5   6   7   8   9   10

Library of Congress Cataloging in Publication Data

Schneider, Ben Ross, 1920–
 My personal computer and other family crises, or,
Ahab and Alice in microland.

 Includes index.
 1. Word processing. 2. SITAR (Computer program).
3. Cromemco Z-2D (Computer)—Programming. 4. Schneider,
Ben Ross, 1920–   . 5. College teachers—United
States—Biography. I. Title. II. Title: Ahab and
Alice in microland.

Z52.5.S57S36 1984   652   84–14392
ISBN 0–02–949610–1

This book was designed by Logoi Systems and by Presentations, Hanover, New Hampshire. The text was prepared by the author on his Cromemco Z-2D computer and transferred on computer tape to Logoi Systems, where it was formatted on an Ibycus computing system and set in London Times type on a Wang/GSI CAT-8 phototypesetter. Layout was done by Presentations.

For Devon, Ben, Nick, and Mackay

With love from Dad

CONTENTS

Illustrations   *ix*

I.   'Twas Brillig   1

II.   All Mimsy Were the Borogoves   11

III.   Cetology   40

IV.   The Jaws That Bite, the Claws that Catch!   68

V.   The Walrus and the Carpenter   99

VI.   Thar She Blows   140

VII.   My Beamish Boy   174

VIII. Sequel: Exit Ahab, Tangled in His Harpoon Line   198

IX.   The Masthead: An Overview   213

Index of Boldfaced Computer Terms   *246*

ILLUSTRATIONS

Mackay McCord Schneider, by Janet Stickney McCord   1

Raths, toves, and borogoves, by John Tenniel   11
Courtesy of Harvard College Library

Whale species from the Norton edition of *Moby Dick*   40
Courtesy of Harvard College Library

Speciation of Word Processors   52

Faces of the rain god Chac, by Frederick Catherwood   68
Courtesy of Harvard College Library

Nicholas Schneider as a child   89

The Walrus and the Carpenter, by John Tenniel   99
Courtesy of Harvard College Library

The view from the porch at The Lake   101

Ahab sighting Moby Dick, by Rockwell Kent   140
By permission of the Houghton Library of Harvard University

Wiring diagram of Z-2D power supply   149
Courtesy of Cromemco Corporation

The family in Spain   167

Ahab enraged with Moby Dick, by Rockwell Kent   172
By permission of the Houghton Library of Harvard University

Jabberwock assailed by Beamish Boy, by John Tenniel   174
Courtesy of Harvard College Library

The Z-2D's memory board, showing patches   179

A cromlech   186
From The Search for Lost America *by S. M. Trento, with
permission from the publishers, Contemporary Books, Inc.,
Chicago*

Alice and Humpty Dumpty, by John Tenniel   198
Courtesy of Harvard College Library

Ishmael at the masthead, by Rockwell Kent   213
By permission of the Houghton Library of Harvard University

Ruben and Carlos, his apprentice, by Sheldon Woodward   240
Courtesy of the photographer

Catherine Mackay McCord, by Carlson   242

Main pyramid at Chichén Itzá in 1841, by Frederick
Catherwood   245
Courtesy of Harvard College Library

CHAPTER I

'TWAS BRILLIG

THE FIRST thing I did right was to marry Mackay McCord. If I had been a professional zoologist, perhaps the keeper of a zoo, and toward the end of a long career had informed her that I found it necessary and desirable to adopt an orangutan, I know she would have resigned herself to it. "If you're absolutely sure that's what you want," she would have said. Actually, according to my sister-in-law, she probably would have preferred an orangutan. Instead, I am a nearly retired professor of English at a small liberal arts college, and I have adopted a computer, and it goes wherever we go, even on vacation. That Kay has adjusted well to this foreign object during the three years it has lived with us will be seen from the tale I am about to unfold.

1

Now why, the reader may ask, would a man comfortably engrossed in the teaching of English Composition, Chaucer, Shakespeare, Milton, and Wordsworth, basking in the afterglow of an interesting and rewarding career, suddenly have an uncontrollable urge to buy a computer?

About four years ago, Kay and I reached an uncertain part of our lives: all four children had graduated from college and were on their own; the four parents in whose eyes we had seen ourselves conducting our lives had reached their eighties and reluctantly died. The houses that we had always called home, though we had never lived in them as a couple, had been emptied and sold. Our parents' belongings had been sorted out and distributed, and their life savings, so carefully preserved in wills, were now in the hands of the banks and the lawyers, whom we must now cajole and harass into releasing portions before they wasted and consumed them all. Our new situation raised serious questions about the meaning and goal of life. In the midst of our confusion, it suddenly came to us that the time had come to do the things we had always wanted to do.

Kay wanted to go places and see things. I did too. But mainly I wanted to write all the articles and books that had been accumulating in my head during almost thirty years of teaching English. In the course of a career, a man stores up a lot of opinions on the subjects with which he has perforce become well-acquainted. This was true of me. It seemed a pity that I should go to my grave without publishing a few pieces of my mind concerning Restoration drama, Wordsworth, eighteenth-century theatre, and, herewith, computers. Now, with a sabbatical coming up, the possibility of early retirement under generous terms, and, who knows, maybe some income from writing, we envisioned a new way of life. We would go places and see things, and I would simultaneously work on my backlog. That's why I needed a computer.

It will occur to my readers that traveling with a delicate, heavy, and cumbersome piece of electronic equipment may be more trouble than it is worth, and I assure them that unless they have tried it, they haven't the power to imagine how difficult it really is. I certainly never did. But, even knowing what I know now, I would do it again. Even so, after hearing my account, some of my wiser readers may decide in favor of the pencil and eraser. Why, then, did I adopt this drastic expedient?

In 1978 was completed an index to every name and title in an eleven-volume reference work called *The London Stage, 1660–1800: A Calendar of Plays, Entertainments, and Afterpieces, Together with Casts, Box-Receipts, and Contemporary Comment, Compiled from the Playbills, Newspapers & Theatrical Diaries of the Period*, edited with critical introductions by William Van Lennep, Emmett L. Avery, Arthur H. Scouten, George Winchester Stone, Jr., and Charles Beecher Hogan, 1960–1968, 8,026 pages. Using a PDP-11 computer made by Digital Equipment Company of Maynard, Massachusetts (hereinafter DEC) and a 360-44 computer made by International Business Machines of Armonk, New York (hereinafter IBM), I produced this *Index*, spending on it nine years of my life and $200,000 of foundation money, with an enormous amount of help from Lawrence University, eighteen student editors, my friends, my children, and Kay. It was an index to the theatre and date of occurrence of every name and title in the 8,026 pages. In the end, there were 500,006 references to 26,264 items.

In the course of this project, which began in the spring of 1970, I became more intimately acquainted with what has come to be known as "word processing" than I hope anybody else ever has to be. In fact my programmer and I actually developed something very much like a modern word processor in 1974, even though we didn't know what a word processor was. It was called "System for Interactive Text-editing, Analysis and Retrieval" (hereinafter SITAR). As it happened, this text-editing software turned out to be very efficient for writing and editing the letters, proposals, memos, guidelines, convocation announcements, course schedules, recommendations, speeches, articles, reviews, bibliographies, notes, and chronologies associated with my work.

I am temperamentally incapable of writing the sentence I want without revising it at least five times. Before I began to use a computer, my typescripts had become so inscrutable from incessant revision that I was forced to read them to a dictaphone, have a typist transcribe the tape, edit the transcription, and have it typed once more, in order to arrive at a fair copy. With a computer I can produce a fair copy as soon as I am content with what I have, because nothing one writes on a computer is permanent. Writing a paragraph is like sketching a scene. It's no trouble at all to move any word or phrase to its optimum position, to change a sentence from passive to active, to try nine different words or sixteen word combinations until one gets precisely what one wants. So, by the time Kay and I decided that we would see the world while I wrote all the things I'd always wanted to write, I had become hopelessly computer-dependent.

It may seem peculiar that an English professor in a small university in Appleton, Wisconsin, should have been entrusted with an expensive computer project like indexing *The London Stage*. It fell upon me by default. George Winchester Stone, Jr., Dean of the Graduate School at New York University and General Editor of *The London Stage*, was looking for a way to provide a general index to it that would open up its vast riches to the scholarly world. He had decided that it was a job for a computer. Some years before, as it happened, I had decided that I absolutely must write a book on *The Ethos of Restoration Comedy*. In the course of my research it became evident that it would strengthen my thesis if I could prove that discrete sets of actors always played the same "type" characters. To do this I undertook to assign 113 commonly observed character traits to all the roles in 63 plays, 1,027 to be exact. During the 90 years when this kind of play flourished, some 200 actors played these 1,027 roles one to thirty-nine times each. Simple multiplication showed me that I would have over ten million facts to sift, even if each actor played a role no more than ten times. That was how I got into computing in the first place.

An offshoot of my research on *The Ethos* was an article called "The Coquette-Prude as an Actresses' Line in Restoration Comedy during the Time of Mrs. Oldfield," published in 1968.

When Dean Stone read this article, he saw a way to get his index. Here was a scholar who apparently understood something about both the London stage and computers. I might therefore be able and even willing to try the index. No other possible candidate then existed, and when he invited me, I leaped at the chance.

I have often wondered what made me think of using a computer in my *Ethos* research. Surely thousands of humanists had by then confronted work for computers and easily resisted the temptation to use them. Perhaps the choice stemmed from the fact that I was in truth a spoiled engineer and that deep inside me was a yearning for technology. My father was a civil engineer, and many were the heroic deeds he accomplished in my boyhood. He once made a map of an island in Canada for the family we were visiting by sighting significant points along a compass bearing and pacing off the distances to them. In the midst of the depression he designed, contracted for, and partially built our summer camp beside a lake in New Hampshire (hereinafter referred to as "The Lake"), using my little brother and me as part of the labor force. It is recognized to be a happy harmony of structure, site, and utility, but he used second grade lumber and whatever windows and doors were on sale. One day he decided to mass-produce six deck chairs, copying the pattern from an assemble-it-yourself kit, but using screws instead of nails. All day my brother and I sawed out the parts, and he screwed them together. At sundown we had six chairs, and we still have two of them.

My father used to say that a man with a good education can do anything he sets his mind to. His own example so well demonstrated this belief that I have inherited a strong urge, whenever a need to build or repair something arises, to do it myself, and I think of recourse to specialists as a form of cowardice.

I guess my father was an engineer because he went to college in the days when the civil engineers were building America. Also, his father's cousin, Herman Schneider, was then Dean of the College of Engineering at Cincinnati. Uncle Herman, the family genius, had invented the "co-op plan" (Cincinnati had it years before Antioch), in which aspiring engineers spend half of their time in the classroom and the other half on the job in the field they are learning. As a "co-op" at Cincinnati, my father built bridges and railroads. When I was about twelve, Father and I visited Uncle Herman in his office, and he explained Einstein's relativity to me on his blackboard. I didn't understand it, and I still don't understand it, but I got an enticing glimpse of unknown modes of being. My three best friends in high school went to MIT, and I went to Williams on the 3−2 plan. Three years of liberal arts at Williams plus two years of engineering at MIT would earn me a Bachelor of Arts and a Bachelor of Engineering. But in my freshman year I confronted calculus for the first time and flunked math conclusively.

Looking back, I think I could have stuck it out, if I'd been a better organized person at the time. But math had always been hard work for me, and English had always been fun. My love of literature dated all the way back to the days when Mother read to me *Mother Goose*, *Aesop's Fables*, *Winnie the Pooh*, *Alice in Wonderland*, *Just So Stories*, *Mowgli*, and *David Copperfield*. With this start, I read *Robinson Crusoe*, *Swiss Family Robinson*, *Treasure Island*, *Tom Sawyer* and *Huckleberry Finn*, Howard Pyle's *Book of Pirates*, *A Boy's King Arthur*, *Ivanhoe*, and so on, much of it still flashing on my inward eye as illustrated or as if illustrated by Maxfield Parrish and N. C. Wyeth. In high school, Robert Keeney, an electrifying English teacher who had taken a class with Robert Frost at Amherst and always brought the Scottish janitor in to read Robert Burns, got me to the point where I was almost totally overwhelmed by Walt Whitman, perhaps mentally ill. When it came time to do my twenty-minute report on him, I gushed on and on for the whole period and still wasn't half done. So, after receiving the news about math in my freshman year at Williams, it took me about ten minutes to become an English major, though I hung on for a second year of physics, for which I have been forever grateful.

In World War II, I went to Signal Corps school and became acquainted with the mystery of vacuum tubes. During the war,

I learned how to trouble-shoot army radar equipment, and I watched over Air Force radio transmitters on the island of Biak, Netherlands East Indies. I became a devotee of Ohm's Law, without which I would be as nothing.

Perhaps the foregoing biographical information will help to explain why this particular English professor reaching the end of his career asked his wife to adopt an electronic word processor. Now many wives object to having a computer for a rival. Many even divorce their husbands for this reason. Certainly after her nine-year wait for my return from *The London Stage* project, my wife might have expected a renewal of normal married life, no longer disrupted by data-processing crises, unexpected dashes to the computer room for unpredictable lengths of time, inability to get one's husband's attention even when he is at hand, nearly total loss of his physical presence on nights, weekends, and summer vacations—the periods when IBM 360s are most likely to be available to literary scholars—engagements frequently broken or interrupted because the computer is down or unexpectedly free, and, if for a weekend or a week she does get him away, a dozen long distance calls to the project to see how it is getting along. But Kay has the patience of Penelope.

Her mother was called Dear Boo, because *her* mother was called Dear Boo, because she used to play peekaboo with her grandchildren. Kay's mother, Catherine Mackay McCord, came from Mt. Carroll, Illinois, where her father was the town lawyer, and she was brought up on a farm near the town. At the University of Michigan she met and later married a medical student, Carey Pratt McCord, of Six Mile, Bibb County, Alabama, where his father, a roving Baptist minister, had paused long enough to marry the daughter of the headmaster of the local Academy. "C. P." McCord was a founding member of the discipline called Industrial Medicine. He was a passionate scientist, and perhaps Kay learned some of her patience from her mother.

Long before Kay and I knew of each other's existence, our fates were intertwined. Carey and Catherine took up residence in Glendale, Ohio, 12 miles north of Cincinnati on the B&O, where my mother, Jean Taylor, was raised and where my grandparents lived. Carey had an appointment at the University of Cincinnati, and since Uncle Herman and he had a common interest in the welfare of American industry, they became well-acquainted. My father, who was born in the anthracite mining town of Summit Hill, Pennsylvania, where his father ran the general store, met my mother when he went to Engineering School at the University of Cincinnati, under Uncle Herman's wing. She was a botany major in the College of Liberal Arts.

There is a pattern in our parentage. Both of our fathers came, so to speak, from the backwoods to the universities where they found their wives, and both married into well-established Midwestern families. It was therefore almost inevitable that as soon as I got my M.A. from Columbia I would get my first job teaching at the University of Cincinnati. And it was inevitable that my grandmother and Kay's mother would arrange for us to meet. The first date was not a success, but the second was. Biography repeated itself. Even though I'd been brought up in a suburb of Boston and my mother was highly civilized, I was fresh from the army and had become an egg-headed hick. Kay dazzled me as Daisy dazzled Scott Fitzgerald. But at first I thought sedate, gracious, old, well-off suburban towns like Glendale were intellectual deserts, and what's worse, I let it be known that I thought so.

And this brings me back to Dear Boo. It is true that she didn't talk much about Herder and Henry Adams, but she had and she transmitted to her daughter a very different and very valuable quality that I had a need to understand. It was Dear Boo and her daughter Kay that converted me to a belief in Glendale. In Glendale, the life of the mind is respected but not adored. Neighborliness comes first, not just as sociability, but almost as deeply as Christ taught it and carried on without display; flowers and trees and lawns come second, not for neatness but for beauty; then tennis, swimming pools, dances, amateur drama, and gracious dining. Husbands' careers come last; they exist simply to make Glendale possible. Glendale is not just another

Winnetka or Bloomfield Hills or Greenwich; it is still, by some accident of real estate, a village, and as far as I know, there is no better village on earth.

What is more precious than a well-knit village? Whales? Sexual parity? Structural criticism? Dear Boo would agree in principle though certainly not in tone with what Swift wrote to Pope while he was working on *Gulliver's Travels*: "I have ever hated all nations, professions, and communities, and all my love is toward individuals." She was always doubtful of grand abstractions like Equality, but her life was one of unstinting devotion to her friends, family, relations, and village, a devotion which no difference of doctrine, dogma, or class could weaken. "Politeness is to do and say / The kindest thing in the kindest way," she told her grandchildren and illustrated the maxim by her every waking act. She turned Thanksgivings, Christmases, Fourths of July, birthdays, and other reunions into big occasions, "putting the big pot into the little pot," as she said, and insisting on ceremonies, projects, and games that enabled and required everyone to participate. Thus she bound us together. And she was an ardent backer of the Cincinnati Smoke Abatement League and the Ohio River anti-pollution drive long before The Environment became fashionable.

When I arrived in Glendale after the Signal Corps and graduate school, a sort of an engineer and a sort of a seeker after knowledge, I needed to know, and I still need to be reminded, that these pursuits are not sufficient unto themselves, so it was most fortunate that Dear Boo and my grandmother were friends in that warm village.

On December 8th, 1979, Kay and I heard that my application to teach at Lawrence's London Campus had been accepted. I suddenly stared a computerless year in the face. Shortly after that, I made my unnatural proposal and began to shop for a computer. When I asked Kay just now, she knowing what she knows now, why she had so graciously acquiesced to my desire, she replied, putting a great many things together, "I am not a feminist."

JABBERWOCKY

'Twas brillig and the slithy toves
    Did gyre and gimble in the wabe;
All mimsy were the borogoves,
    And the mome raths outgrabe.

"Beware the Jabberwock, my son!
    The jaws that bite, the claws that catch!
Beware the Jubjub bird, and shun
    The frumious Bandersnatch!"

He took his vorpal sword in hand:
    Longtime the manxome foe he sought—
So rested he by the Tumtum tree,
    And stood awhile in thought.

And as in uffish thought he stood,
    The Jabberwock, with eyes of flame,
Came whiffling through the tulgey wood,
    And burbled as it came!

One, two! One, two! And through and through
    The vorpal blade went snicker-snack!
He left it dead, and with its head
    He went galumphing back.

"And hast thou slain the Jabberwock?
    Come to my arms, my beamish boy!
Oh frabjous day! Callooh! Callay!"
    He chortled in his joy.

'Twas brillig, and the slithy toves
    Did gyre and gimble in the wabe;
All mimsy were the borogoves,
    And the mome raths outgrabe.

CHAPTER II

ALL MIMSY WERE THE BOROGROVES

I HAD visited computer stores before, but never with intent to buy. Once, at the first computer store in Appleton, I had looked longingly at an Altair microcomputer. I saw it just before that pioneer venture overreached itself by trying to capture an unready business market and in consequence went out of business itself, and well before I had a real need for my own computer. But now that I was ready to shop, our plans for Christmas, made some months before, prevented me from the swift satisfaction of my appetite for knowledge of the field. Early in the fall, I had committed myself to attending the annual meeting of the Modern Language Association of America between Christmas and New Years in San Francisco. Kay had never seen that fabulous city. So when I announced my intention of attending the meetings, it wasn't long before she had hit upon the idea of transferring Christmas to San Francisco, which was an easier trip for two of our children than Appleton and an extra incentive to make the journey for the other two.

As soon as the Christmas vacation began, we would fly to Tucson, where son Nick (number three) was doing a Ph.D. in planetary science at the University of Arizona; get in our old green Ford station wagon, now his, and drive to San Francisco to join son Ben (number two), who was doing a Ph.D. in political science just across the Bay at Berkeley; rendezvous there in due course via air transport with daughter Mackay (number four), a junior at Earlham College, Indiana; daughter Devon (number one), environmental planning consultant, Chicago; Aunt Janet (Kay's brother's widow), housewife, painter, and gravel-pit fighter of Clarkston, Michigan; and Nephew Chris, her son, finishing up a B.A. in arts, social sciences, and philosophy at Michigan. We would all spend Christmas together. Then I would go to my meetings for two days, missing the last. After that as many as were free to go would get into the green Ford and explore northern Mexico, because it was so close.

It all worked very well, except that we could not lure Devon away from a pressing engagement in the East. The sister of an Appleton friend helped enormously by graciously going away for Christmas and leaving us her spectacular San Francisco apartment on the top floor of an extravagantly Victorian hill-climbing house. Thanks to her, we were able to appreciate the full flavor of the city. I even managed to pay a ten-minute visit to a computer store, which I left unedified but holding a manual for the Microsoft BASIC programming language.

Mexico was enchanting, with its startling landscape, its hellish buzzards, its colossal cacti, its charming aborigines, and its patina of Old Spain. We penetrated it as far south as Guaymas, on the eastern shore of the Gulf of California. I remember most a great white moon that seemed close enough to touch, rising up behind the black silhouette of an unearthly volcanic mountain shaped like an immense thumb. Nick, the astronomer, said that the large size of the rising moon was an optical illusion, but the rest of us insisted on believing our eyes. There were no computer stores in Guaymas.

Mackay and I left the excursion in a six-passenger plane the day after New Year's to return to our respective classrooms. In the spring would come the first term of my spread-out sabbatical leave—one term per year for three years, skipping the year at the London Campus. When Kay returned from Guaymas, we decided that we would begin that first free term with a three-week excursion to Mexico, which now drew us as a magnet. Then, after some weeks in Appleton of organizing and packing for London, we would go to The Lake in May and stay through July, when my brother's family began their tenure. Then we would fly to London from Boston.

In short, I had to buy my computer before April, when we went to Mexico. I could not buy it during the summer—even though Boston, certainly a hub of the computing universe, would not be far away—because I had big plans for that summer. I was going to hire son Nick, the best programmer I knew of that I could afford, to convert SITAR, as developed for *The London Stage* Project, from Lawrence's PDP-11 computer to whatever machine I bought. I had to have a computer by May 22nd, when Nick would be free of courses until the middle of August. It probably wouldn't take him all summer, perhaps, but it was not safe to assume it wouldn't. For I wanted to take to England with me not only my own computer but also my own word-processing software.

I visited computer stores in San Francisco, Tucson, Chicago, and Appleton and Neenah, Wisconsin. Sometimes they were downtown, sometimes they were in the mall, sometimes they were on the strip, but they were all the same. You enter a large, white room, and brilliant cold fluorescent lights beat mercilessly down on you. There aren't any counters; in fact there's not

much at all, considering the size of the room. Maybe a desk over
in a corner, maybe occupied by a blonde who is talking on the
phone and looking at her fingernails. Maybe a magazine rack partially loaded with old issues of *BYTE* magazine, *Business Week*,
treatises on *How to Choose a Personal Computer* by Apple Computer, Inc.; *Programming Made Easy* books; brochures for printers, desk chairs, and disk drives; documentation for general
ledger, inventory, herd management, and Space Invader programs; boxes of floppy disks; announcements of last year's Computer Fayre; and somebody's raincoat.

The room is sparsely furnished with compact and bulky
computers. At the keyboards of some of these, children, teenagers, or full-grown men are banging away as if they have been
there all week and plan to be there all next week. Some computers are operating themselves. On one, green missiles are forever
flying across a yellow screen and sometimes hitting blue rocket
ships, causing red fireworks. Another flashes its name in full-
screen letters, and afterwards boasts its virtues over and over
again in words that slide across the screen:

```
. . . . . . ADVANCED LSI TECHNOLOGY . . . . . . . 16K RAM . . . . . .
BASIC IN ROM . . . . . . PROGRAM IT YOURSELF . . . . . . .THE LEADING
EDGE IN MICROCOMPUTING . . . . . . MENU DRIVEN . . . . . . WORLDWIDE
SERVICE . . . . . . EASILY UPGRADABLE . . . . . . ONLY $1595. . . . .
ADVANCED LSI TECHNOLOGY . . . . . .
```

No one comes forward, smiling politely, and asks, "What
can I do for you today?" I go over to a man banging away at one
of the bulky computers and wait for him to reach a stopping
point. He is copying the contents of about forty pages of 8½ by
11 paper, each consisting of seven columns of handwritten numbers. He does not reach a stopping point. I cough and say,
"Excuse me ... I'm interested in buying a computer." "Huh?
... , Oh," he says, as if he'd never thought of that before, and
then, "I'm just doing some work on this one. Ask her." I go
over to the desk and wait for the blonde to finish her phone
conversation. She doesn't. I lean on the desk and look at her.
She says, "OK, Lucille, I'll call you back. There's somebody

here, oK? What was it you wanted." I repeat my interest in buying a computer. "OK, I'll see if Bob is in there, oK?" She wheels 180 degrees and shouts through an open door into a gloomy space, "Bob, there's somebody here, oK?"

In a little while, Bob comes out, squinting a bit while his eyes adjust to the light and looking a bit like an absent-minded Phil Silvers: "What was it you wanted?" he asks. I reiterate my interest in computers. "What did you want it for?" I can read his mind, as plain as day. He is thinking, "What is an old guy like you going to do with a computer?" I search frantically for something important-sounding to say, like "general ledger," but finally decide I had better come clean: "I want to write books with it." He looks very seriously to the right and down, as if he has suddenly discovered a hole in the floor.

After a long pause, he says, skeptically, "I suppose . . . you would want . . . lowercase . . . "; then, brightening, "This one over here is what we sell for a word processor. It has full-screen editing, automatic centering, proportional spacing, autowraparound, autorepagination, global search and replace, DP capabilities, math pack, and KorrectoSpell. Oh, yes, and full-page scrolling. That ought to do it for you." The device in question is a gray desk with a gray videoscope sitting on it and a gray computer where the drawers would be. "How much?" I say. "Well, including the furniture and the spelling, twelve-nine." "Too much," I blurt. "Well, without the hard disk and the desk and the spelling, you can have it for $6,995," he says, not very well hiding his contempt. "How about that?"

Having gone this far, I decide to plunge all the way in. "Can you insert a page into a book with it?" I had decided that this would be my test. "Of course," he says, obviously offended by the question; "you can do anything with it. Shall I give you a demo?" In a few seconds, he flicks some switches, slaps in some disks, bangs some keys, and has it going. It flashes a business letter on the screen. "Now suppose you want to center this title on this page. All you have to do is highlight it," his hands all the while playing expertly on the keyboard. "See?" Now suddenly

"Fiscal Policy" glares out with double intensity. He plays the keyboard some more. "Then we hit this key here and there . . . it . . . is!" Right in the center.

"Want the next page?" Bang: first page vanishes and next page sweeps down the screen, spread like a sheet by a chambermaid. "Want the first page again?" Bang: first page.

"Fantastic," I say, very sincerely. But I press on: "Now, perhaps you have a fairly long piece of text. Could you put that into your machine and insert a page from somewhere else into it?"

"Nothing to it," he says. "Now watch me insert a new footnote, and it autorenumbers the rest." More Victor Borge keyboarding, and it autorenumbers indeed. I reiterate my request; and now he shows me how easy it is to personalize a form letter. He then wheels around in his chair and says, giving me a straight look, "Well, what do you think? You get a 90-day warranty and free software update support for a year." I would see. Perhaps he could lend me or sell me an operator's manual so that I could look up the specifications for insertion and deletion. He puts his hands on his knees and looks again at the hole in the floor, which now appears to be growing larger.

"oK! So you would like to see how we move a page into a page. O . . . k." This time his keyboarding is a bit rough, and when the magic moment arrives to deposit a page into a page, the videoscope goes "Bleep, bleep, bleep," and flashes the following message: "PAGE FULL." Not disconcerted, Bob says brightly, "You see? The system is fully idiot-proof," not seeming to mind what that makes him. Then he looks at the hole in the floor again but doesn't seem to notice it. Finally these words issue forth. "O . . . K! I'll be up front with you, . . . Sir; I'm the hardware man here; I don't actually have the expertise with this software. You should talk to our software specialist." He wheels toward the front of the store: "Hey, Bob, come over here a minute."

On this signal, a gangly teenager at one of the compact terminals bangs out some finishing touches, unfolds himself, ambles over, and leans on our gray desk. He smiles benignly at me and says, "What can I do for you?" Lamely, I reply, "Your boss says you can show me ... ," only to be gleefully interrupted by the original Bob: "Oh no," he chortles, grinning a big Phil Silvers grin, "Bob is *my* boss."

Just then the telephone rings, and the blonde says that it's California wanting to speak to Bob, provided that it's OK. Software Bob now ambles into the back room, where I can dimly perceive him describing the battle scene of *Star Wars* with one hand, banging away at a computer with the other, and carrying on an animated conversation with the telephone tucked between his shoulder and his neck. It is now nearly dinner time, and I realize that this phone call shows no signs of termination. I ask the blonde when would be a more convenient time to talk to Bob. "Mornings," she says. "About when?" I ask. "Any time after eleven-thirty. He's usually in by then. If he's not out on a call. Call first, OK?" All this approximates my experience of computer stores, but it didn't all happen at the same time or place.

After a few such visits, I knew I was not going to find out much about microcomputers at computer stores. Each one sold three or four kinds, and that exhausted the possibilities as far as they were concerned. A few brushes with such systems analysts convinced me I must heed my father's legacy and consult only myself. Casting about for better information, I began to collect issues of *BYTE*, "The Small Systems Journal," as I passed from store to store. I soon knew that I had found the right place to shop. My clue was that *BYTE*, a monthly, was three-quarters of an inch thick. It was thicker than most issues of *Datamation*, the principal journal of the whole computer business. And a half-inch of this was advertisements. Something very important was going on in *BYTE*, if so many merchants wanted their wares to be shown in this particular marketplace.

The articles in *BYTE* weren't much help: "Program those 2708s!" Was I supposed to have one? "Build a Low Cost EPROM Eraser." Would this gadget erase an EPROM, or was it an eraser made out of EPROM? In the former case, what was wrong with the EPROM? In the latter case, how was EPROM better than rubber? "An Overview of Long Division." I already had a hazy idea of that. "An Animated Slot Machine in Color." Not my line. "A DC to DC Converter." Something like converting Swiss francs to Swiss francs? "Model of the Brain, Part 3." I'd never be able to make up the lessons I had missed. Clearly the readers of *BYTE* articles were a great deal more advanced than I.

The ads were more down to earth: "Low cost hard disk computers are here and field proven." "Call on Monday ... your North Star computer will be DELIVERED by Thursday." "To-day, hundreds of thousands of microcomputers run with Micro-soft software." And much plain dealing: "Atari 800 $899.00"; "New Centronics 737 Printer Wow! $799.00"; "32K Static Ram Boards $469.00"; "Magic Wand Word-Processing System $400." In fact, the most important difference between *BYTE* and all the other computer journals I had previously known was the univer-sal presence of the bottom line. You never saw a price tag in *Datamation*, the *large* systems journal. In *BYTE*, computing had deserted the elite society of yachtsmen, where if you have to ask, you can't afford one, to mingle with the hoi polloi, who won't even look at a thing until they know how much it costs. I found this heartwarming. And it certainly did save a lot of time wasted trying to worm the price of whatever high-class device it was out of "my local dealer," who like as not dwelt in Atlanta.

Still, *BYTE* society had its own brand of chic. There was an unmistakable atmosphere of college humor. A computer called Superbrain advertised itself by means of a picture of a computer wearing a mortar board. A printer called itself The Paper Tiger, completely destroying the metaphor. A color videoscope, boast-ing extremely high quality, called itself MicroAngelo, ruining my whole day. Another painful punster sold hardware known as "Thinker Toys," a bad mistake, too, because "toys" are what you call the other fellow's merchandise. There was also a very strong smell of rock culture. Outfits like Smoke Signal Broadcast-ing, Radio Shack, Pickles and Trout, Apple, Orange, Electric

Pencil, Lifeboat Associates, Jade, and Novation Cat expected us to take their products seriously while they put us on.

J. R. R. Tolkien and Stanley Kubrick had also taken their toll. Commodore, Ltd., had given its PET computer model number 2001. Most *BYTE* covers evoked outer space, like the one showing astronauts on the moon discovering stone tablets on which lines of programming code were inscribed. Infinite, Inc., sold software. Magic Wand was the name of a word-processing system. Exidy, Inc., called its computer The Sorcerer. And so with games: if the aim was not to zap Klingons, it was to slay dragons and escape from dungeons. In this vein also, Mad Hatter Software presented itself, incongruously including a picture of Alice with the White Knight.

I had not turned many pages when I became aware of certain curious words continually hovering about. They were "S-100," "Z80," and "CP/M": "With an S-100 bus adapter, you can add a ten megabyte disk." "The most fully S-100 compatible CPU on the market." "Established leader in S-100 interfaces." "Catch the S100 Bus, Inc." "Fast Z80 processor." "We all know how powerful that Z80 chip can be." "Runs on any Z80 system." "WHATS-IT? (Wow! How'd All That Stuff Get In There?) The Query System for your CP/M machine." "Opens up the whole world of CP/M software." "Requires CP/M or derivative." "Utilizes the powerful CP/M operating system." In fact—I have since counted—in the ads of the August 1979 issue "S-100" occurs 84 times, "Z80" 41, and "CP/M" 31. I got the distinct impression that nothing mattered as much to the readers of BYTE as S-100, Z80, and CP/M.

Clearly, I had to know what these ubiquitous terms meant, for they might have significant bearing on my choice of a microcomputer. There ought to be a glossary in such magazines just to explain the ads. Now, years of trying to figure out what Wordsworth and T. S. Eliot meant came to my assistance, and I began to read between the lines. "S-100" was a selling point for hardware; "CP/M" was a selling point for software; "Z80" might turn up in either context.

S-100 was a **bus**. I knew that the term "bus" was used to
describe a thick strip of metal in an ordinary electrical service box
that carried electric current to the circuits of one's house. It was
indeed a sort of "omnibus" on which the circuit breakers of the
household rode. I knew busses were important in computer design, because I had heard that an engineer in a very big company
had left because they wouldn't adopt his bus and had founded
another company on basis of that bus, which then became a very
big company too. If I supposed that computer busses, like house-
current busses, were the basic conductors common to all parts of
the computer, the definition seemed to work in the various advertising environments of the term S-100. The bus was apparently
the computer's way of communicating with its peripheral devices:
that is, the units of memory, the videoscope, the printer, the disk
drives, the burglar alarm, the telephone, the environment, the
laboratory, the factory, or whatever else you might want to plug
in.

Putting the computer modules mentally into an electrical
service box, I dimly perceived the bus of a computer to be a set
of parallel metal strips to which every module of the computer is
attached. Perhaps it could be compared to the cerebral cortex and
the spinal column, which interconnect arms, legs, ears, eyes,
brain, and memory in the human system.

If a device was "S-100 compatible," then, one must be able
to plug it into the bus of an S-100 computer, like a house circuit
into a service box, and expect it to work. If one could, in order
for a device to work on a given bus, it would be necessary for its
manufacturer to know in advance which strip of the bus the
computer would use for which purpose: which strips would go to
memory, which would connect to the power supply, which would
talk to peripherals. Working on this premise, I concluded that
"S-100" would be some kind of a convention or manufacturer's
agreement about the function of each strip on the bus.

Now the ads began to make better sense. There had been
many references to **slots** on **motherboards**. A computer board,
often called a **card**, I knew to be a rectangular piece of plas-

tic about four inches by eight inches with an electronic circuit printed on it, with electronic components (chips, resistors, condensers) soldered to it, and with several dozen contacts attached on one side. In *BYTE* usage, a computer's "mother" board seemed always to consist of so many "slots," into which one could plug as many "boards." I deduced that "motherboard" was the name for the board bearing the bus. "Why 'mother'?" I wondered. Was it because the motherboard "bears" all the other boards or because all connectors are either male or female and the "mother" board happens to be female? Or both? The idea was almost poetic. John Donne couldn't have invented a better metaphor.

The reason, then, for the frequent mention of the S-100 bus was that both makers of computers and makers of components found it advantageous to advertise their compliance with the standard. It was almost the only bus one heard about, because those who didn't comply apparently kept mum. So widespread was the convention that one could buy an S-100 motherboard from one manufacturer, a power supply from another, a central processor from a third, memory from a fourth, and printer and videoscope interfaces from a fifth and sixth. It was just like plugging together a turntable, a pickup, an amplifier, tuners, mikes, and speakers from six different manufacturers to make up one hi-fi. It came home to me that the owner of an S-100 computer would have his pick of most of the computer components on the market not only then, but probably forever, because widely adopted standards in a free market eventually force compliance. Who would be so foolish as now to manufacture a radio that ran on 175 volts, 72 cycles AC? Thus I determined that my computer would have an S-100 bus.

I understood **CP/M** better. The ads clearly identified it as an **operating system**. Having had a good deal of experience with both DEC and IBM computers in my *London Stage* days, I knew pretty well what an operating system was. In the case of the IBM 360, it was OS (Operating System), the supervisory program that interpreted one's job cards, found one's data, ran one's programs, and printed out one's results, or found it impossible to interpret one's cards and flushed them out, printing instead numbers referring to errors one had committed. In the case of the DEC PDP-11, it was **RSTS** (Resource Sharing Time-sharing System), the interactive supervisor that let you into your account, gave you access to its programs, your programs, and your data, filed your files on its disks, and unfailingly remembered where it put them.

I also knew that a program written to run under one operating system would not run under another. From the ads in *BYTE*, I gathered that a great many microcomputers used CP/M (Control Program/Microcomputer) and that a great many programs were written to run under CP/M's supervision, including the most-advertised word-processing programs. Many makes of computers used CP/M. Those that didn't had their own private brands: AppleDOS for the Apple, TRSDOS for the Radio Shack TRS-80. CP/M was the product of an independent software house, Digital Research, not a maker of computers, so it must have made its way in the market on its own merits, not, as with AppleDOS and TRSDOS, by virtue of its monopoly on a particular computer. I felt I could believe what CP/M said of itself:

> CP/M is the industry standard operating system for small machines. With thousands of users throughout the world, it's the most popular and widely used. It's the original, hardware-independent 'bus' for users working with a broad array of languages and word processing and applications software available from scores of suppliers at affordable prices. . . .

If this were so, a person whose computer could be run by CP/M might choose from a "broad array" of the software on the market at that time, and undoubtedly for a long time to come. CP/M was to software what S-100 was to hardware—a universal "bus." I determined that I would have a CP/M computer.

The **Z80**, the contexts made evident, was a "computer on a chip," one of those things no bigger than a domino that has electrical circuits equivalent to the wiring of a small city. The Z80 was a **central processing unit** (hereinafter **CPU**): the part of the computer that computes; the part that reasons, calculates, decides, and communicates, as distinct from its memory and its peripheral devices—videoscope, printer, disk drives, and so forth. For though we customarily refer to our whole conglomerate of components as a "computer," if we spoke strictly, we would reserve that word for the CPU only.

There were a great many brands of personal computers, but all of them used the same half-dozen CPU chips. The Z80 was easily the most commonly used, and makes which didn't use it tended to keep silent about what they did use. I learned from *BYTE* articles that the Z80, made by Zilog, a division of Exxon, had superseded the 8080, on which the microcomputer industry had been founded, but even though it had bettered the 8080 in speed and efficiency, the Z80 accepted programs made for the 8080 because it was **upward compatible**; the new breed did things differently, but they were the same things. So CP/M, originally made for the 8080, could run on a Z80 too. Since I must have CP/M, then, I would prefer a Z80 microprocessor, which I took to be the best chip that CP/M could handle.

Although the landslide toward S-100, CP/M, and Z80 that was going on in *BYTE* seemed bound to sweep me along with it, this pressure could nevertheless not avail with me if the resulting configuration in any way hindered me from mounting my beloved SITAR. Lots of word processors were advertised to run on CP/M machines—Wordstar, Magic Wand, and Electric Pencil, to name a few—but I stubbornly preferred my own concoction. At this time, I had no sure knowledge of any other word processor than the TECO that ran on Lawrence's PDP-11 and some others like it. These systems were incredibly hard to use. On this flimsy evidence, my instinct or my arrogance or my ignorance told me that SITAR would work better for writing books than any product of contemporary computer technology.

It had been my experience that computer technology was a closed circuit whose purpose was the satisfaction of its own ends, the main one being to perpetuate itself. It could accomplish miracles in its closet but never seemed to get the point of what it was doing. It could fabricate brilliant gadgets that failed to serve their purposes. It couldn't see the forest for the trees. It preferred the complex to the simple, the clever to the easy. Evidence of this point abounds in the story I am about to tell, and I shall have more to say about it in my conclusion, but in the winter of 1979–80, when I shopped for my computer, I simply had a hunch that SITAR would serve my purposes as well as any existing word processor, and probably better than most. Besides, I thought transferring SITAR to a microcomputer would be easy.

I was egged on by a rumor that circulated around the Lawrence computer center at this time to the effect that Anton Chernoff, a mathematician, genius, and brilliant programmer, who had left our campus some years before to work for DEC, strongly disapproved of SITAR because it was too rudimentary. Now, Anton Chernoff was the designer and programmer of TECO, which was then and still is the principle word processor on DEC machines. TECO was a programmer's dream: not only could you correct errors in text with it, but it was itself a programming language in which you could write an infinite number of fiendishly clever programs to edit and manipulate text automatically. Therefore it was referred to in computing circles as "*the* most powerful text editor." I simply thought it was ridiculously difficult to use. If Anton Chernoff's approach to word processing was typical, as I confidently believed it was, then nothing as simple as SITAR was going to materialize in the whole wide world of computing.

Having convinced myself of this premise, I began to look for the shortest way to put SITAR on a computer of my own. It was written in the programming language BASIC-PLUS, developed by DEC to run under its interactive RSTS time-sharing system. If I could buy a microcomputer that ran under RSTS, my problem was solved. SITAR would run. If I couldn't, the best solution would be a microcomputer on which a language exactly like BASIC-PLUS would run.

Once there was a man who called up a business associate at home. "Hello, this is the Smith residence," said a small voice.

"May I please speak to Mr. Smith?" "I'm very sorry, he isn't here; may I take a message, please?" "Yes, please tell him Mr. Brown called." Long pause. "Excuse me, how do you spell Brown?" "B-R-O-W-N," answered the businessman. Another long pause, and then the small voice, very small: "How do you make a B?"

That was one of Dear Boo's favorite jokes. We never tired of hearing her tell it; she was so amused by the little boy. I tell it now because the little boy is very much like a computer, and the man on the telephone is very much like a programmer. The man has to teach the little boy how to do the task at hand, a very little bit at a time. The story nicely illustrates the three levels on which we can communicate with a computer: with a **high-level language**, **assembly language**, and **machine code**. "Brown" is high-level, "B-R-O-W-N" is assembly language, and the strokes necessary for making a "B" are machine code.

A computer's memory may be thought of as consisting entirely of little boxes, which are called **bytes**. Each byte contains eight switches, called **bits**. The CPU can flip any of the switches in a given byte on or off, and it can also sense which switches in a given byte are on or off. And every byte in memory has an **address**, enabling our CPU to find it. I suppose that when a CPU senses a bit at a given address, it switches on a wire to its address. If current flows, the switch is on. If current doesn't flow, the switch is off. In order to cope with these bewildering arrays of bits in bytes, human beings resort to binary arithmetic—in which 10 means two and 11111111 (eight bits full) means 255—and pretend that off is 0 and on is 1. But the computer doesn't care what we call them; it's just a mess of wires and switches.

The really important thing is that by turning certain bits on and off in a byte, we can make up a set of codes that will convert the computer to a giver and receiver of information. The eight-bit code that computers use is nothing more than a variation on Morse code, with on's and off's instead of dots and dashes. As long as all parties understand the code, it works. With eight bits, there are 256 separate codes, enough to represent every character on my keyboard and then some. When I strike a character, my terminal converts it to the eight-bit code corresponding to the character and sends that code to the address in my computer's memory that is waiting for it. Because it doesn't know how to make a 'B', my terminal sends it '01000010'; if I retrieve that byte later on, my terminal converts it back to a 'B'. When my computer puts my words on a disk, it converts each byte to magnetic bits.

Getting action from the CPU is another matter and involves an altogether different set of codes. These codes are **instructions** to the CPU, like "add addresses 0180 and 0181" or "put 'B' in address 0185." **Instruction sets** vary from chip to chip. To operate a Z80, one uses a very different set of instructions from those one uses to operate a 6502. That's why Apple programs won't run on a Z80 computer (or almost any other). Instruction sets proliferate because every chip maker thinks he has a better idea of what instructions are most needful. Instruction codes are called **mnemonics**, because they are supposed to be easy to remember. Thus "LD A,L" means to a Z80 "load the contents of address A into address L." By using the instruction set's mnemonic vocabulary according to strict rules, one may write an **assembly language program**. This program must of course be converted to eight-bit codes before the Z80 can understand it. One does this automatically by means of an "assembler" program. When a program in assembly language is "assembled," it comes out in zeroes and ones or machine code. At the top of page 27 are assembly-language and machine-code versions of a high-level routine called PAGE that reads the screen of a video terminal.

Breaking up a process into the minute operations available in an instruction set is very hard work, and a very simple process may involve dozens of instructions. High level languages evolve because certain clusters of mnemonics get used over and over again. Why not give names to all the clusters of instructions that a person might ever want to use and write programs with the names alone? The computer itself can do the work of interpreting the myriad operations represented by each name. It can just substitute the appropriate pattern of zeroes and ones whenever the name for

```
PAGE::  PUSH    HL
GET:    LD      E,0FFH
        LD      C,06H
        CALL    5
        LD      B,A
        CP      0
        JP      Z,GET
        POP     HL
        LD      (HL),B
        INC     HL
        LD      A,B
        CP      13
        JP      NZ,PAGE
        RET
        END

111001010001111011111111100001110
000001101100110100000000000000101
010001111111111100000000011001010
000000000000001111000010101110000
001000110111100011111110000001101
110000100000000000000000011001001
```

that cluster occurs. The names can be English words that indicate what each cluster does. Two questions remain: what is the best set of clusters to use, and what is the clearest way of expressing and combining them? There must be a grammar as well as a vocabulary. So high-level languages spawn and seek their fortunes.

To sum it all up, let us consider the following analogy. If I ask my wife, "Please make my breakfast," she goes to the kitchen, squeezes me an orange, makes my oatmeal, brews me a cup of tea, and sets out honey and milk. My wife and I communicate in a high-level language. But if I ask my daughter just home from college to please make my breakfast, she doesn't know what my breakfast is these days. I have to interpret "breakfast" for her: squeeze an orange, make oatmeal, brew tea, and set out honey and milk. She understands assembly language. If, however, I ask a neighbor child who doesn't know how to do any of these things to make my breakfast, I have to interpret again: "Boil the water, put the tea bag in the cup, pour the boiling water over it . . . ," and so on. I have to break each operation into little bits. The child understands machine code. The higher the level, the greater the ease of use, but the definitions of terms, "breakfast" in our example, must be agreed on in advance. BASIC-PLUS is a high-level language.

My problem would have been simpler if there were only one BASIC. But every manufacturer of microcomputers had its own

idea of what features were best for the market, or, if it were
striving for economy, which features its machine had room for.
Some BASICs were tailored for business, others for math, others
for games. Which was best for SITAR?

I am an old maker of Heathkits; my monophonic Heath hi-fi
amplifier, made in 1954, still blasts away, and my Heath tuner
keeps on tuning. Heath people have been friendly about advice
and parts. So, when in 1977 Heath came out with a personal
computer, I said to myself that if I ever bought one, theirs would
be it. And when I finally did decide to buy one, Heath's H11
became my first candidate. When I found out further that the
H11 was not just a copy of DEC's LSI-11 but used the very same
computer, licensed to Heath, I was overjoyed. Maybe BASIC-
PLUS would run on it. Heath's software advisors couldn't tell
me on the phone if or how much H11 BASIC differed from
BASIC-PLUS. So I immediately ordered all the H11 manuals.

My joy was short-lived. I knew that **string functions** would
be crucial. SITAR was littered with string functions. In computer
talk, a **string** is a set of any number of characters. Even a space
is a character, character number 32 in many computers. At first,
we find this practice difficult to believe, but on second thought,
we realize that it must be so. Like a period or a comma, a space
is punctuation, and without spaces we can't read a sentence. "To
be or not to be," spaces included, is a string, "ghxycd" is a
string, "3.1416" is a string, and *War and Peace* is a string. A
"string function" is a word in a programming language that does
something to a string.

Much to my dismay, as I checked H11 BASIC's vocabulary
against that of BASIC-PLUS, I found that the words LEFT,
RIGHT, MID, and INSTR were missing, and filling in the gap
were strange things called POS and SEG. In BASIC-PLUS, LEFT
goes to a given string in memory and comes back with the "leftmost substring," how much of a substring being determined by
accompanying specifications. In this sentence, the leftmost seven
characters are "In this" (the space counts). RIGHT does the
same for the rightmost string. MID finds a string somewhere in

the middle, exactly where to be specified concomitantly, and, most important, INSTR will find a given substring, let's say "Out, damn spot," in a given string, let's say, *Macbeth*. It's not hard to see that such capacities would be very useful for writing a word-processing program. I rushed over to Jim Evans, redoubtable professor of chemistry and director of computer services at Lawrence and a world class Grand Master of software, to find out just how bad for my purposes H11 BASIC was. "We-ell," he said taciturnly, with a slight trace of Maine accent, "Looks like RT11 BASIC to me-e. You can do all these things with their POS and SEG, but it would mean a lot more wo-ork. Besi-ides, you need record I/O."

Just possibly, somewhere out there was a BASIC with all the right string functions and record I/O, whatever that was. Maybe it was Microsoft BASIC. Anyone who paid the least attention to the buzz created by the Rise of the Micros had heard "Microsoft . . . Microsoft . . . Microsoft . . . " whispered over and over in the breezes. Full page ads on expensive pages of every issue of *BYTE* made plain its prominence in microdom. "In 1975, Microsoft made the first BASIC interpreter for the 8080. Today hundreds of thousands of microcomputers run with Microsoft . . . BASIC interpreters for 8080, Z80, 6800, 6809 . . . Language features above and beyond any other BASIC have made Microsoft BASIC the world's most popular interpreter." "Get Microsoft . . . and get serious with your (Radio Shack) Model II."

I remembered the Microsoft manual I had picked up in San Francisco and rushed back to my office to look up the string functions. There they were—LEFT, RIGHT, MID, and INSTR. Back in a trice to Jim's office, I asked how he liked them. "Ye-es. This is more like it." He leafed back and forth a bit and then said. "And it looks like they've got some kind of record I/O, too." I wondered how he thought it would work for SITAR. "I'd say it's worth a try, anyhow." That was about as positive a comment as you could get from a computer veteran on the probability that anything would work, and it was downright enthusiasm coming from a Yankee.

My hopes rose. Microsoft might be the answer. And the best thing about it was that, according to their ads in *BYTE*, Microsoft had a **compiler**. "The Microsoft BASIC compiler has the fastest execution times of any BASIC available," they claimed. I knew that a compiler made a difference because SITAR ran many times faster on Lawrence's PDP-11 when it was compiled than it did when it was merely "interpreted." An **interpreter** is a program in machine code that feeds a high-level program to the computer, translating each line into machine code as it goes. A compiler feeds nothing but simply makes a complete translation of the whole high-level program, ready to run on demand. Since the work of translation has been done in advance, once and for all, a compiled program runs much faster than the same set of lines running through an interpreter. It's the difference between having a printed English translation of a French book and looking up each word in a bilingual dictionary. Speed was important to me, as I knew from experience with SITAR on slow and fast PDP-11s. It could mean the difference between waiting two minutes for the page you want to revise or two seconds.

Now my choices were narrowing. If I used Microsoft BASIC I would need to have a computer that used CP/M, because Microsoft was made for the CP/M operating system. The Z80 chip seemed to be the best that CP/M could operate. And, to keep as many hardware options as possible open, I should have an S-100 motherboard. By now I had brochures describing the prominent microcomputers, and I started to eliminate.

During my browsings in *BYTE*, I became aware of a recurrent message between the lines. An article would be entitled: "I/O Expansion for the Radio Shack TRS-80, Part 1." Hmmm, I thought, the TRS-80 needs more I/O. "Recently," says the author, "my mail has been dominated by owners of the Radio Shack TRS 80 Model I thirsting for hardware expansion by means other than Tandy Corporation equipment." Hmmm, these do not seem to be very loyal customers. The author continues to the effect that in the old days computers had sufficient I/O, but things had changed: "Most importantly, the Radio Shack

TRS-80, the Apple II, and the Commodore PET were introduced." Hmmm, he doesn't like these brands. Such hints were
reinforced by the amount of equipment actually being offered in
ads and articles to owners of Radio Shack, Apple, and PET by
manufacturers other than those. "PERCOM Low-Cost Add-On
Storage for your TRS-80. ... Systems include Percom Patch Pak
1 [which] de-glitches and upgrades TRSDOS." Hmmm, Radio
Shack's operating system is downgrade and has glitches. **Glitches**
are unexpected events, usually unpleasant and often disastrous,
that should not happen to a computer in the normal course of its
daily work. Sometimes the message was unequivocal. Here is
Ohio Scientific, on *BYTE*'s outside back cover: "The C4FP has
execution speed that is twice as fast as Apple II or Commodore
PET and over THREE times as fast as TRS-80." Hmmmm!

I ruled out Apple and PET anyhow, because neither had the
S-100 bus or CP/M. Radio Shack's most advanced model could
run Microsoft, but it didn't have the S-100 bus either. Ohio
Scientific's candidate was disqualified for having the wrong bus,
its own operating system, and its own version of BASIC. The
North Star Horizon was tempting, with a Z80 chip and "Ex-
tended BASIC," but the literature said nothing about CP/M.
Zilog, I thought, ought to have a good candidate, being the
developer of the Z80 itself, but it also had private software and
cost a fortune. Heath had the wrong bus, the wrong operating
system, and the wrong BASIC. I probably should have looked
into Altos, but their ads at this time pushed bigger computers
than I could consider. The only reason I ruled out the rest was
that either they didn't stand out or that I didn't like the cut of
their jibs. I wouldn't feel comfortable at my age banging away at
something called Smoke Signal Broadcasting, Superbrain, or Exidy Sorcerer. This language did not inspire confidence.

Besides, there was one kind of computer I haven't mentioned yet: Cromemco. It could afford the first two pages of
nearly every issue of *BYTE* and even sometimes the first two
pages of *Datamation*, the marketplace of giants. It was seriously
in business, and it must be good. Cromemco offered a Z80,

S-100 computer. But its operating system was CDOS, not CP/M. Could it by any chance run Microsoft BASIC? My local Cromemco dealer, Computerlab (not Computer*land*) in the neighboring town of Neenah, told me that it would. Talk is cheap. I bought the CDOS manual and scanned it frantically, hoping to find verification in writing. Sure enough, on page 88 I found the following good news:

> The Cromemco Disk Operating System (CDOS) is an original product designed and written in Z80 machine code by Cromemco, Inc. for its own line of microcomputers. However, due to the large number of programs currently written to run under the CP/M operating system, CDOS was designed to be upwards CP/M-compatible. ... This means that most programs written for CP/M ... will run without modification under CDOS. This also means that programs written for CDOS will not generally run under CP/M.

In sum, CDOS contained all of CP/M, but CP/M didn't have all of CDOS. But I didn't like that "most" in "most programs written for CP/M ... will run on CDOS." Was Microsoft BASIC one of the exceptions? I had to know. I called the source of Microsoft itself in Bellevue, Washington, and got through the order department to a software consultant. "It should run on CDOS," he said. Nobody promises anything in computerland. That answer was as much as I could hope for.

A Cromemco Z-2D computer, which was then the bottom of their line, came with two 5½-inch floppy disk drives, a 21-slot S-100 motherboard, a DC power supply with enough power to handle boards in all 21 slots at once, and four S-100 printed circuit boards—the Z80 central processor, a disk controller with a video terminal interface included on it, a printer interface, and 64 kilobytes of memory. I would have 17 slots free for any more boards I might some day need. If I expanded the memory to the computer's limit, 512 kilobytes (commonly known as "512K"), I would need seven more boards. A communication interface for conversing with big computers and databases would need another board. That made twelve. In the back of my mind there was also the thought that my own computer might be the ideal ultimate home for *The London Stage* Information Bank. What controllers and interfaces that would take, I couldn't guess, but it looked as if that S-100 bus could handle it.

A **kilobyte** is 1,024 bytes; a byte is eight bits of zeroes and ones. It takes eight bits to store a character in memory. That last sentence took up 0.050 kilobytes; this paragraph takes up 0.270 kilobytes. This page takes up approximately 2.37 kilobytes, 2.37K bytes, or 23.7K bits.

Think of me with 64K bytes of my very own memory! Thirty-two pages! The IBM 360 on which I'd processed the 8,026-page *London Stage* and which occupied a whole cellar had only 128K, and that system had cost $150,000. And here was Cromemco offering me a system that, expanded to 128K, would cost a total of $5,575. With 64K, they were asking $3,990, $500 less than the components would cost separately. It was an offer I found impossible to refuse. I weighed it against commensurate packages from other manufacturers. That set of components with surprising regularity came to just about that price, whoever packaged them. It was a good offer, and some of those 21 slots were a bonus. The question, "Which computer?" seemed to have been answered.

By now I knew pretty well which video terminal, because I'd been combing the magazines for information on these too and I already had a collection of manufacturer's specifications. I scanned brochures from Ann Arbor, ADDS, A-J, Beehive, Conrac, Courier, Delta, DEC, EECO, Hazeltine, Human Designed, Incoterm, Infoton, IBM, Lear, Sycor, Teleray, Western Union, and Zentec.

SITAR is finicky about terminals. It requires an **intelligent** terminal with **block send**, cursor positioning keys, and wraparound. A terminal with block send can send a block of text from its screen to a computer, all at once. Unintelligent (known as **dumb**) terminals can't. With block send you can call a piece of text from the computer to the screen, switch the terminal off the wire to the computer (**off-line**), and revise text on the screen of the terminal without the computer's help. All the computer does is, so to speak, send rough text to the terminal and get it back smooth from the terminal. Dumb terminals can't do anything off-line because they have no brains.

Because it edits with the terminal's intelligence instead of the computer's, SITAR needs a terminal with its own cursor-positioning keys, by which one may move the **cursor**, usually a bright mark of some sort, up, down, left, and right. The cursor indicates at what point on the screen any editing action will occur. SITAR also needs a terminal with **wraparound**. When I position the cursor at some point in the text on the screen and insert some words, all the characters beyond that spot on the screen or "page" must move out of the way. If I delete a character at that point, all the text beyond that point must close up. An insertion pushes, and a deletion pulls. "Wraparound" is simply what they call this push-pull effect.

ADDS, Beehive, and Lear-Siegler met SITAR's stringent requirements, but only Beehive's DM20 met them comfortably. SITAR had been using a Beehive terminal since 1973 and a DM20 since 1978, during which time I had developed a good deal of confidence in the manufacturer. But could a DM20 interact successfully with a Cromemco Z-2D?

Now an odd intervention of chance did me a good turn. While inspecting a Cromemco computer at my local dealer's, I did a double take. Wasn't that a Beehive it was using? No, it was brown and had "Cromemco" written on it. It should be gray and have "Beehive" written on it. Then I made a gestalt switch: I turned off the color and the label, and it was unmistakably a Beehive. "Hey," I said to Alex (for that was my local dealer's name), "isn't that a Beehive?" "Yes, it's a Beehive," he said, as if anyone knew that. "It's an **OEM** version." That means, literally translated, "It is an Original Equipment Manufacturer version." This meant, I hazily understood, that Beehive had made it for Cromemco to sell under their own label. Well and good, but is Cromemco the OEManufacturer because they sell it as their own original work (in which case it should be PEM, for Plagiarized Equipment Manufacturer), or is Beehive the OEM because they originate it for Cromemco, not themselves, in which case it should be UEM (Unlabeled Equipment Manufacturer)? I suspect that nobody knows precisely what OEM refers to. I'm sure nobody cares.

At any rate, Cromemco was putting modified Beehive DM30's on their computers and selling them for $1,995. I wondered if the modifications would hamper SITAR. DM20s did work with SITAR, and they cost $400 less. Why should I put up with someone else's tinkering and pay $400 extra for it too? "But can I use a DM20 on a Z-2D?" I thought out loud. "Sure," said Alex. "How do you know?" said I. "Because I've been using one," said he. He forthwith took me out back and showed me a DM20 hooked up to a computer. "That's not a Cromemco," said I. "But I've been using it on a Cromemco," said he. I could ask him to plug it into his Z-2D and show me, or I could take his word. I saw no reason not to take his word, it came so spontaneously.

"But you may not be able to use the Cromemco screen editor with it. They've changed the cursor-positioning keys." Well, I theoretically didn't need the Cromemco screen editor, but it might be handy until I got SITAR going under Microsoft. I assumed it would be another sort of TECO. Then suddenly Alex ran out into the front of the shop and began banging away on the DM30. "It's OK," he said. "They didn't disable the old cursor keys. You can use them." He meant that I could use a set of **control characters** to move the cursor with Cromemco's screen editor, instead of the up, down, left, and right arrows on the keyboard of a standard, labeled Beehive, which wouldn't mean anything to Cromemco's editor.

All conventional terminal keyboards have a CONTROL key. It's a sort of superSHIFT that turns the letters of the alphabet into special computer codes. Thus upon receipt of a CONTROL/U from a terminal, most computers will obligingly forget what you just said, and upon receipt of a CONTROL/C they will cancel a program that you just started. Alex had discovered that CONTROL/W, CONTROL/Z, CONTROL/A, and CONTROL/D caused Cromemco's editor to move the cursor of the DM30 up, down, left, and right. Any terminal could make those codes, including a DM20. "So you're all set," said Alex. I wanted very much to believe it, so I decided to believe it. The terminal would be a Beehive DM20.

What about the printer? A great deal of my antipathy toward the computer establishment has been built upon their failure to put "descenders" on their printers' p's, q's, y's, g's, and j's. You see here how nicely these letters descend below the line. Well, up until recently most makers of computer printers have dispensed with descenders and made these letters stand ridiculously *on* the line. For instance, observe the following sentence, typed without descenders on a standard DECwriter,

```
Inequality reigns uppermost upon my beggarly quagmire.
```

and note how much its legibility improves when printed the way you expect it to look: "Inequality reigns uppermost upon my beggarly quagmire."

Redesigning the alphabet like this is high-handed contempt for the common reader. Any deviation in the way we habitually see words forces us to look twice and puzzle out the letters. Funny-looking letters are eye-catching, as the ad-makers know, but we don't want our eyes to get caught in ordinary text; we want them to glide smoothly through, pausing only to reflect. And for a long time the makers of computer terminals didn't even give us lowercase letters. Adding insult to injury, Texas Instruments a while ago had the gall to bring thousands of printers into the world on which the small letters were simply small capitals. They thus missed the whole point of lowercase. We don't read letters, we read words and phrases, and when the words don't look familiar, we stall and stall. "THE" doesn't remotely resemble "the", if the words are taken as a whole. Here is a prime example of man's inhumanity to man. My printer would have true lowercase, of course, and on that lowercase, true descenders.

Cromemco offered a choice of three printers with their computer, OEMs no doubt. A slow **dot-matrix** for $1,495, a faster dot-matrix for $2,995, and a "typewriter-quality" for $3,195. These prices were ridiculous. All sorts of dot-matrix printers, any reader of *BYTE* knew, were selling for less than a thousand. Dot-matrix printers make all characters by means of one tiny rectangular matrix of pistons the size of the biggest letter, say capital 'M'. A 7×9 dot-matrix printer can print 63 pixels—small dots—with these pistons—or hammers—in a space. When the head gets to a place where a given letter belongs, it fires the pistons that make the pixels that comprise the letter. With 63 potential pixels to a space, printer manufacturers can design a fairly good font of type, with descenders if they please, in which the individual dots are almost indiscernible, and because they need only nine hammers to pass across the width of the matrix, they can make them cheap. Even though the designers of dot-matrix printers clearly had no inkling that type design is a high art, I could make do with a matrix printer—if it had descenders.

Using *BYTE* ads, I had written away for literature on printers, specifically asking for samples of print. I got brochures from Anadex, AXION, Centronics, MicroTek, NEC, Paper Tiger, and Printerm. Only AXION sent a sample—no descenders. But Paper Tiger sent a picture of their machine in action. With a magnifying glass I could discern p's, q's, y's, g's, and j's standing clumsily on the line. Printerm showed a blowup of a square inch of beautiful print that included no p's, q's, y's, g's, or j's. They *were* hiding something, I discovered when their local dealer innocently sent me a more inclusive sample. NEC was too expensive. The illustration of the MicroTek machine made me very suspicious, by showing a blank sheet of paper.

Centronics offered a model 737 which they claimed had "print quality suitable for text processing . . . ideal for microcomputer-based small business systems." They offered 18 other models, they had been in business since 1968, and their literature was straightforward. I pursued the matter. Hamilton-Avnet, a nationwide electronic supply house with a branch in Milwaukee, was advertising the Centronics 737 in *BYTE*. I called the 800 number in the ad, and one Tom Suzda quoted me $900. What's more he sent me a sample of print, as he said he would, after he hung up. Centronics had managed to make characters that didn't show the dots. Better still, they had designed them with **proportional spacing**, that is, spacing proportional to the actual width of each character. Unlike the letters on a typewriter, each of which occupies an equal amount of space, these letters occupied only what they needed: an 'i' took less than a 'w' and an 'n' took less than an 'm'. Therefore, print from the Centronics 737 looked almost like that of a book or magazine. And of course there were descenders. I was sold. But would a Centronics printer plug in to a Cromemco interface? In my *BYTE* browsing, the words "standard Centronics interface" were often repeated. I consulted myself, and my opinion was that the printer would indeed match the computer.

The catalog specifications of the Z-2D and DM20 indicated that they could be converted for 220-volt, 50-cycle AC operation in England, and Tech Support at Centronics assured me that by replacing the ribbon drive motor and the power transformer with parts available from them I could convert the 737.

As I ransacked my brains for every possible hitch in my proposed acquisition, I realized that one major prerequisite to the conversion of SITAR was the power to transfer the original program from Lawrence's PDP-11 to my new computer. It was absolutely necessary to work from an exact copy, because we knew it worked. SITAR consisted, all told, of 2,727 lines of cryptic words, arbitrary symbols, and punctuation, as many as contained in three books of *Paradise Lost* and even more complicated. To think of typing it into the Z-2D would be madness, and even if by chance it might be an exact copy, the suspicion that it wasn't would spread the locus of possible errors over the whole 2,727 lines, not just the lines Nick had changed, thus immeasurably complicating the task of debugging the conversion. Nothing but transfer by computer could guarantee accurate copies. It couldn't be done by mounting a disk or tape made by the PDP-11 on the Z-2D, because the PDP-11 could make no floppies and the Z-2D could read no tapes. Direct transmission by wire from one computer to the other was the only way. Alex said that a Cromemco could do it.

There remained the question of memory. Would 64K be enough? I needed enough memory, I thought then, for the compiler itself and the largest SITAR module it would have to compile. The largest module was 12K, but how big was the compiler? By phoning Microsoft, I found out that the compiler used 30K. Since 42 was well under 64, I decided that a Z-2D with 64 kilobytes of memory would serve my needs. The system I wanted, with $500 off for the Cromemco package, and a good price for the Beehive terminal would come to about $6,000. "Kay," I said, "this computer is going to cost six thousand dollars." "Six thousand dollars," she replied, batting an eye. "Are you sure you need that much?" "Yes," I said; "probably seven thousand before we're done." "Well," she said, "if you're absolutely sure that's what you want, why not?" But we both knew that we had left the life we had known and entered an unknown territory. I was bringing a computer into the family. Kay and I, and the Z-2D, the DM20, and the 737, and CDOS, Microsoft, and SITAR were going to travel together, and I was going to write. While there was life left in us.

On Thursday, the third of April, 1980, I crossed the Rubicon. I ordered a Cromemco Z-2D with 64 kilobytes of memory and a Beehive DM20 from Computerlab of Neenah, Wisconsin. On the 4th, I ordered a Centronics 737 printer from Hamilton-Avnet in Milwaukee.

CHAPTER III

CETOLOGY

Already we are launched upon the deep. ... It is but well to attend to a matter almost indispensable to a thorough appreciative understanding of the more special Leviathanic revelations and allusions of all sorts which are to follow.

MY OWN dazed and desperate hunt for the archetypal word processor, one pursued with no inconsiderable disruption of the regular economy of the household that I coerced and wheedled into cooperating with me, seems at times to reflect some small glints of Ahab's quest for the Great White Whale, Moby Dick. It may therefore be fitting that I, as Melville did before me, pause, before getting irretrievably lost in in my narrative, to attempt a rough taxonomic survey of the great class of computing machines to which the quarry I seek belongs.

To take as large a view of the matter as I can comprehend, I shall begin at the beginning; that is, with the word. Some time after man began to speak, he invented writing so that he could keep certain words for future reference. This writing at first took the form of pictures suggesting the thing or idea contained in the word, as exemplified by Egyptian hieroglyphs, Chinese characters, and international public information signs announcing dead end, men's room, filling station, and so forth. But evolution for the most part passed ideograms by and took the route opened up by another invention, the alphabet. This ingenious system represented the sounds, not the ideas, of the words it signified. With signs for only a few sounds, twenty-six in our case, people could write the words for millions of things and ideas. With writing thus simplified, movable, reusable types became feasible; Gutenberg in due course used these and a printing press for producing multiple copies of documents, and publishing came into being.

Centuries later, the linotype speeded up typesetting a notch or two by enabling one to set a piece of type by touching a key. The linotype saved the trouble of hunting for the right piece in a box, picking it out, and fitting it in by hand. The typewriter is essentially a linotype that makes only one copy. Typewriters enable anyone who can hit the right keys to produce writing that looks almost as good as printing. With carbons and stencils and Xerox machines, a typewriter can generate multiple copies. But all these devices are simple extensions of the printing press. After Gutenberg, the next great leap forward, in some ways the greatest leap forward since the invention of writing, was the introduction of the computer, which freed man from the burden of rewriting, resetting, or retyping his documents whenever he revised them.

What happened was something like this: writing found a new medium of expression. It was no longer carved in stone, scratched on clay tablets, or inscribed on parchment. A text became one single long line of characters, written on a perfectly elastic electronic medium that stretched for insertions and contracted with deletions. It was a long thin string of warm taffy, even easier to cut and splice than taffy is.

At first, computers were used very crudely. During the 1960s, almost all text was fed into computers on punched cards ("IBM cards"). The earliest method of inserting, deleting, and writing over was to find the card that needed changing and repunch it the way it should be. A better method was to have the computer itself find the place in the electronic image of the text and make the change according to instructions about what to do where— such as for instance, "change the second letter of the fifth word in the 52nd line to a 'p'," only much abbreviated. Under this system there were three ways to make the text worse than it was before: one could specify the wrong place, the wrong operation, or the wrong insertion or replacement. Because computer time was very expensive, economy dictated the submission of all known changes to a text in one single stream or "batch."

Using a computer this everything-at-once way is called **batch processing**, and for a long time batch processing was the only kind there was. In the late sixties, a better way of keeping a computer busy, called **time-sharing**, came into being. In this mode a number of people could use a computer at the same time. Or so it seemed to each one. Actually, the computer was visiting each user in turn for a few microseconds at a time, doing part of his job, asking him a question, or getting an answer, like a very busy waiter taking and filling orders at several tables so fast that you have the illusion that he's your waiter exclusively. Time-sharing is much more efficient than batch processing. Carrying on the waiter analogy, suppose the waiter serves one table its whole dinner, one course after another, and doesn't start another until that table has paid its bill. That's batch processing. It is immediately evident that he will spend a lot of time waiting for each course to be prepared, waiting for the diners to eat it, or waiting for them to ask for the check. If several tables share a waiter simultaneously, he can attend to one while he's waiting for the others. That's time-sharing.

Along with time-sharing came **interactive computing**. Since it always had work to do, the computer could afford to give you time to think. It even had time to prompt your thinking. Instead of getting a big batch of cards ready to submit, you simply sat down at a terminal of some sort and typed, "Hello". The computer then, typing back on the same terminal, asked who you were and what right you had to use its services. If your answers qualified you, it gave you access to its programs, your programs, and your data, which it kept in storage. The computer was all yours, and you could go to work.

Interactive computing can greatly simplify the process of revising text, because the computer waits on the editor, asking him for one element of the editing process at a time, pointing out errors, and giving him a second chance, eliminating the all-or-nothing batch approach. I can illustrate by describing the behavior of the program with which I am writing this book—that is, SITAR. Once admitted to the computer, I type, "Run SI-TAR", and after a bit, SITAR erases anything on the screen of my Beehive and types a question mark in the upper left-hand corner, inviting me to put my next request there. There are twelve different word-processing operations that I can bring into force at this time, but editing is the mode for composition, so I type, "EDIT", and press a button. SITAR answers, "What file?" and I type, "CETO", for that is what I have named the file of data that contains this chapter. Then it asks me what part of the file I wish to edit, and by quoting a key word, I tell it. It forthwith writes the designated passage on the screen.

Now I can make changes when and where they occur to me, free from the regimentation of the batch method. After I've inserted and deleted until I'm satisfied with what I have, I press a button, and the passage goes back into CETO, replacing the old version with the new. If at any point I make a mistake—misspell something, give a file name that doesn't exist, ask to see a place in the file that isn't there—SITAR in each case tells me what I have done wrong and gives me a chance to clarify the matter before taking the next step. All contemporary word processors are more or less interactive.

The first interactive systems for revising text evolved from program editors. Programs are written in lines decreed by computer law not to exceed a certain number of characters, usually less than eighty, each line containing at least one step of the program. To revise a line, one simply wrote the line number and followed it by the corrected version of the line, and the new version took the place of the old. This system might work well for poetry, but it was not very good for prose, where a change in the length of one line affects the arrangement of others. By making it possible to insert and delete material at a specified place in a line and to allow lines to grow several times beyond their official boundaries, and by writing another program to straighten out the ragged edges of the revised product, software magicians did manage to give these primitive program editors the unlimited power of insertion and deletion that prose processors have to have. All the same, text was always stored in lines, so that a large part of the program was devoted to undoing what need not have been done in the first place. For the logical unit of prose is the paragraph, not the line, and paragraphs can have any length you like.

But the biggest drawback of these systems was that, even if they were interactive, they didn't use video screens. You could make any change you wanted to, but you couldn't see what you were doing while you were doing it. Because they were made for interactive typewriters, there could be no living image of the text, showing the changes occurring as fast as they were made. The text was in the computer, and there was no way to look at it but to print it out on paper, a very slow process. Thus, it took three steps to make a change. First you asked the computer to print the line or lines in question. Then you gave instructions for the change. Then, to be sure you'd made the change correctly, you asked the computer to print the line again. Such systems of course could be operated from video terminals, but they used them simply to print before-and-after results, the same as if the screens were paper in a typewriter.

A good example of an early line-oriented interactive text-editing program is TECO, still going strong on thousands of DEC computers. TECO's commands to the computer consist of one or two characters each. They are "mnemonic characters" to the degree possible, selected so as to help one remember what they do. Some commands are preceded or followed by what programmers call an **argument**, which merely supplies further information for the computer to use in executing the command. Thus "I" means "insert," and "D" means "delete." "I" must be followed by an argument providing the string to be inserted, and "D" must be preceded by an argument giving the number of characters to be deleted. TECO has 151 more or less mnemonic commands. It uses an imaginary pointer to designate the place in a text where a change is to occur. You can't see this pointer because it exists only in the computer's memory. To find it when you have lost it, you may issue a command asking TECO to type everything on the current page up to the pointer.

Now let us suppose that I wish to remove the word "chapter" from a TECO page and replace it with "Cetology." The pointer is at the beginning of the page.

> Step 1: Put the pointer in front of the word "chapter." I must first know where on the page the word I want to change occurs. Since it probably occurs more than once, I had better type out a copy of the page. If I command "HT", TECO will type out the page. Having located on it the word I want to change, I may then either count the lines preceding the word and advance the pointer that many lines, or I may ask the pointer to search for the word "chapter." I take the latter course. On inspection, it appears that the word I want is the third instance of "chapter" on the page. To get to it, I command "3Schapter$." If the third instance of "chapter" is indeed the one I want, we have completed step one.

> Step 2: Make sure that this is the right place by having TECO type from the pointer to the end of the line: "T$"

> Step 3: Make the change by deleting all the letters (I must count them) in "chapter" and inserting "Cetology": "7DICetology$"

While programmer's tools were aspiring to be prose editors down in the computer center, up in the office typewriters were trying to become word processors, with even less success. By putting an ordinary tape recorder on an electric typewriter, you could record what you typed. When you played it back, the typewriter could automatically type what you had just written. If, while it played back, it also transferred the text to a second tape, you could stop it and write changes onto the second tape. To insert new matter, here's what you would do: play back tape one, transferring its contents to tape two and monitoring your progress on the typewriter; when the point of insertion arrives, stop the tape recorder; turn on tape two; type the new material onto the paper and onto tape two; continue transferring from tape one to tape two. To delete: when the typewriter gets to the point of deletion, stop the tape recorder; turn off tape two; turn on the first tape, and let it type out what you wish to skip; stop; turn on both tapes and continue transferring. Proceed in this fashion until the end of tape one. Tape two is the revised version.

Again, the difficulty of verifying a change as soon as it is made is a major problem. Did we transfer when we meant to skip, or skip when we meant to transfer? Did we forget to start tape two before making an insertion? For when we skipped, tape two should have been off and tape one on, and when we inserted, tape two should have been on and tape one off. Wait and see. Yet so great was the demand for the power of insertion and deletion that many thousands of such machines were sold, most of them IBM MT/STs—Magnetic Tape/Selectric Typewriters.

True word processors came into being when makers of business machines put video screens on a species of MT/ST so that one could watch what was happening to the text, took the keyboard away from the typewriter and gave it to the video screen, programmmed a computer to decide what tapes should be on and off during insertion and deletion, and used the keyboardless typewriter to print the recorded product of the interaction between the keyboard, video screen, and computer.

IBM, the self-designated leader of the industry, was unable or unwilling to make this quantum leap, even though it had the computers, the videoscopes, and the MT/STs, perhaps because its office products division was totally independent of its computer division. Its philosophy held that computers and videoscopes belonged in the computer room and that typewriters, however sophisticated, belonged in the office. To allow computers and scopes to proliferate into offices would weaken Data Processing's hold on computing. That way lay chaos.

But in the mid-70s chaos came anyway, brought on by competitors. IBM did not bring out a true word processor until the next decade, at least fifteen years after they had developed all the pieces of one and needed only to assemble them. This was nine years after the first true word processors were introduced by Lexitron and Linolex (and seven years after SITAR was assembled). By the time that IBM brought out its first true word processor, more than fifty different brands of word processors had infiltrated the offices of the nation; IBM had lost its grip. Soon after introducing its Displaywriter in 1981, IBM merged its computer and office products divisions.

When one surveys the species of word processors that came into being during this era, certain fundamental differences stand out. As I define it, a word processor consists of a videoscope— **Cathode Ray Tube, Video Display Terminal (CRT, VDT)**—a computer,[1] a keyboard, a medium[2] of permanent storage, and a printer. The videoscope of a word processor displays writing for inspection and revision. The keyboard is the means by which the writer puts his words on the screen and commands the computer. The computer alters and arranges the words on the screen at the behest of the writer. The medium of storage, usually a magnetic disk, keeps the writer's product for future reference. The printer, at the writer's request and under the computer's control, types on paper bodies of text that have been stored on the medium, following a format decreed by the writer.

In a typical session at the keyboard, the writer calls a unit text from disk storage, specifies segments of it for display on the screen, alters these segments to his liking, and then stores the

[1]The computer is often built into the CRT, but it is, nevertheless, always an entity and always present.

[2]In saying "medium," I fly in the face of current usage, by which any medium is called "a media," but as an English teacher I feel obliged, for the sake of accuracy, to preserve the singular form of the word. I confess that I want to scream when the marketer of a medium advertises under the slogan "Our media is our message."

improved version on the disk, perhaps making a printed copy of his work. If he is creating new text, he simply writes on a blank screen, revising as he goes, if he has the need.

CLASSES: Thus defined, word processors may be divided into two classes, depending upon whether their computers are enslaved or free. In the first case, the computer is entirely dedicated to one word-processing system; in the second, it can do anything else a computer can do, as well as process words. I call a word processor free if its owner is free to write his own programs on it or run ready-made ones that are sold on the open market. Word processors mounted on dedicated computers are often called "**stand-alone** word processors," but, alone or not, they stand only by virtue of a computer inside them.

ORDERS of word processors emerge when we discern whether a species gives a "full view" of a page of text or restricts the writer to a "window" through which he can see only part a page. For practical purposes, a full-view word processor may be defined as one whose screen holds at least fifty-six eighty-character lines. A window shows between twenty and twenty-four eighty-character lines. It seems axiomatic that the more text one can see at a time, the better one can revise. I rule out of consideration here "electronic typewriters" that display only one line at a time and some brands of microcomputers (like Apple II) that display only forty characters to a line. Such limited machines cannot qualify as word processors.

FAMILIES: In order to identify the family to which a word processor belongs, one must ascertain whether it is **page-oriented** or **document-oriented**. In computer lingo, "orientation" means something like "how we expect (or hope) the device will be used." Some systems assume that the *page* is the unit of words that will undergo processing and that a document, if desired, can be made by concatenating a certain set of pages. Other systems assume that the whole *document* is the unit that will undergo processing and that this document can be cut up into pages whenever pages are desired. As I define the term, we have document-orientation only if the system will *automatically* absorb any insertion for which there is space on the disk. One can reasonably expect to insert a page into a page or a chapter into a chapter. On the other hand, we have page-orientation if the system, by setting a physical limit to the size of a page and treating a document as an assembly of pages, will not absorb a large insertion unless the user performs a laborious multistep cut-and-paste operation. Page-oriented systems simply do not foresee large insertions.

GENERA emerge when we distinguish whether a word processor's editing powers are active or dormant. There are three powers of editing: insertion, deletion, and overwriting. I call these powers dormant if the number of key depressions required to insert, delete, or write over one character exceeds the theoretical minimum. Once the cursor is positioned, the minimum number of keystrokes for deleting a character is therefore one, and the minimum number of keystrokes for inserting or writing over a character is one or two, depending on which of these two functions happens to be already in force when either operation is desired. Unless writeover must be disengaged, only one keystroke is needed to insert or delete one character. With this exception, there is no reason whatsoever for extra keystrokes that some systems use to turn insertion or deletion on or off. When a word processor needs no extra keystrokes, it has what I call active editing powers.

At this point, some of my readers may be wishing to interpose an objection to the effect that I am splitting hairs in a peripheral concern. "If it takes a few extra keystrokes to do a thing," they may say, "what does it matter, as long as it can be done?" If so, I ask them to reflect seriously upon the question of why we have word processors in the first place. Is it so that we can have our right-hand margins straight instead of ragged? Is it so that our headings can be perfectly centered and our footnotes can be unerringly numbered? Is it so that the computer can check our spelling, decide where to hyphenate our words, and choose the best place to start a new page?

Except for making straight right-hand margins, a good typist with an old-fashioned typewriter can do all of these things, and a common, ordinary computer, without being watched through a screen, can straighten margins, center headings, check spelling, and terminate lines or pages in the proper places. What even the best typist cannot do is insert and delete without having to retype at least a page to get get perfect copy. If it were not for the power of insertion and deletion, could anyone justify spending eight thousand dollars to replace a typewriter or two? These powers are by no means trivial.

Furthermore, extra keystrokes are distracting. Imagine what it would be like if all we had to do was look at a point on a page of text, wish a word inserted, and find it there. We have not reached this point yet, but we are getting close. When the method of pointing, inserting, and deleting is as simple and efficient as it can be, we approach a state where these operations take place subliminally, as they do when we shift for capital letters. We can almost think a change into a text.

Some readers may also question why I have fixed on so few differentiae as a basis for identifying species. A recent survey lists 60 features by which to measure word processors and not one of those that I do.[3] My reason for the narrow focus is the universality, irrelevance, or inconsequence of said features. Some of them have to do with how many different ways you can delete. I pass them by because one good way is enough. I pass by "block move"—the capacity to move a block from one place to another in a text or from one text to another—because it is standard. For the same reason I ignore "word wraparound," by virtue of which whole words are "wrapped" from line to line when insertion or deletion threatens their integrity.

Neither do I consider any features that have to do with formatting the finished product. Since all **formatters** at least cut a

---

[3] "*Infoworld*'s Guide to Word-Processing Programs," January 17, 1983.

text into lines, paragraphs, and pages while they justify, indent, and center, we can safely ignore those features. I ignore automatic placement of footnotes at the bottom of the page and automatic production of double columns because they are luxuries. But the main reason I rule out formatting features is that I believe they pertain to printing, rather than editing.

What boots it if our word processor can generate proportional spacing, multiple fonts, multiple type sizes, multiple alphabets, special symbols, underlining, boldface, italics, and so on, if our printer can't achieve them? On the other hand, supposing we do have a printer that can do all of these things and our word processor can indeed generate them, what boots it if its editing system is inadequate? Only if we see the formatter as an adjunct of the printer can we think sensibly about word processors. Many word-processing systems provide the formatter as a separate program, thereby recognizing its essential autonomy.

Any editing system can prepare text for any formatting and printing system, however elaborate, because the basic principle of formatting by computer is very simple. One merely establishes a set of codes by which to signal the beginnings and endings of fonts, alphabets, type sizes, paragraphs, vertical and horizontal spacing, and so on. The writer, using the editing system, embeds these codes in the text. The formatting software translates the codes for the printer as it feeds the text to the printing device, and the printer responds with the proper fonts, alphabets, and spacing as it hammers out the text. Printing devices range all the way from an ordinary typewriter to a computer-driven phototypesetter with a theoretically infinite set of fonts, alphabets, sizes, and so on. Furthermore, by virtue of the fact that text is easily transferable to other computers, by telephone or by a magnetic medium, any printing device is available to any word processor. Therefore, it would be short-sighted to put much emphasis on a single word processor's built-in formatting capacity.

I also rule out another much cried-up feature: whether "you see what you get." You see what you get if you can see on your video screen what you will get when you print. But since what you

EVOLUTION OF WORD PROCESSING

WORD
Speech
Writing
Alphabet
Manual Typesetting
Mechanical Typesetting
Computer Typesetting
Interactive Editing
Screen

Linotype
Typewriter

Tape to Tape Editing MT/ST
Batch Editing

No Screen
TECO

WORD PROCESSORS

Slave — Free

Slave

Full View — Window

Page — Document
Dormant Active — Dormant Active
Jacquard — Dictaphone
Magna SC
Vydec

Page — Document
Dormant Active — Dormant Active
CRT — Xerox

Free

Full View — Window

Page — Document
Dormant Active — Dormant Active

Page — Document
Dormant Active — Dormant Active

Window

Page — Document
Dormant Active — Dormant Active
IBM — Vedit — Syntrex
Lexitron — Wang- — DEC-
Magcard — writer — mate
SCREEN — Word- — SUTPR
Scripsit — star

52

get depends on your printer, seeing what you get is another relative matter. What good is it that your system can display 180 characters to a line if your printer can't print that many? Or, if your printer is going to be a phototypesetter, who can afford a video system to match its infinite capacity? Such a device could cost five figures. Therefore, I consider here neither formatting nor video display of formatting. We want to know whether a species is a bird or a fish before we begin to discuss the shape of its dorsal fin.

We are now in a position to catalog several of the most commonly observed species by means of the differentiae I have laid down. Since my data were collected in the fall of 1981, the reader is warned that by the time he reads this chapter some of these species will be extinct, numerous mutations will have occurred, and many new varieties will have evolved.

CLASS, slave; ORDER, window; FAMILY, page-oriented; GENUS, dormant

Lanier No Problem Typewriter: In its physical appearance the Lanier machine, with its screen molded to its keyboard, does suggest a typewriter.[4] But on close inspection one finds the analogy imperfect. The screen is restricted to a twenty-eight line window of a full page which doesn't behave at all like a piece of paper. Not until the typist has written 29 lines on stationary video "paper" does the No Problem Typewriter scroll like a typewriter, and then the top of the page begins to disappear.

---

[4] The typewriter analogy is carried further in the *Operator Training Manual*: "At first glance the Screen and Keys of the No Problem Typing System may remind you of a computer. A computer! For people who are not 'into' computers, the first reaction can be one of mistrust. Let's create a more accurate image. Your new typewriter is, quite simply, two things. First, it is an obedient servant that will relieve you of tedious, repetitive chores. For instance, if you make an error, you don't have to get out the correction fluid. Backspace to the error and it will vanish! ... Also you don't have to worry about carriage returns. The typewriter can tell when it's needed and will do it automatically. The second feature is that your typewriter has a memory. ... "

The analogy to a typewriter holds better when one comes to consider the No Problem's page-orientation. When a typewriter page is full, it is full, and so is the No Problem's.[5] To insert more text when the page is full, one may execute the following cut-and-paste procedure, essentially splitting the page in two, writing the insertion as a new page, and then adding all three pages to the original document in the right order:

1) Record the overflowing page on the magnetic medium under a new name (press keys marked FILE and m; write "Full Page", or whatever name you wish to give it; press the key marked EXEC). 2) Recall Full Page to the screen (press FILE and r; write "Full Page"; press EXEC). 3) Delete everything on Full Page that follows the point of insertion (position your cursor anywhere after the point where you wish to make the insertion; press SCREEN and R; position your locator at exactly the place where your insertion is to begin; press EXEC). Because the R (Remainder) command deletes only what shows on the screen, any unscrolled text below the screen will have to be scrolled up and treated to one or more repetitions of step 3. 4) Record what's left of Full Page by repeating step 1, but this time name the file "First Part", to help you find it again later. 5) Repeat steps 2, 3, and 4 on Full Page, but this time delete everything *preceding* the point of insertion and record it under the name "Last Part". 6) Write your insertion on the screen, and, repeating step 1, record it as, let's say, "Insertion". 7) Delete the original page from the disk (press FILE, DEL/CHAR, and p; write "Page 7", supposing that was its name; press EXEC). 8) Insert "First Part" into the old document after page 6 (press FILE, INSERT, and t; write "First Part" and "Page 6"; press EXEC). 9) Repeating step 8, insert Insertion and Last Part into their proper places in the original document. If you wish, you may at this point repaginate the whole document to even up the page lengths, but perhaps it would be better to wait until all possible insertions and deletions have been made.

Minor insertion and deletion on the No Problem require at least one more keystroke than the mimimum theoretical num-

---

[5] The No Problem's page can, admittedly, be 99 lines long, but that limit is nevertheless absolute.

ber. After an insertion one must press a CANCEL button, which realigns the text. Hence no deletions may take place while insertion is in force.

CLASS, slave; ORDER, full view; FAMILY, page-oriented; GENUS, dormant

AM Jacquard J425: The outstanding feature of this species is its full page display screen. The statement in *Datapro Reports* (August 1981) that "total storage of one document is 6,656 characters" (about 80 lines) must be in error in the light of the system's apparent design. "Total storage of one *page* is 6,656 characters" would make better sense. If my emendation is correct, the system must be page-oriented, like the No Problem Typewriter, and, like that machine, would require some sort of cut-and-paste operation for a major insertion. For minor insertions the J425 requires two more keystrokes than the minimum theoretical number to reform the text, thus falling into the genus dormant.[6]

A B Dick Magna SL: This species may easily be identified by its singular full-page display screen, which is bounded by two video rectangles, one inside the other. The outside rectangle delineates the edges of the paper on which the text will actually be typed, and the inside rectangle delineates the space that the text will occupy on that page. If insertions cause the text to overflow the bottom margin, this species beeps, signalling the writer to correct the problem. Overcoming this page boundary requires a cut-and-paste procedure similar to that outlined for the Lanier No Problem Typewriter. Minor insertions and deletions require more than the theoretical minimum number of keystrokes because

[6] Based partly on a telephone conversation with Joe Roloff, local representative. AM (Addressograph-Multigraph) International, which has marketed the Jacquard 425, filed for Chapter 11 bankruptcy on April 14th, 1982 (*New York Times*, 15 April 1982).

they leave irregular line lengths requiring the action of a CLOSE UP button. In a fully active system, realignment would be automatic.

Exxon Vydec 1800: This species is distinguished by a large display screen 60 lines long and 100 characters wide, capable of showing side-by-side segments of two documents at once, either of which can be revised. When a page overflows, this species' screen "wiggles" and rejects further typing, according to Judy Keenan, customer support officer at Vydec's Milwaukee office. Recovering from the full page condition requires a cut-and-paste process like that described for the No Problem. In order to make a minor insertion, one must disable the power of deletion and vice versa, so that the system requires more keystrokes than the theoretical minimum.

CLASS, slave; ORDER, full view; FAMILY, document-oriented; GENUS, dormant

Dictaphone Dual Display: This one is recognized by its dual display, the videoscope showing a full page of text in green characters, and a single-line display on the top of the keyboard showing in 37 orange characters what is currently being typed or advisory messages from the computer. It also has a ZOOM button that magnifies the text on the screen. Because it holds the text as one continuous document, up to 256 potential pages long, until one presses a pagination button, this species belongs to the document-oriented family. After pagination has been invoked, the system continues to be document-oriented as far as the operator is concerned. It now simply repaginates the whole document automatically whenever a given page exceeds or falls short of the declared page length. Insertion and deletion each require two extra keystrokes, one to get into the desired mode and another to get out of it.

CLASS, free; ORDER, full view; FAMILY, page-oriented; GENUS, dormant

CPT 8000: In the interests of computer science, I shall describe this fantastic machine in considerable detail, for I fear it to be in danger of extinction. This species emulates a typewriter more perfectly than any other word processor I have observed. It shows what looks exactly like a piece of white 8½ by 11 typing paper on its black screen. As one types, the letters appear in black, and the top edge of the video paper rolls up a line with each carriage return. At the bottom of the screen is a black rule, calibrated to show where each letter will fall, which has simulated white tabs and margin stops on it that can be slid back and forth on the rule by means of the margin and tab keys. All typing takes place on a line just above the rule. A white pointer, indicating where the next letter will fall, travels across the rule as one types. The ERASE key leaves blank space in the text, just as if it were typist's white-out fluid, and there is even a margin release key, in case one wants to type past the margin. And, as with a typewriter, whenever one wishes to make a change in text that has passed above the rule, one rolls the line to be changed back down to the rule.

However, in handling strikeovers and minor insertions and deletions above the rule the machine does and does not behave like a typewriter. There are no INSERT and DELETE keys, just as there are none on a typewriter. When the machine is in its normal state, any character we strike goes onto the paper above the pointer, and the pointer moves one space to the right, just as with a typewriter. If we backspace and strike a character, it goes on top of the character at the pointer position, just like a typed character, but unlike a typed character it obliterates the one underneath, a distinct concession to the electronic medium.

To allow insertion and deletion, the machine again deviates from the model, but it does not let go altogether. With most typewriters, it is possible to hold the carriage still and type in one

place. CPT adopts a typewriter-like HOLD button but endows it
with special properties that enable electronic insertion and deletion. If we type in HOLD mode, the pointer will hold the rest of
a line, pushing it out of our way as we type. If we backspace in
HOLD mode, the pointer holds still and sucks the rest of the line
towards itself as the backspace key deletes characters that appear
over the pointer. Thus we accomplish minor insertions and deletions.

When we come to making substantial changes, the simula-
tion yields again in several respects. Let us suppose that we have
left out a sentence that has passed above the rule and we want to
put it back in. Here's how we might insert the missing sentence:
By striking LINE and then DOWN as many times as it takes to
get there, we roll the place of insertion down to the rule, just as
we might do with an electric typewriter. But suppose that the
new sentence must go into the middle of the line. The 8000
meets this difficulty by allowing us to move less than a full line
up from below the rule. In order to use this facility, we must
move the line containing the place of insertion below the rule.
On a typewriter we can't see below the rule, but the 8000 con-
cedes three lines of visible text down there. Now, looking at the
line we wish to break, we bring the first part back up by striking
WORD and then ADJ as many times as there are words to bring
up. We now have blank paper to the right of the place of insertion, and we can type on it, so we write in the missing sentence.
But suppose there isn't enough space on the line for the whole
sentence? The machine solves this difficulty by having its carriage return always produce a new blank line, in essence stretch-
ing the paper while it holds the rest of the text in a vise-like grip
below the rule. Thus we can write our new sentence above the
rule without disturbing what we've done already. But suppose the
insertion ends short of the right margin, throwing off all the line
endings below the rule. Fortunately, as we ADJust the rest of
paragraph, it reforms to fit the margins in force above the rule.

We can make major deletions below the rule by means of a
SKIP button that enables us to skip a word, line, paragraph, or

page, before we ADJust succeeding, words, lines, paragraphs, or pages to the "paper" above the rule.[7]

Now, what happens if our insertion is too long to fit on the page? In its response to this problem the CPT 8000 hedges a little in its commitment to the typewriter model. When a typewritten page is full, it is full, and there is no way to add any more except by cutting and pasting. So also with the 8000. The *Operator's Manual* (Revised Edition, 1981, Appendix A) tells what steps to take if the message "SCREEN IS TOO FULL" appears above the page: "Action: 1. Record the page. 2. If the system has locked, remove all disks, press the RESET button and insert the program disk." The manual does not tell us one hard fact: that when we press the RESET button, our whole page will disappear from the face of the earth. But that is an unfailing consequence of resetting a computer.[8] If, however, we do record the page before the computer locks, that still does not solve the problem of an insertion that would force the page to exceed its limit. To handle this condition, we proceed with a multistep cut-and-paste routine similar to that used with the Lanier machine.

The main differences between the CPT 8000 and a typewriter, then, are that the HOLD button enables insertion and deletion, that we can see below the rule, that new white lines occur above the rule whenever we hit a carriage return, that we can move up less than a whole line from below the rule, that lines moving up adjust to the space available above, that we can skip any material below the rule, and that the computer will repage the document after we cut and paste.

The CPT 8000's computer recently became free. By adopting CP/M as an alternative operating system, it can use any of the

---

[7] In the 8000's way of handling insertions and deletions, one detects a vestige of the MT/ST, on which we revise by skipping and inserting as we transfer text from one tape to another.

[8] By means of a three-step, fifteen-keystroke process, we can preset a "line limit" so that the system automatically records a full page and sets up a new blank page when the declared limit is reached, but if we neglect to do so, we must suffer the consequences of "SCREEN IS TOO FULL".

large stock of programs available for CP/M, including dozens of word processors. This mutation may temporarily suspend its extinction, but its very success in simulating the typewriter, itself a doomed species, will soon select it for the fate of the dinosaurs.

CLASS, free; ORDER, full view; FAMILY, document-oriented; GENUS, dormant

Xerox 860 Information Processor: For less money, this system may be had with a window on the page instead of a full view. For more money, one may have the benefit of an ingenious cursor-positioning device called CAT, a compass-like pad beside the terminal. To position the cursor, one puts a finger on the perimeter of the pad at the bearing of the desired spot. By putting two fingers on the perimeter, one can make it move faster.

The user may choose whether he wants a document paginated or not. If he does, pagination occurs automatically after any change affecting page length. Any amount of text may be inserted, up to the capacity of the disk on which the document is filed. Because insertion and deletion both require two steps, these powers must be declared dormant. The owner of an 860 is free to write his own programs in the 860's form of BASIC.

CLASS, free; ORDER, window; FAMILY, document-oriented; GENUS, dormant

IBM Displaywriter: The keyboard of this species is attached to the videoscope by means of a coiled cord, and it is sometimes observed in the operator's lap. Since the standard CP/M operating system is available for this machine, enabling it to use the thousands of programs and dozens of programming languages written for CP/M, the computer is free. The Displaywriter can hold text either as a single document or in pages. In either case, the system silently absorbs major insertions without any help from the operator.

The Displaywriter's designers decided to omit entirely the capacity to write over text, so that any character typed on the keyboard is inserted at the cursor position. Since the capacity to write over a string entails mode-changing keystrokes and causes errors due to confusion of modes, this omission may be an advantage. If one substitutes a large word for a small one, he will have to insert some letters anyhow and might better use an insert/ delete operation instead. Another acute recognition of text-editing reality is the Displaywriter's special deletion key, which causes the computer to remove all text on the screen from the cursor position up to the next character struck on the keyboard. Hence, by striking a space, one deletes a word at a time; by striking a period, one deletes the rest of the sentence. But since one cannot delete any characters at all without pressing a key to enter DELETE mode and then pressing another to return to INSERT mode, its powers of insertion and deletion must be considered dormant.[9]

Lexitron 1303: Although this species has a twenty-two-line screen, it manages to simulate the sixty-six-line page of a typewriter by showing the top, bottom, left, and right margins as lines on the screen. When, through the window, we look at the top of a page, we see the top and sides; when we look at the middle, we see just the sides; and when we look at the bottom, we see the bottom and sides. Like a typewriter, it keeps its typing point on one line, seven lines from the bottom of the screen. It also provides a button that displays a reduced but untouchable full page, as if through the wrong end of a telescope, to enable inspection of page layout. In its orientation, the 1303 entirely ignores its presumptive model, for after any amount of insertion or deletion, it automatically repaginates the whole document.

[9] The backspace key deletes and closes up text as it backspaces. But although active deletion while backspacing is useful, deletion in front of the cursor, some form of which is almost mandatory, is the differentia in effect here.

Its mode of insertion is archaic, taking three steps to accomplish: (1) open up the space needed, (2) write the text to be inserted, and (3) reform the paragraph. Deletion also takes a reformatory step. This species is relatively free, because the owner can create his own special-purpose programs in Microsoft BASIC and run any programs in this language that are sold on the open market.[10]

Peachtree Software Magic Wand or PeachText: Hitherto, we have observed stand-alone word processors, some of which could behave as computers if necessary. With Magic Wand, we come upon a hardier form—the parasitic word-processing program that can adapt to many different kinds of host computers. Magic Wand solves the problem of page limits by not establishing any pages whatsoever. When the document is finished, Magic Wand paginates it while feeding the printer. Minor insertions and deletions require no extra keystrokes, but because the system takes an inconvenient amount of time to reform text after revision, its powers of insertion and deletion must be considered dormant.

Cromemco SCREEN: This exemplar is a piece of software made exclusively for one make of microcomputer, the Cromemco. But, although the word processor is enslaved to Cromemco, the computer on which it runs is free to operate under any programs created or purchased by its owner, including any programs written for CP/M. SCREEN holds a document as a single entity until it is printed. Insertion and deletion are dormant because the system doesn't recover instantly from an insertion and because both require two more keystrokes than necessary.

Radio Shack TRS-80 Scripsit: Like SCREEN, this species works only on one make of computer, but that computer may also be

---

[10] Probably because their device requires a special version, Lexitron sells Microsoft BASIC for $3,500 (*Datapro Reports*, June 1981). The market price for the standard version hovers around $300.

the host of hundreds of programs that have been written for this machine. Although Scripsit holds a document in pages, it is truly a document-oriented system. When, for example, page 3 overflows, the extra material automatically goes onto page 3.1 and then onto page 3.2 or 3.3, if necessary, up to page 3.9. Because Scripsit understands these numbers, it can automatically repage or print a document with pages and subpages in the proper order. But because minor insertion is encumbered by two extra keystrokes, Scripsit falls into genus dormant.

Compuview Products VEDIT: Another parasitic word processor. In respect to all four characteristics under consideration here, VEDIT differs little from Magic Wand. It is a piece of CP/M software.

Wangwriter: This species may be identified by the tiny dots between all the words on its screen. It is sometimes important for the operator of a Wangwriter to know whether he or she has a space or nothing at the end of a line, and the tiny dot tells which is the case. The system holds a document as a document unless one wishes to break it into pages by pressing a pagination button at some time. Otherwise one may wait for the system to do the job as it prints. Even if the document is paginated, any Wang "page" can hold "126 screenloads" (manual, p. 90), which is about 40 pages, long enough for most insertions one might have in mind. Wangwriter's powers of insertion and deletion are dormant, however, because deletion requires two steps and insertion three. Nevertheless, a Wang word processor won a John Henry contest with TECO a few years ago, in which four expert editors entered a short memorandum, modified two business letters, and corrected an excerpt from a text on philosophy. With the same expert operators, TECO averaged 47 minutes for the four tasks, and Wangwriter averaged 24.[11] Because CP/M can

[11] Roberts, T. L. "Evaluation of Computer Text Editors," Ph.D. dissertation, Department of Computer Science, Stanford University, November

take over a Wangwriter, it is a free computer as well as a word processor.

Micropro Wordstar: This parasitic species first flourished on CP/M computers but has migrated to many other kinds. It achieves document orientation by means of "dynamic page breaks" which are always adjusting to insertions and deletions. They exist simply as lines on the videoscope until the document is printed. Although Wordstar can be set up so that any character struck will be inserted, and its delete key is always active, its insistence on dividing text into lines makes it impossible for it to display the final effect of editing without extra keystrokes. As text is entered, Wordstar obligingly puts a carriage return at the end of every line for us and wraps any incomplete words onto the next line. But if we move back into an already completed paragraph and make insertions or deletions, these carriage returns, now embedded in the text, are pushed into the middle of the next line or drawn back from the margin so that now, because a carriage return always starts a new line, we have very ragged right margins. To reform the paragraph, we must type CONTROL/B and wait until Wordstar, undoing what it just did, puts the carriage returns back on the ends of lines—for the time being. In any case, wraparound materializes so slowly on the screen that a burst of typing speed at the end of a line will beat it, and if we want to see what we are doing, we will have to wait for wraparound to catch up. These characteristics put Wordstar in category dormant.

CLASS, free; ORDER, window; FAMILY, document-oriented; GENUS, active

Syntrex Aquarius (marketed by Olivetti): The Aquarius word processor is mounted on a computer that is free (as of May

---

1979, and Roberts, T. L., *Xerox Research Report* SSL79-9, described in *Computing Surveys*, March 1981, p. 43ff.

1982) to operate under CP/M and use all the computing power that CP/M entails. It is page-oriented only to the extent that one may call for any page by number, but its pages are not poured in concrete. For moving blocks of text from one place to another in the document under revision (or to another document), Aquarius has two keys called CUT and PASTE. One simply marks the block to be moved and strikes CUT to take it into temporary storage. Then one marks the point where it is to be inserted and strikes PASTE to complete the operation. Upon pasting in the block, the computer repaginates the whole document. Because INSert and DELete keys are always active (unless one wishes to write over something), Aquarius achieves the theoretical minimum number of keystrokes for these operations and easily qualifies for genus active.

Digital Equipment Corporation DECmate: This species holds text as a single document until it is printed, at which time it paginates as it goes. As with the Displaywriter, insertion is permanently active, disabling the possibility of writing over text segments. Though insertion and deletion are active, DECmate retains a vestige of Anton Chernoff's TECO. Editing action is restricted to one line of the screen, as with the Lexitron and CPT systems. It may be easier to move a cursor to the place to be changed than to move a whole screenful of text so that the place to be changed lands on the action line. DECmate is also a DEC computer, free to make use of a vast library of programs in DEC BASIC that has been growing for more than a decade.

"SITAR": I put the name in quotations because some features of it belong to the SITAR I wish I had instead of the one I do have. In its actual form, this species is so rare that no more than a hundred people have ever seen it. It can be observed only on Lawrence University's PDP-11 or on my own Cromemco Z-2D. In all its incarnations, it has used a free computer, and it will work on DEC's RSTS, Cromemco's CDOS, and CP/M. It belongs to the document-oriented family of word processors, treating a text as one long single string until it is broken up into lines, paragraphs, and pages by a formatter. On RSTS, the formatter is Jim Evans's RUNOFF, and on CDOS, it is Cromemco's FORMAT. It has no CP/M formatter at present, but it could use Magic Wand's or that of any other CP/M word processor whose formatter is a separate entity.

The SITAR that is supposed to be would have active powers of insertion and deletion. At present one must hold down the CONTROL key during deletion, and that step constitutes one more keystroke than the minimum. The original SITAR, using a 1973 Beehive, did not require this extra keystroke. Thus its current dormancy arises from a regressive mutation in its hardware, not its original design. It also lacks two desirable features common to almost all word processors today: block move and word wraparound. As it is now, I must transfer a text file to Cromemco SCREEN in order to move a block of text from one place to another. And my DM20 wraps around character by character to compensate for insertions and deletions, instead of word by word, leaving broken words at the beginnings and endings of lines.

The facts in this survey have been accumulated from *Data Pro Reports on Word Processors*, operator's manuals, live demonstrations, and telephone conversations with dealers. To the best of my knowledge, these analyses fit the facts available in the fall of 1981. I have tried to be absolutely sure about the way the machines work, but the manuals are sometimes obscure, marketing personnel often use terms loosely, demonstrations can mislead, and it isn't always easy to communicate accurately by telephone.

I hope that my readers now have some small inkling of the long slow march toward modern word processing, the almost explosive proliferation of species that has occurred in less than one decade, and the numerous, various, and curious specimens that had found comfortable or uneasy habitats in the homes and offices of our world by 1982. If I had the means, the patience, and the time for such a pursuit, I might have attempted a more encyclopedic survey, but my little inquiries have uncovered the existence of so many types that even Audubon might have despaired, had he studied word processors instead of birds. Add to the disheartening immensity of the task my apprehension, abetted by rumor and confirmed by the annals of the marketplace, of the futility of recording so many species that are doomed to imminent extinction, and the even greater futility of describing exemplars that can mutate almost on the instant of an executive whim. The class at least will survive and flourish. It is better, then, that I should proceed with my narrative.

CHAPTER IV

THE JAWS THAT BITE, THE CLAWS THAT CATCH!

THE DAY after I ordered my computer system, Kay and I flew to Yucatán to begin the first term of my sabbatical leave. Eastern Airlines dropped us in Mérida, the capital city, in the early middle of the night, and a mad taxi driver threaded us through a labyrinth of narrow streets to our hotel. Unable to settle down, we went out into the street and sat on a cement bench in front of a very old church and watched a restaurant close and straggling traffic rattle by. Some students (they had books) seemed amused at something: was it us? The scene was absolutely foreign. The people were short, wide, black-haired, and copper-colored, and we were tall, thin, and somewhat gray.

Next morning it was hot, and we were in the middle of an immense, flat, thickly packed city, where everyone was selling panama hats and hammocks, in Spanish mostly. Only a block from our hotel was the *zócalo*, the large, tree-shaded main plaza, with a round stone platform in the middle of it, where a great many people seemed to be wasting time, if not shining shoes or selling hats or hammocks or ice cream. On one side of the *zócalo* was the house of the Montejos, who had conquered Yucatán. In case you forgot it, they had framed their door with two long thin stone knights about fifteen feet tall standing on two short wide heads without bodies. A very old tall thin pallid direct descendant showed us around the magnificent dilapidated formal rooms of this house for a few pesos.

Across the square was the statehouse—a large colonnaded courtyard four stories high, the grand staircases and galleries painted with many huge murals depicting the heroic agonies of the Maya in their struggle against Spanish and Mexican oppression. On the other two sides of the square were the cathedral, four times bigger and thicker than anything else in sight, and the handsome city hall, whose tower told the time.

Beyond the Montejo side of the square, we found the marketplace, an endless maze of tiny shops, selling stationery, piglets, doves, statues of saints, limes, papayas, rum, pots and pans, lassos, embroidered shirts, fish, chickens, blue jeans, very hot food, raw meat, blouses, watermelons, toilets, hats, TVs, hammocks, auto parts, comic books, everything costing less than they told you first, the haggling generally accompanied by bottles of icy Coca-Cola or Montejo beer—"The taste that conquers"—and loud zero-fidelity Mexican music.

It could have been Chandni Chowk in Delhi, but instead of saris, the tub-shaped women wear brilliantly embroidered blindingly white knee-length tub-shaped dresses, over lace petticoats showing four inches below, with a dark silk shawl about six feet long looped variously on the neck and shoulders. They can feed babies, sit on the curb, or eat watermelon without ever getting dirty: for us, that was the miracle of Yucatán.

After a week of churches, museums, and hot walks among the sisal planters' run-down 19th-century French mansions—a fine preamble to cool evenings by the hotel pool watching the setting sun hit the cathedral towers while sipping icy martinis, amid occasional gusts of rain—we decided that we were ready to conquer Yucatán. Aunt Janet had arrived, and we had made trial sallies in an air-conditioned rented car to scorching ruins at Dzibilchaltún and Uxmal. Our itinerary would be Uxmal again, Chichén Itzá, Cancun on the east coast, and a beach between there and Felipe Carillo Puerto to the south; altogether we drove 1,000 miles.

Fortunately, we were forced to stay in first-class hotels, there being no second-class ones. Best of all was the Hacienda Uxmal: colonnades surrounding a spacious courtyard full of exotic trees and giant forms of American house plants, no two alike, some flowering, and warbling screeching whistling birds, surrounding a large pool dive-bombed by crazy wheeling swallows, drinking on the wing; scores of laughing Mayan waiters and waitresses in spotless white; antique decor, palatial rooms, drinkable tap water, cakes of clear ice.

It wasn't easy to appreciate the ruins properly, to imagine smooth marble roads where now lay only dusty beaten paths and see solemn parades of brightly feathered totem-bearing Mayas where now walked only tall thin white people (getting pink) using the ruins as background for pictures of each other.

But I think we saw for ourselves what the textbooks had led us to expect. Uxmal was the authentic Mayan site: it illustrated a Greek love of order and balance, buildings framed by other buildings, using countless faces of the rain god Chac four feet square—with beetling brows, popping eyeballs, fishhook noses, stuck-out ears, hissing cat's mouths—arrayed in vertical and horizontal rows to form borders, frames, and corners, so that from a distance they made an abstract design, even though only one face in a hundred still had every one of its parts. And pyramids built on pyramids until they became so steep that climbing them was a death-defying experience.

Chichén Itzá, the work of barbarian invaders, was randomly laid out and totally lacking in restraint: temple columns made to look like fanged rattlesnakes coming down over something; two hundred square columns carved in bas-relief representing people doing things in gorgeous costumes, now very hard to make out; a platform as big as a ferryboat faced entirely with stone skulls and used for storing real ones; a bas-relief in the soccer field showing the grand climax of the game—a fountain of blood gushing from a beheaded competitor. Inside the main pyramid, at the top of a steep tunnel discovered by archeologists, in a dank inner sanctum left behind when the Itzás built upwards, remained a reclining humanoid Chacmool glaring straight at us and a jade-decorated jaguar—workbenches for human sacrifice, not in times of dire necessity as with the Maya, but day after day, in shifts. Chichén Itzá gave me nightmares in which I was trying to behave splendidly while being skinned alive so that a priest could wear my skin like a shirt—as I had seen illustrated in a book.

Fleeing the unsettling experience of Chichén Itzá, we hastened to the beaches. Cancun offered little more than a hundred thousand seaview bedrooms to accommodate airline package deals. We searched the coast and came to Akumal (Turtle Bay) sixty miles south of there, once a center for deep sea treasure-hunting. The sea was crystal clear and turquoise, the sand was pure white, cool, and powdery. A great coral reef calmed the waves, and a grove of coconut trees lined the beach. At the hotel you could stay in half of an enlarged Mayan hut, or you could have a handsome modern living room by the surf which slept five and had an icebox. We chose the latter. The hotel dining room was round and served a hundred people in grand hotel style under an enormous conical thatched roof. After being asked once, the Mariachi band played Las Palomas for us every time we ate dinner. Under water, using snorkels, we saw enough strange and wonderful fish and coral to fill several *National Geographics*, and cannons and anchors too. That's all there was at Akumal except for twenty-odd ocean villas whose fanciful architects must have been given a free rein.

In the midst of the marvels of Yucatán, I was sometimes, waking in the middle of the night from dreams of human sacrifice, plagued by nagging doubts. Refusing to abide by conventional wisdom, I had rejected Cromemco's printer, terminal, and software in preference of my own choices. And while all kinds of word-processing software costing only one or two hundred dollars were easily obtainable for microcomputers, I insisted on converting my own SITAR, designed and written for a PDP-11, to this far different system. Not only must all these diverse entitities concur with each other, but they must all agree to perform at 220 volts in England—if not destroyed in transit. Was my father's spirit of self-reliance leading me out of my depth?

We returned to Appleton on Sunday, the 27th of April. I now had a month in which to make sure that my computer worked before we took it to The Lake, where Nick would convert SITAR. By now the computer certainly should have arrived, and naturally the first thing I did Monday morning was call Computerlab. Alex said that the Z-2D was there but that it hadn't been checked out. As for the Beehive, it was still on its way; he would check on it. I didn't mind that delay so much, because I could borrow Lawrence's DM20, but expressed my utter dismay that the computer wasn't ready and did my best to bring it home to him that quick delivery was mandatory.

My printer, being in scarce supply, was not expected for another week, but just to make sure everything was all right, I called Hamilton-Avnet in Milwaukee. Tom Suzda, who had sold me the 737, wasn't there, but Jim Strand said he'd try to find out. What he found out after a long inquiry was that there had been a hitch at the factory, and Hamilton-Avnet's shipment of 737s would not arrive in Milwaukee for another month. This would not do. I told Jim that Tom Suzda had promised me delivery by next week, that I was leaving for New Hampshire in three weeks, that I must have it. He put me on hold for several more minutes and then came back to say that Hamilton-Avnet would not get delivery for another month.

I couldn't wait. I determined I would bypass Hamilton-Avnet and buy the printer direct from the factory, if I could. I then called the Centronics factory in New Hampshire, not far from The Lake, told them my story, and asked what was the fastest way to get a 737. My interlocutor replied, after only a brief check, that Hamilton-Avnet should have received their 737s by now. I relayed this information with considerable heat to Jim Strand in Milwaukee. He could only reiterate that as far as he could find out, it would be another month.

At the top of my agenda, however, was trying out the Z-2D. A day went by without word from Alex, so I called Computerlab again and this time got Angelo. Computerlab was a partnership, I had begun to realize, of Alex and Angelo, in which Alex covered software and Angelo hardware. Alex never had a care in the world, but Angelo's brow was often troubled. Angelo now told me that my computer was uncrated but that he hadn't had time to assemble it yet. It hadn't occurred to me that microcomputers came from the factory in pieces, but if so, so be it, as long as I would soon have my Z-2D.

Angelo obviously did not feel my sense of urgency. At the end of the week the computer still wasn't quite ready, and when I called on Monday of the next week, Alex said it would be ready Tuesday. Tuesday morning Angelo said he'd have it for me by four. I told him I'd be there at four, and he gave me directions for finding their new store. Computerlab, I discovered, had just moved out of its dingy downtown location into brand new quarters in a shopping center.

When I arrived that afternoon, Angelo had just put in the circuit boards and was attaching cables to the disk drives and the sockets for the printer and Beehive. After a few minutes he stood back and looked proudly at his handiwork: "That ought to do you, Ben." He carried it out to the car for me and put it in the trunk. It was just about as big and heavy a thing as a man could carry, and Angelo, who was not puny, staggered under its clumsy weight, but I pushed that aside. Kay was in the car, very happy to see the the great thing at last. "Didn't you say you were going to keep the boxes?" she said. "To ship it to London?" True, I had asked Angelo to save them. "How about the boxes?" I asked. Angelo assured me that he had them at the old store and would have them available here soon. But for me right then, the main thing was that at last I had my Z-2D.

It was too late to try it that day, but I at least proved that even with my bad back I could get it up to my office on the fourth floor of Main Hall—by driving the car on the sidewalks up to the building, borrowing a dolly from Science Hall, trundling it down to the basement on the wheelchair ramp and up the elevator. I slept fitfully that night, dreaming endless cyclical dreams in which the black box of the Z-2D came and went.

Next morning my initiation into microcomputing took place. I commandeered the Lawrence's DM20 and prepared a cable with which to plug it into the Z-2D. I was all atremble, like a man about to drive a brand new car or a woman inaugurating a new dress. Trying out an expensive new thing is one of the greatest thrills that life provides. But I had never operated a microcomputer, and I hadn't the faintest idea what difficulties and hazards it entailed. Eagerness anulled caution, and I plunged ahead precipitously, a maestro of machines. After all, I had once brought a cellarful of IBM 360 into glorious action all alone, in an empty building late at night, facing down that fearful control panel of red and blue buttons whose captions are still meaningless to me, following scribbled directions on a sheet of paper to press this, load that, write precisely this on the console keyboard, load the tape so it wouldn't spew all over the room, mount the disk so as not to cross the threads, and put the cards in the card reader 9-edge down.

I do not remember hooking up the Beehive or plugging in the computer. But I remember that it wouldn't come to life. I had on the table a black box a foot high, a foot and a half wide, and almost two feet deep, with two vertical slots for disks on the right side of the front, marked "A" and "B". On the back were a red button marked "RESET", a white on-off switch, and receptacles for my printer and terminal cables. Alex had said to put the CDOS disk in drive A, press the RESET button, and hit the RETURN key of the terminal four times to start the computer.

I slid the disk into drive A and snapped the door shut on it. I struck the RETURN key 4 times. Nothing happened! I struck it many more times: still nothing. I reinserted, RESET and RE-TURNed over and over again. Nothing. I checked things: Z-2D on (fan humming). Beehive on (fan humming). But not ON LINE, not switched onto the computer!

I took care of that. Now when I struck RETURN four times, I got a welcome sign of intelligence. My computer wrote "Cromemco RDOS1" on the screen of the Beehive, did a carriage return, and put down a semicolon. But there it stuck. Whatever keys I struck, all I ever got was another semicolon.

Now everything blurred. Frantically I moved plugs, turned things on and off, RESET, RESET, RESET, tried every key on the keyboard, said "hello", as to a PDP-11, reloaded the disk, put it on the other drive, put everything back the way it was. No matter what I did, the computer would do nothing more than print another semicolon. Only that and nothing more.

I called Alex at Computerland: "Alex, it won't start up. When I hit the RETURN key four times, all I get is 'Cromemco RDOS1' and a semicolon." "That's the boot load prompt," he said drily. "Give it a 'b'." "A '*B*'?" "Yes, so it will boot up." "Uppercase or lowercase?" "Doesn't matter." I struck the 'b' key. The red light on drive A went on, the drive made rattling noises, and the computer wrote

```
CDOS version 2.17
Cromemco Disk Operating System
Copyright (c) 1978, 1979

A.
```

I reported the result to Alex, waiting on the other end of the line. "You're in business," he said. "Sorry, Alex. Thanks, Alex," I said, ashamed.

The letter "A" followed by the period, I deduced, must be the CDOS "Ready" signal, and it was an "A" because it was assuming that any programs I wished to run would be found on the disk in drive A.

At no time during this untowardly display of panic did I once think of consulting my manual. When I came to myself and did so, I found out that RDOS1 was my Resident Disk Operating System and **bootstrap loader**, that it consisted of **ROM**, or "Read Only Memory," that it was a computer program on a chip that knew how to get the CDOS operating system from disk A and put it in the Z-2D's memory—if you gave it a 'b'. It was called a "bootstrap loader" because it was the means by which the computer pulled itself up by its own bootstraps, and Alex's terms "boot" and "boot up" clearly derived from this idea.

Until a computer is booted up, it has no character at all; when RDOS1 puts CDOS into the computer's memory, the Z-2D assumes the character of CDOS. Whatever character a computer has comes from the programs that run on it. It is a Galatea whose programmer is a Pygmalion, a Liza Doolittle whose programmer is a Henry Higgins. The manual told me that on the circuit board of my disk controller was an "autoboot" switch that would cause RDOS1 to load CDOS without asking for a 'b'. I switched on autoboot and implemented my Galatea's first personality change. I no longer had to boot her into action. A few gentle carriage returns would set her stirring.

Now, desirous of getting better acquainted, I began browsing in the CDOS manual. I saw that there was a "DIR" command that gave me a DIRectory of all the files on a disk. I wrote DIR and pressed RETURN. No operating system will even look at a command without a signal that says, "That's it." For CDOS, the signal was RETURN, and in three seconds it produced this report:

```
CDOS      COM    15K        INIT    COM    10K
CDOSGEN   COM    28K        STAT    COM     8K
XFER      COM     4K
```

I knew from PDP-11 experience that "COM" was an **extension**, designating a type of file, and that COM meant it was COMpiled and would run whenever I named its name. But something was wrong. My manual's list of CDOS commands did not jibe with my directory of programs to execute them. My disk didn't contain "ATTRibutes," "ERAse," "REName," "SAVE," "TYPE," "BATCH," or "DUMP." It didn't even have DIRectory, which I had just finished *using*. I went back to the manual.

It said that ATTRibutes (to make a file unreadable, unerasable, or unchangeable), DIRectory (as illustrated), ERAse (to erase files), REName (to change the name of a file), SAVE (something to do with programming), and TYPE (for typing out a disk file) were "intrinsic"; and that BATCH (for running any set of these programs in a batch), XFER (for transferring programs from one disk to another), DUMP (for displaying a disk file in computer code), INITialize (for preparing a new disk), and STATus (for making a more thorough analysis of a disk than DIR) were "Utility Programs." My directory listed none of the "intrinsic programs," and of the "utility programs," I was missing BATCH and DUMP. I had, on the other hand, two programs not listed in either category, CDOS and CDOSGEN. And I significantly did not have Cromemco SCREEN, which I had expressly ordered with the computer.

If DIR was really there but did not show up on a directory, what did "intrinsic" mean? Intrinsic: underlying, like an assumption. Equality is *intrinsic* to democracy. I combed the manual for clues. It said only that these commands were "intrinsic to the operating system." But what exactly is the operating system? Everything in the manual, if I could trust its title.

I will not bore the reader with further castings about, though I did a good many. The truth was that these unlisted programs were not underlying assumptions of anything; they were simply parts of CDOS.COM, which was listed but not categorized. And the operating system was not one, but two things: (1) CDOS.COM by itself and (2) everything in the manual. When one booted up, RDOS1 automatically loaded the intrinsic programs into memory as part of CDOS.COM. The so-called "utility programs" (weren't all of them utility programs?) had to be specially loaded from the disk every time they were used.

I still didn't know the whereabouts of BATCH, DUMP, and SCREEN. As soon as I could get him on the phone, I notified Alex. "Alex," I cried out, "where are BATCH, DUMP, and SCREEN?" "That disk doesn't have those," he said. "Some time when you're over here, I'll give you the rest."

The next order of business was to **configure** or adjust CDOS
(the program) to my particular collocation of hardware. According to the manual, I must first **initialize** a new disk, then copy all
of CDOS (extrinsic and intrinsic), and finally generate a new
CDOS system suited to my hardware.

I approached initialization with considerable excitement, because it would be a thoroughgoing test for both me and the
system. With trembling hands, I put a new disk in drive B and
wrote "INIT" on my terminal. The Z-2D then wrote five lines at
a speed that left me dizzy. Like whitewash against a wall, the
following text splatted on the screen:

```
Initialize Disks version 02.15
Press: RETURN to supply default answers shown in brackets.
     CTRL-C to abort program and return to CDOS.

Disk to initialize (A,B)
```

When I recovered from this display of virtuosity and decided
to tackle the "default answers" instead of abort, I turned my
attention to the final question. Strictly speaking, I didn't have a
disk A or B, I had a *drive* A or B, but I thought I knew what they
meant. The disk was in drive B, so I wrote "B," and was
instantly informed

```
Testing Drive:
```

Before I could quite register that, it said,

```
Completed
```

leaving the ominous announcement,

```
Initialization:
This portion can destroy all data on a disk with no chance of recovery.
Press ESC during initialization to abort the process.
```

for me to mull over. Before I could conjure up what data might
be on my disk, it wrote

```
Single or double sided (S/D)?  [S]
```

It was telling me, I deduced, that I was allowed to answer "S" or
"D", but that it supposed I wanted "S", for "single-sided," and
that if I defaulted, reneged, or copped out by striking RETURN,

that's what it would give me. I was much afraid to contradict my computer. Maybe it knew something I didn't. But I knew I'd bought disk drives for double-sided operation and wrote "D", fearing the worst.

Not in the least ruffled by my intransigence, it shot back

`Single or double density (S/D)?" [S]`

I had no idea about density. The manual told me simply to decide but not on what basis. So I gambled that the computer was right and pressed RETURN.

The worst was to come:

`First cylinder (0-27H)? [0],`

This question was utterly beyond me. Although I knew that **cylinders** were parallel recording **tracks** on a multi-layered disk, the term seemed a bit grandiose for a floppy disk. Even worse, the default answer was "Track 0." If you asked the average person where Track Zero was, he'd say, "Nowhere," but my computer believed that it really existed. What could I do but cop out? It then wanted me to state my

`Last cylinder (0-27H) [27]`

and I copped out again. My interrogation still wasn't over, though. Now my computer asked me

`Surfaces (0, 1, or Both)? [B]`

indicating that it thought $0 + 1 = 2$.

I hit RETURN, wondering how long this grilling was going to last. And now CDOS put on another display of virtuosity. While disk drive B went "Thunk, thunk, thunk, thunk … ," its red light brightly shining, the computer produced something like an odometer ticking off mileage on the space ship Enterprise:

`Cylinder, Surface: xy,z`

While z changed twice per second from 0 to 1, x stood at 0 and y increased like this: 0,1,2,3,4,5,6,7,8,9,A,B,C,D,E,F; then

x changed to 1, and y went from 0 to F again; then x went to 2
and y went from 0 to 7, leaving me with 27 for xy. I realized,
with a shiver, that my computer had been counting in **hexadecimal**, a mystical, base 16, new math system I knew of but never
could master. It can count to sixteen in a one-digit space by
starting at zero and using the first six letters of the alphabet after
it gets to nine. That was why CDOS thought 0 and 1 made 2. As
a flunker of college math, I have always shunned hexadecimal,
and I still do. They tell me that "hex" is necessary for stuffing
computers to the brim, but I would like to see it abolished.

Anyway, when my computer got to the "27th" cylinder of
disk B (really the 40th, as ordinary people count), it saw that it
was good, turned off the red light under disk B, and rested.

I will not tire the reader with my similar perplexities in
generating a new operating system with CDOSGEN.COM, which
my manual told me I must do if my system was to match my
hardware. The questions left me even more in the dark. Once,
the manual told me to "answer the last two questions with 'B:'
and 'B:CDOS'," when I had no way of knowing when I had
reached the last two questions. It was like being told to turn left
two miles before you reach the Mobil filling station.

By writing as if my computer were a human being, I have
been trying to convey its personality. I do know it is a machine.
If it has any personality, it is the personality of its Pygmalion, its
Henry Higgins, its programmer, its designer. And of course this
Pygmalion isn't one person. It isn't even Cromemco, because a
whole history of hardware and software contributed to its character.

How shall I describe thee, Z-2D? Austere, in your big black
box. Pedantic, in your display of esoteric knowledge. Inconsiderate, perhaps, in your demands, but certainly not sadistic, like the
IBM 360. Indeed, eager to help, wanting to be friendly, but
sometimes offering aid that isn't much use. Wanting to communicate, but not much good at words. Once I broke two bones in
the back of my hand by fending off a tree with my fist while

skiing. As the doctor and I looked at the X-ray, I noted, "Looks like that bone is pushed down." "Yes," he said, "depressed." I noted further, "Looks like that bone is shoved into that one." "Yes," he said, "impacted." If the Henry Higgins who created my computer system has ever talked to a typical doctor about medical matters, he knows what it's like to talk to his creation.

And withal, a challenging competitor, an enthralling companion, a deep mystery. Somewhat like a chess opponent, but more like a Rubic's cube, passively puzzling; or like nature to the scientist, tantalizing him with revelations, but evermore hiding deeper secrets.

As a result of my first exercise with my new computer, I felt quite well-acquainted with it and pleased with my success. Cromemco's CDOS was much more comfortable than IBM's OS and perhaps even easier to get along with than DEC's RSTS, but the really exhilirating aspect was that it was all mine.

Bright and early the next morning, I went to my office to rearrange the furniture and improve the computer's work space. The ways of commerce are inscrutable. Soon after I arrived, I received a phone call from a friend in Physics, asking if the Centronics printer addressed to the Physics Department from Hamilton-Avnet was by any chance mine. "I'm sure it is," said I. It had gone to Physics presumably because that department had an account with Hamilton-Avnet. Soon the printer that wouldn't be delivered until next month was out of its box and sitting on my desk.

It was a beauty—neat, clean, and compact, and if plastic, substantial plastic. But my joy at seeing the printer I had despaired of was short-lived. Although I had specified one in my purchase order, there was no cable with which to hook it to the computer. What I needed was not the standard 25-pin plug used throughout Lawrence's computer system but what I soon came to know as a 40-pin edge connector. I had to find a socket that would fit the 40 contacts on the edge of the printer's circuit board.

Our electronics shop didn't have one; perhaps Computerlab did. So, wanting the software they still owed me, I drove over there after lunch. Angelo had a 40-pin connector that looked as if it would fit. He also drew me a chart showing which pin on the printer connected to which pin of the computer interface board. Alex lent me a disk from which to copy the programs I needed, with the stipulation, "Don't copy what you're not supposed to have." He also found a SCREEN manual for me to take. I rushed back to hook up the printer, only to discover that Angelo's connector would *not* fit.

Just then the telephone rang. It was Kay telling me that there was water all over the cellar floor. Guessing what had happened, I rushed home. In preparation for England, we had just converted our furnace from oil to more dependable gas. In order to fill the system with water after the conversion, it was necessary to open the air cocks on the radiators, one by one, until each radiator was full of water. While home for lunch, I had opened two radiators at once in order to speed up the process. In my hurry to get back to my printer, I had closed only one. The water from the other had run down the radiator pipe into the cellar, where quite a lake had developed by the time Kay discovered it. It was easy to stop the water, but I spent the rest of that day mopping up the cellar.

Next morning, Friday, I ordered an edge connector from Hamilton-Avnet. I couldn't expect to have it until Monday. I set to work copying my missing software from the disk Alex had given me, using my extrinsic utility XFER. SCREEN was there, and all the utility programs I already had. But neither BATCH or DUMP. Nor did I have SCREEN's companion FORMAT for printing a text file, without which SCREEN was not much use. When I tried out SCREEN, I discovered that it had an editing command—BEAUTIFY—not covered in the manual. BEAUTIFY would reformat a page on the screen with smaller margins, perhaps to show how it might look when printed. Apparently Alex had given me an obsolete manual. There was only one program on Alex's disk that I wasn't supposed to have. To my amazement, he had given me Cromemco BASIC, which would have cost me $295. I didn't copy it, though I was sorely tempted to.

The 40-pin edge connector arrived on Monday. It didn't fit. When I called Hamilton-Avnet with this news, Jim Strand said I would have to talk to Tom Suzda, but he was away at a show. I'd just received a circular from Hamilton-Avnet announcing a show in Appleton at a dance-hall called the Country Aire. "Not the one in Appleton?" I asked Jim. It was, so I called Tom Suzda at the Country Aire, and, lo and behold, I got him right away, wondering what he could do for me. When I told him, he replied, "I know what connector you need, but I don't have one here. Tell you what I'll do. I'll call Milwaukee right now and tell them to send you the right one." That connector arrived so fast it left me breathless—the next morning—and it was a perfect fit.

But it had been made to go on the end of a forty-wire flat ribbon cable, not an ordinary round multiwire cable. I could renegotiate with Tom Suzda, call the factory for a complete cable assembly, or try to solder a round cable to the tiny little knives that were supposed to pierce through the insulation of the ribbon cable. I decided to ask the opinion of Leroy Frahm, Lawrence's electronic technician. Leroy not only thought it feasible but volunteered to do it. I gave him Angelo's wiring diagram and soon possessed as tidy a 737 connector as I could have wished. It was now my task to solder a standard 25-pin plug onto the other end. I did an awful job, but I checked it carefully against Angelo's diagram for shorts and open circuits, and it was perfectly sound electrically.

Now to try it out. I had trouble feeding paper under the platen. Something was askew. In haste to get to the bottom of the problem, I started taking things apart. It was much easier than I thought, and suddenly I had removed the whole mechanical assembly. The trouble was a loose screw. I eagerly reassembled the printer, plugged it into the computer, and turned my system on. Then I smelled the smell, the dreaded smell of burning insulation. I broke into a sweat. No, it couldn't be true. I went ahead with the test.

I booted up the computer and then gave directions for it to print a directory, by writing DIR and pressing CONTROL/P for

Print, following directions in my manual. Now I was, like Oedipus once, on the brink of frightful knowing. I struck RETURN. And now I knew. Nothing happened. I punched more keys. The computer was DEAD. By rebooting I could get it back, but any attempt to print killed it again. Again and again I rebooted and tried to print, but it was hopeless. My nose had already known it. But what had burned out, the printer or the printer interface in the computer? My nose led me to the computer. I unscrewed the lid, pulled the interface board out of the bus, and held it to my nose. It was obviously the source of the smell.

I could not pursue the matter further at this juncture, however, because I had an appointment with a doctor. As part of our preparation for England, we had undergone physical examinations. As a result, this afternoon I was to visit a specialist to get his opinion on blood tests pertaining to the performance of my liver.

On looking at me and the blood tests, the doctor informed me that I might very well have a most interesting hereditary disease called hemochromatosis, in which one's liver, heart, and other organs collect iron from iron-saturated blood. Since the cure is rather drastic—draining a pint of blood out of the patient every week for a year—he must be sure I had hemochromatosis by doing a liver biopsy. This was a routine procedure, in which, under a local anesthetic, he would stick a needle with a little snipper in its nose into my liver and pull out a piece of tissue for pathological analysis. He would be happy to do this tomorrow morning at ten o'clock. He would do it in a hospital room, and I would remain under observation there until the next morning.

I was lying naked under a sheet in a hospital bed at ten o'clock when the doctor and his nurse arrived. The local anesthetic was not so bad, nor was the needle, though I couldn't help seeing that it was six inches long and an eighth of an inch thick. He pushed it with considerable force against my numb chest. After a minute of this, he said, "Now I'm going to snip it. You may feel a little twinge."

I felt a very sharp sting. When the needle came out, he said, "Darn it. I don't think this will do. A piece of duct or something."

The sharp sting rapidly became a greater pain than I had ever felt or imagined possible. I told him I thought I could not stand it without a shot of something. I think he said, "This never happens . . . only once in a thousand." I don't remember much after this.

The drug didn't help much. I remember telling Kay some time in the afternoon that I thought something bad was happening inside me. I felt as if I might vomit, and I didn't think I could stand it. That was the only time during what ensued that I actually had a sense of my life slipping away.

I remember going into the operating room and then waking up afterwards. "Is it over?" I asked the surgeon. "Yes," he said. "Then I must be all right," I said, reasoning that I had survived the operation. He gave me a long, serious look and said, "Yes," not as firmly as I had hoped he would. Nevertheless, except for that one awful moment when I feared I would vomit, I never subsequently felt anything except that I was getting better or that the next thing they did would make me better.

Except for nightmarish visions of dim hospital rooms in the long night during which wraithlike nurses came and went, and an awareness of having had tubes in my side, arms, neck, and nose—once I counted seven tubes—and perhaps some dreams in which a Mayan priest was tearing my beating heart out of my chest, I retain little else of the next two weeks. But having gotten the reader so far, I think he deserves to have a fuller account than I can give unaided. Fortunately I have good testimony from other sources. I have Kay's diary, the doctor's reports on the several states of my health, and notes taken by my four children, who watched me in shifts.

On the fateful day, Kay had no idea that the biopsy had gone wrong until she paid me a routine visit during the afternoon. She was greatly distressed to find me in a frightful state, with a cleaning woman bending over me, trying to make me comfortable.

Upon discovering me so unlike my self, she went directly to the doctor and insisted that I be placed in intensive care immediately. This was done. A surgeon was called in, and the doctors discussed opening me up to find out what had happened. They decided to operate the next morning. Kay wanted immediate action, but they thought it better to wait and see if I improved. Nevertheless, as the evening progressed I got worse, and they called the surgeon out of his house. At ten o'clock he operated.

> Under general endotracheal anesthesia, after application of plastic drape, a right subcostal incision was made, the rectus muscle transected, and the abdomen opened. Immediately apparent was a large amount of golden bile, extending in particular in the right gutter but also extending over the anterior portion of the omentum and down into the pelvis. As much as possible of this bile was aspirated, and we then mobilized the liver, and high in the right lobe we were able to see a small puncture wound of the liver biopsy, and a small amount of bile was still continuously trickling out through this opening. No gross blood was observed. Using an 0 Vicryl transfixion suture, we placed a piece of surgical gauze over this and tied the suture over the gauze to cause good compression and apparently control the drainage. . . . Postoperative condition was good. The tachycardia noted preoperatively gradually slowed during the procedure from 150 down to 110.

But when Kay arrived the next morning, my blood pressure was dangerously low, and drastic measures were required again. My body had used up most of its liquid component in trying to repair the damage done by caustic bile in the abdominal cavity. An open-heart surgeon was called in. He reported that the situation was indeed serious, but that "The patient . . . denies any particular distress elsewhere and states that if the abdominal pain was gone, he probably would feel very good. He is alert and not at all confused." He then pushed a "a central venous pressure subclavian line" into the base of my neck. It was just another tube to me. By means of this and two or three other tubes in the veins of my arms they pumped fluid and antibiotics into me all day, and towards evening I reached solid ground. Kay tells me that the really hard part of this day was that they couldn't give me any pain-killer for fear I would lose what blood pressure I had.

All I remember was some of the ceremony of inserting the subclavian tube and my joy at having reached this day. For Kay, who knew what was going on and could see how I looked, this was a greater ordeal. In her diary she wrote volumes in the narrow space allotted for the two days:

> This is a page I would like to leave blank. Ben had a liver biopsy, and everything went wrong. Bile seeped from his liver & burned his system, & bacteria from bowel infected his blood. Surgery at 11:15 stopped seepage, but blood was already infected. All vital signs slowed & almost halted, but Ben pulled through. . . . God was with us.

On Sunday I continued to improve. Devon, the environmental consultant, flew up from her base in Chicago to strengthen the support forces. She was our first-born, named for the English county in which she was conceived. She takes after her grandmother, Dear Boo, and her mother, and all three are regarded as beauties. She had now reached her late twenties, and we wished that she would marry. We liked her present suitor, and we waited expectantly. Devon was an efficient businesswoman, and I soon found business for her.

Son Nick, my programmer, now at an astronomical congress in Hawaii giving a paper on the plumes of Jupiter's moon Io, was due to arrive in four days to begin work on SITAR, and I didn't have the Microsoft BASIC compiler. We had hesitated over the purchase of the compiler because Nick, who had made extensive investigations, preferred the superior string-handling capacity of Cromemco's version of BASIC. We couldn't compile Cromemco BASIC, though, and fearing it would be too slow, I now arbitrarily decided against it and asked Devon to order the Microsoft compiler over the telephone from a software broker in New York named Lifeboat Associates. She would pay for it by giving them my MasterCharge number and have it sent to us by Federal Express, in time for Nick's arrival.

The reader may wonder how, with my known prejudices, I could bring myself to deal with a company having such a frivolous name as Lifeboat Associates. Well, their name actually made some sense. Microsoft Corporation, I had discovered earlier, would supply their software only on 8-inch disks. If I wanted the compiler on a 5¼-inch disk, they had told me I would have to get it from Lifeboat Associates. I had heard of this house before but had not understood its raison d'être: it rescued people whose hardware or software prevented them from using the standard release. A drowning man does not question the name of the boat that is about to rescue him.

Encouraged by my wife and daughter, I continued to improve during the week. When Nick arrived on Thursday direct from Hawaii, where we had been unable to reach him, he was abashed to hear that but for the grace of God he might have been attending my funeral. But by then I had left intensive care, had no more tubes in me, and was beginning to eat soft food.

Nick, number two, had always been a builder: of bobsled runs for tennis balls in sandpiles, of sandcastles on the beach, of paper-folded origami birds and beasts, of cut-out and glue-up cathedrals, and of Heathkits. He had graduated from Dartmouth a year before, where he'd majored in physics and astronomy.

Dartmouth was a pioneer in the development of interactive, time-sharing computing, and John Kemeny, first a math professor, then president, had created Dartmouth BASIC with Thomas Kurtz. Especially designed for interactive use, it was the patriarch of all BASICs. As a student, Nick applied the computer to problems in astronomy. He invented a planetary model that made it possible to view the solar system from any planet. And he won the prize for the best program written by an undergraduate by submitting a program enabling astronomers to interpret telescopic data by interacting with the computer. He might have become a computer addict, the fate of too many undergraduates

these days, but he loved friends, frisbee-throwing, and female companions too much. Nick's childhood ambition was to go to Mars, and I don't think he has entirely given it up.

While I lay in the hospital recovering, Nick became my proxy at the Z-2D. I gave him three projects immediately: get the printer running, transmit the SITAR modules from the PDP-11 to the Z-2D, and start converting them to Microsoft BASIC. The day he arrived I pushed a scratched-out list of chores into his hands: Go to Computerlab. Return Alex's disk. Find out how I clean the read/write heads of my disk drives. Find out what has happened to the Beehive I ordered. Get my shipping boxes. Why don't I have FORMAT? Where is the word-processing package I ordered? Why don't I have BATCH and DUMP? Why doesn't my SCREEN manual say anything about BEAUTIFY? How do I modify the Z-2D for 220-volt operation? Take the printer inter-face, and find out if it's burnt out.

The next morning Nick paid a visit to Computerlab and returned with the following answers: Don't clean the read/write heads. The Beehive is delayed because the factory is out of stock. The boxes are still at the old store. The word processor will arrive in a week. It will include FORMAT, a more current SCREEN manual, and the complete operating system, including BATCH and DUMP. There is a double-pole double-throw switch in the Z-2D which sets it for 220-volt operation. The printer interface is burnt out: a new one is $195; a rebuilt one is $75, with trade-in.

Putting the evidence together, I could now form a hypothe-sis to explain why my software had not matched my manuals. Alex had not ordered my software by the time I returned from Yucatán. When I wondered where it was, he ordered it. To keep me happy until it arrived, he had given me whatever utilities and manuals he found lying around the shop. These did not match. BATCH, DUMP, and FORMAT were not lying around the shop.

It was now Friday, and the doctors thought I might be out of the hospital next week. Devon flew to The Lake for a holiday with her young man.

On Saturday it began to appear that my recovery had reached a plateau. My intestinal tract refused to move any food through me. The large wound under my right rib cage was festering, and eating produced abdominal pain. It was Memorial Day weekend, and I came under the care of duty doctors. Kay was unsatisfied with my condition and urged me to stop making light of my aches and pains, as I had been brought up to do. I tried to do a better job of reporting my symptoms, but the duty doctors saw no cause for alarm. They said, "You have experienced an ex-tremely severe shock to your system, and you cannot expect to snap right out of it." They prescribed enemas. These produced all of the appropriate gyrations and contractions, a great deal of pain, and no results. Fortunately I was allowed to have some pain-killer every four hours.

As part of our campaign to impress the doctors, I began to record my symptoms as I had them, but they were somewhat randomly and incorrectly set down on the page:

No colon power
weakness
Respiritory games?
Didn't take a walk after dinner
11:30 Hot stomach
11:10 Perkodan
1AM Dry
11:15 sweaty
3:15 walked, tiring
Afraid to eat Graham Crackers?
Intake — very slowly: soup water 7up? sherbert Milkshakes
   Maalox juice fruit

On Monday my handwriting and clarity deteriorated:

hiccups
vision not very accurate
12:00 chest abdomen exray
12:30 coffee sanka
stiff neck
tv guide
Straw Sherbert pulls down?
pain pill 1PM xtra pain in side after
hiccoughs
bloated
Is rash associated with R-try?

On Tuesday, the weekend over, the medical men appeared to be in doubt as to what to do about me. Kay was not: she went to the chief doctor and told him that I must be flown to the Mayo Clinic in Rochester, Minnesota, at once. In our part of the world, the Mayo Clinic is famous for medical miracles, but the quality of local medicine is so high that Appletonians only rarely resort to it. No Schneider had ever been there. So, when it was decided to send me there, I felt a little bit as if a priest had been called to give me extreme unction. But I was so sure I was getting better that I instead concluded that the family was merely overreacting. And if it made them feel better, perhaps the experts up there could get me off this plateau, which even I suspected was beginning to slope the wrong way.

Soon I was bouncing through the clouds in a six-seater "air ambulance," draped across a mattress that had been thrown diagonally over collapsed back seats. A nurse was sitting sideways behind the pilot and copilot. I knew I wasn't going to like this arrangement at all, and I told them so, because it bent my back the wrong way and put just the wrong stress on my tender stomach. As the flight progressed and my prediction proved true, I became furious with all three of them and remained so all the way to Rochester, Minnesota. After we landed, I refused to let any of them touch me. Fortunately, a Rochester ambulance crew was waiting, and I petulantly submitted myself to their ministrations, reiterating all the while that they should not bend me the wrong way.

At the hospital, I immediately missed Kay. Who would tell them what was wrong with me? How could I get any attention? Why weren't they doing something about this pain in my stomach? I think I spent some time in a large room with several other stretcher cases. A young doctor came by, felt my pulse, took my temperature, and said (I'm told), "You'll be all right for a while," at which (I'm told) I flew into a rage and did what came to be known as my "King Lear act," in which I spluttered out, "My wife tells me I am too much of a stoic. I am not being a stoic now. I am in terrible pain, and you've got to do something about it instantly."

Soon, I think, a nurse came with a shot, and I felt much better. After that, a tow-headed young surgeon looked at my incision and said, "Yuk." "Is that what you always say when you look at wounds, or is it cruddy?" I said. "It isn't what I always say," he said. Then I was wheeled off to a room by myself.

Now the curtain falls. I am told that I picked up the telephone and somehow called Kay's brother Jimmy, a doctor in Cincinnati, whose number I do not keep in my head, and the faculty secretary in Main Hall of Lawrence University. I demanded of both of them that they find out where my wife was and tell her to get here immediately. The Lawrence telephone operator says that I threatened her with the combined wrath of the English department if she did not accept my collect call to the faculty secretary.

Kay, of course, was making the five-hour drive to Rochester with Nick. I didn't know that the Appleton doctors had cast some doubt on whether I would arrive in Rochester at all. During the trip she tearily wondered if a panama hat she liked on me in Yucatán might not appropriately sit on top of my coffin. While I was in the air, the whole family, tied together by telephone, was waiting to hear whether to go to Rochester for my last words or to Appleton for my last rites. Kay's brother Jimmy was to monitor the hospital in Rochester and relay the word to the rest. As they drove to Rochester, Kay and Nick stopped frequently to call Jimmy. Not until they were halfway there could he tell them not only that I had arrived but that I had personally announced the fact.

Devon was the first to arrive, flying in from Chicago on her return from her rendezvous at The Lake, loaded with questions for the doctor:

1. Did you talk to the Appleton doctor? What did he say about Dad's condition today?
2. What happened on the trip? What is happening now? What is being done?
3. What is the problem? Will they have to operate? When will they know?
4. Drs. names on the case? Where can they be reached? When?
5. Visiting?
6. Do all the nurses & doctors know Dad's history? Who is the head nurse?
7. Get medical terms for Uncle Jimmy to explain.

When the world came back into focus again, the tubes were all back in me, and the whole family was there. What it means when whole families gather from the ends of the earth to watch over a parent's sickbed never struck my mind. I just thought how considerate it was of them to drop what they were doing and come to cheer me up. I silently wished Nick were back there working on SITAR.

Ben III, number two, had broken off cramming for imminent Ph.D. exams. And Mackay, number four, was missing the last week of classes in her junior year at Earlham. When Ben graduated from college, where he majored in political science with special emphasis on South America, he went to Washington and indicated to the appropriate agencies his willingness to help out that continent in any way he could. They told him, "We can get Ph.D.'s to do that," and so he went off to get the required document. Despite the fact that his politics are pretty far to the left, he is the *boulevardier* of the family. He always calls his younger brother "Nicky" because Nick prefers "Nick," and he has stunning girl friends. He arrived in Rochester with a just-purchased medical dictionary and a book entitled *This Is Your Stomach*.

Mackay is named for Kay (which is really short for Mackay) but is called "Bibs" by her brothers and sister, who won't let her forget she's the baby, and her brothers have elaborated this to "Bibseltoid." Like most Earlhamites—it's a Quaker college—she is very cheerful and at the same time very earnest about leaving the world better than she found it. There have been times when we thought she might give all she had to the poor and follow Jesus. Her specialties at college were chemistry and German, and she was looking forward to a summer as a lab technician at Oak Ridge National Laboratories, Tennessee.

My problems were an infected wound, peritonitis, general blood poisoning, pneumonia, and malfunctioning intestines; and the treatments were antibiotic powder on the wound, antibiotic fluid intravenously, pulmonary exercises, no food, and a suction tube through my nose, through my stomach, and into my intestine. Horrible green and yellow matter was pumped into a glass jar. I was soon on the mend.

The family had gotten into the habit of monitoring the doctors during my Appleton mishaps and now continued the procedure. The children took careful notes on my condition, watched every needle and tube, tabulated my blood pressure, followed my chart, and peppered the doctors with questions.

Nick watched me carefully while he kept up with medical technology:

> X-ray showed tube did not enter intestine
> All fluid was from stomach.
> 2:00 Doctor uncoiled tube in stomach (pulled it out some) and is waiting for tube to find exit.
> While sleeping, Dad's fingers moved as if working at a terminal
> Dad must stay on right side until 4:00
> Dad said he was "ready to pack it in" around X-ray time today, feels "miraculously better."

Mackay kept a log:

> — sweating a lot
> — Nick wants to know why fluid is green when it was yellow
> — in WI Pa had a laparotomy (sp?) larapotomy

I remember the first time I saw the doctor in charge of my case, a native of Quebec whose name was Jean Perrault. He appeared in front of three or four residents, whom he proceeded to brief in a decided French accent. The children, all of them better linguists than I, were much delighted by my imitation of this episode in French of a quality superior to any that had ever before passed my lips. I am supposed to have mimicked him thus: "Voici, mes enfants, un malade de sexe male, âge soixante ans, poids cent soixante-six, température normale, pression de sang un peu élevée, qui souffre un grand mal à l'estomac. . . . " I don't know how long I went on or how I could have dredged up

as much French as they say I did, but I believe I had practiced. I
must have imagined him to say "mes enfants" because my father
in his World War I stories used to tell us that that was the way
French officers addressed their troops.

Benny quizzed the doctors:

9:30 Father broke wind — hooray
9:30 Doctors arrive
— Bowels moving stuff slowly, has been since he arrived
— cultures haven't shown anything. He probably doesn't
  have pneumonia.
— more likely lungs just have built up fluid. Antibiotics are
  precaution, prevention.
— unlikely bile is still leaking — only way to tell is to open
  him up
— if they performed surgery now it would only be to drain
  fluid.
— don't know where tube is. X-rays later today
— more — wait & see attitude

By Friday, two weeks from the day the biopsy needle opened
a bile duct, my white count began to dive towards normal, and
on Saturday, medical opinion gave out that Benny might return
to Berkeley and take his exams. To crown the good news that I
was out of danger, Devon announced to me her engagement to
the young man, and the wedding was scheduled for the fifth of
July at The Lake. When I later rose dramatically up out of bed to
announce this news to the rest of the family, they thought at first
I was hallucinating. This time I wasn't. Now our emotional roller-
coaster started to climb again.

But it was another week before my alimentary canal began to
function, and by then I had lost thirty pounds from living off my
own protein. They would have to keep me another three weeks
before I'd be strong enough to leave. But this was no reason why
Nick should not go back to Appleton and get cracking with
SITAR, and I sent him home to work.

I kept track of Nick's progress by telephone. He spent a good part of the time left to him in Appleton finding out what combination of software and hookup would persuade the PDP-11 to send SITAR to the Z-2D. The annals of SITAR are littered with evidence of Nick's failures to accomplish communication between the two machines. Alex's ideas didn't work. Jim Evans's ideas didn't work. Rewiring connectors didn't work. And seven different Z-2D programs to read SITAR as it came over the wires did not succeed. He couldn't just sit down and deduce a way that had a chance of working because nobody seemed to know just how computers communicate with peripherals anyhow.

The trick was to make the Z-2D think it was receiving data *from* a terminal and make the PDP-11 think it was sending data *to* a terminal, both of which statements were lies, and get both set up to act out the lies at the same time. Eventually Nick succeeded by carrying both the Z-2D and the Beehive to the computer room, running a program that prepared the Z-2D to receive a stream of data from the Beehive, unplugging the Beehive, plugging in instead a cable to one of its terminals from the PDP-11, and from a second PDP-11 terminal commanding the PDP-11 to copy SITAR to the pseudoterminal that was now the Z-2D.

Still reluctant to reject Cromemco BASIC, he admired its string-handling so much, Nick tried to persuade me to adopt it. As for its speed, he'd talked to software specialists at Cromemco, and they guaranteed that programs written in their BASIC ran much faster than those in any other BASIC interpreter's, because they could be partially compiled. I was willing to reconsider, but we needed proof, and Alex had unwittingly given us the way to get it.

Before Nick had returned Alex's disk to him, he had copied Cromemco BASIC from it, telling himself that if we ever used it for SITAR, we could buy it. Meanwhile, we could at least test drive it, or, in computer lingo, make a **benchmark** test. A benchmark is a task used to test the relative speed of similar software. The task we chose to test the Cromemco interpreter against the Microsoft compiler was to run a simple but hard-working SITAR module that rearranges a file on a disk. Nick wrote this module in Microsoft and Cromemco BASIC and raced the products against time. Microsoft's compiler beat Cromemco's fast interpreter decisively, finishing the task in three minutes, fully nine minutes ahead of Cromemco's interpreter. We never used Cromemco BASIC again.

Having thus cleared the air, Nick bent his mind to the discrepancies between Microsoft and DEC BASIC. Computerlab made its contribution to progress by delivering us a rebuilt printer interface.

I left Rochester to fly to The Lake on the 24th of June, having nothing to show for six weeks out of commission but proof that I actually had hemochromatosis. In the course of my laparotomy, the surgeon had excised a sample of liver suitable for conclusive diagnosis, and it proved that my liver was indeed laced with iron. Bloodletting would start in London in the fall.

The course was clear. Now, onward to The Lake and the conversion of SITAR.

CHAPTER V

THE WALRUS AND
THE CARPENTER

"It seems a shame," the Walrus said,
   "To play them such a trick,
After we've brought them out so far,
   And made them trot so quick!"
The Carpenter said nothing but
   "The butter's spread too thick!"

IF IT WERE on the ocean, it would be a *cottage*, but any summer home on fresh water in New England is a *camp*. The camp my father built on the big island in our lake in southern New Hampshire sits in the midst of a forest of pine and hemlock on a granite ledge fifty feet above the water. Through the boughs of the trees, from the shaded front porch, one glimpses a bright expanse of water about three miles long and a mile broad. From there a series of strategically placed stepping stones leads down past a giant boulder in the approximate shape of a six-foot cube, dropped there how and when we sometimes try to guess, to the floating dock. The camp is a rectangular two-story frame building whose long side runs along the top of the granite ledge. It is painted dark brown with green trim, and it sleeps twelve, counting the porch swing. Although there are 14 camps on this island, not one can be seen from any of the others or from the lake, so big is the island and so thick is the forest. We call it "The Lake," because no one—mother, father, son, or grandchild—has ever been capable of thinking of it as Forest Ledge, Pine Cliff, Hemlock Crest, Granite Nest, or any other appropriate but typical name.

It isn't in the forest primeval because Governor Benning Wentworth deforested the island in the 18th century and planted pastures, but two hundred years is time enough for two full growths of pine. If it weren't for the Governor's stone walls crisscrossing the woods, you could believe that the native Americans once roamed this identical forest. Now there are occasional deer and foxes, a few porcupines, raccoons, lots of red and gray squirrels, and even some flying squirrels; screech owls and horned owls at night, kingfishers, cranes, a visiting loon or two, blue jays, chickadees, nuthatches, and, deep in the woods, hermit thrushes playing their distant flute songs; black snakes, garter snakes, toads, salamanders, bull and leopard frogs, and painted and snapping turtles; bass, trout, pickerel, shiners, horned pout, perch, sunfish, eels, blood suckers, snails, and mussels; water lilies, pickerel weed, dogwood, Indian pipes, mushrooms and toadstools, moss, lichens, checkerberries, blackberries, raspberries, blueberries, trailing arbutus, and, in June, hundreds of pink ladyslippers where the sun lights up the rust-colored pine needles.

I went to The Lake to restore my health and discover whether my software could be made to work on my computer. Having lost thirty pounds, I had a lot of health to regain, and by the implementation of SITAR, I would avenge the insult done to my body. As the mariner of infinite wisdom and sagacity said upon leaving the whale's throat, in the *Just So Stories*, "By means of this grating, I will stop your ating."

Week One

Kay and I arrived by plane and rented car several days before the great machine, because Nick, who was transporting it by car, visited Dartmouth friends in New York and Boston on the way from Wisconsin. There was not much we could have done with it anyway, because we were concentrating most of our energy on preparations for Devon's wedding. There were guests to put up, roles to review and practice, the house to clean, catering to arrange, and decorations to plan and acquire.

We expected Devon and her intended on the 29th of June, a week before the wedding. On the afternoon of that day, Devon called to say that they were delayed and would not arrive in Boston until late in the evening. They would rent a car and drive up. Kay and I went to bed but slept only fitfully in expectation of the first bride and groom in our family. Some time after eleven, Devon called from the airport. Had we been able to arrange for Nick to pick her up, or should she rent a car? We told her to rent a car. Somehow we dozed off and did not awaken until Devon's dark form entered our sleeping porch. We were overjoyed to see her at last, but I couldn't figure something out. "How's the groom doing?" I asked. Kay found the light. "He's not here," Devon said, without any expression. "When's he coming?" I asked. "He's not coming." Then she sat on the bed, and I had to hold her very tightly because she was shaking.

For Kay and me, this news was a disappointment. We had been anticipating this first wedding in our family like children looking forward to Christmas, and Christmas had been cancelled. Even worse, we were the parents of a child whose Christmas had been cancelled, and we were helpless. We could not stop it. Nothing but family solidarity stood between us and the bottomless pit as we tried to find out where the future was and how to get there. It helped for us to realize that her chosen one's withdrawal was all for the best. And it was in its own way magnanimous, because he must release her from any further obligation to him on the strength of their happy companionship of several years' standing and face an utter emptiness in his own life. Nor could he in any way hint to her this sense of deprivation without compromising the freedom she must now undertake for her own good. So we became convinced that we must thank our stars that he had made his hard decision instead of taking the easier course, at this point, of drifting into reluctant husbandhood.

Now two of us were healing our wounds at The Lake. While she supported me on my teetering constitutional walks, I listened to her evaluate what had happened and build an attitude on which a future could stand. And, just as they had in my dark time just passed, gathering around like white corpuscles surrounding an infection, the rest of the children soon gathered at The Lake.

Though assuredly they had expected to attend the wedding, the unfortunate eventuality, far from leaving them to pursue their own affairs, all the more moved them to come: Mackay from her chemical analysis at Oak Ridge, Benny from his political studies at Berkeley, and Nick, bearing the computer, from his last stop in Boston. Aunt Janet, whose principal activity these days was driving the operators of gravel pits away from the country north of Detroit, and Nephew Chris, philosopher, anthropologist, naturalist, and pot-maker, also arrived according to plan, and Vicki, a student of business and Benny's lovely girl friend.

On Tuesday, the first of July, Nick arrived with the computer and a new printer interface. We installed the Z-2D and its peripherals in an upstairs bedroom, where it was arrayed on benches, tables, and desks against a range of windows overlooking the lake. Lifting up my eyes from the video terminal, I was often surprised to find myself in the treetops of a forest of pine and hemlock with water glinting through the branches far below and sky opening up above.

The day after Nick arrived, I rewired the plug for the printer, using the pin assignments in the 737 manual instead of Angelo's, and connected it to the computer. But even with the new interface, the printer still did not work. The printing element bucked and buzzed as if it wanted to print, but it could not travel across the page. It was stuck.

Today was Kay's birthday. Aunt Janet, Nephew Chris, all the children, and Benny's girl Vicki were getting ready for a big celebration.

It could be my wiring again, or it could be that I'd burned out the printer that bad day in May along with the board. . . . The factory was now only fifteen miles away. I could just run over there with it and have it checked. I called the factory and was told I wanted Technical Support, to which they would connect me. The telephone went dead. So I called the factory again, and this time made my way to Technical Support, who told me I wanted Service, at another number. Service told me that they did not service anything there. I would have to take the printer to the Walk-In Depot nearest me, and where was I? The Walk-In Depot for me was located in Woburn, Massachusetts. That was 35 miles away, almost in Boston.

Now it was time for lunch. When Nick came down from the computer, he reported that he had accidentally wiped out our only duplicate of BASLIB and that he had been unable to make a new copy from the original disk without registering a number of errors. BASLIB, meaning, I guess, "BASic LIBrary," is the file in which the compiler looks up ready-made routines in machine code as it converts a Microsoft BASIC program to zeroes and ones. We had to have a perfect copy of BASLIB in order to eliminate it as a possible cause of the many programming errors that would inevitably occur.

So, right after lunch, I called Lifeboat Associates in New York and asked them what to do about this. I was referred to a pleasant fellow in Tech Support named Gary Sawyer, who told me that Lifeboat would be happy to replace the faulty disk free of charge. I asked him to send me one immediately by Express Mail to expedite a major programming project. For this purpose, he referred me to the order department. "I'm sorry," they announced, "but for security reasons we are not authorized to send out a replacement disk until the original has been returned to us."

The nearest Express Mail depot was at Lawrence, Massachusetts, ten miles away. I announced to those assembled that I was on my way to Lawrence with the faulty disk. This idea was immediately ruled out on the basis that I was too feeble. How that package did get to the Lawrence post office in the middle of Kay's birthday amidst children, cousins, aunts, and girlfriends, swimming, sailing, water-skiing, fishing, cooking, walking, conversing, catching up, and celebrating, I do not know, but I have a receipt for it that proves it did. I do not remember what I gave Kay for her birthday, nor does she. It must have been a promise of some sort.

It was now the middle of the week ending in the Fourth of July, and all serious work in America began to slack off. I decided I would postpone getting the printer fixed. But, I thought, why not try to get the 220-volt transformer and ribbon drive motor that I would need for London while I was so close to the Centronics factory? I did manage to order these on the telephone, but the order clerk was not sure that there was a way I could pick them up at the factory, and delivery would be approximately a month anyhow, so I directed that they be sent to Appleton. Amid fireworks and lobsters, steaks and tennis, Nick made some progress in ironing out the purely syntactical divergencies of Microsoft BASIC from DEC BASIC.

In order to understand and appreciate the task Nick had before him this summer, the reader will need to know more about SITAR than I have hitherto set forth. The fundamental design of it came to me one spring afternoon in 1972 during a tour of the Rhine and Mosel with Mackay and Nick while Kay and the children steamed up and down the river and I stayed in the hotel to work. In the midst of a sabbatical year, I was trying to attract foundation money to *The London Stage* Project. On this afternoon of our Rhine tour, I got to the point in my grant proposal where I had to explain how I was going to standardize the the text of *The London Stage* by means of computer-aided editing.

Once there was a corporation called Viatron, based entirely on a "data entry" system that used a four-line video display, cassette tapes, and "large-scale integration"—chips. It was, but did not know it, the first word processor. Viatron intended, by virtue of this large-scale integration, to undersell every other data entry system in existence, in particular the universal IBM keypunch. And by virtue of its video display, it was going to outperform every other data entry system, especially that same keypunch. The year was 1970, in the "dark backward and abysm of time" when video terminals first began to appear on the face of the earth.

During the first exploratory months of *The London Stage* Project, I once had seen a demonstration of this machine at Viatron's salesrooms on Boston's Route 128, the cradle of American computing. Here my astonished eyes beheld text-editing on a video terminal for the first time. In the practiced hands of the typist who showed it off, the Viatron device performed insertion and deletion perfectly and effortlessly. The display was too small, it wrote capital letters only, and it did not have wraparound, but all the basic concepts were there. But Viatron failed because its bankers lost faith in it after it went only 20 million dollars in debt.

I was one of the last to see Viatron alive. But for me that venture was not a total loss. In their waiting room, my eye fell upon a copy of *Electronic Engineer* announcing on its cover a review of display terminals, and, leafing through it, I discovered that there were actually scores of video screens on which text might be edited. As I departed, I paused to write down the name and number of this journal for future reference. "Take it," said a member of the firm, perhaps thinking that it would be one less thing to throw away.

It was thus I found out about Beehive Medical Instruments of Salt Lake City and their model III text-editing terminal, which could, way back in 1972, instantly insert and delete using the theoretical minimum number of keystrokes. By then Lawrence had installed a PDP-11, and all the ingredients for SITAR were at hand but the software to make the computer and terminal interact.

It was upon the design of this software that I ruminated that spring afternoon on the Rhine. The terminal, unaided, took care of revisions in the text; all the computer would have to do was display the desired segment of text and put it back where it came from after it was edited on the screen.

There remained the problem of retrieving the section of text desired. Working instinctively from the notion that a text was one long single string of words divided up by various types of punctuation, and having a natural antipathy to artificial and arbitrary locators of any sort like line numbers or page numbers, so easily disarrayed by additions or deletions, I hit upon the notion of finding the passage desired by simply quoting it, using ellipses (three dots) in the conventional way to indicate text omitted from the quotation but present in the source, and confining myself to key words or strings. To specify how much of the source to display, I could quote the beginning and ending of the desired segment, using words or, better still, the natural punctuators and demarcators of ordinary text: periods, commas, indentations, spaces. The quotation would be a skeleton, template, archetype, or **pattern** of the segment desired. For instance, to call up a sentence mentioning Viatron, assuming that the text used the common two-space sentence demarcator employed by most typists, I could quote the pattern:

```
"  ... Viatron...  "
```

(two spaces, ellipsis, key word, ellipsis, two spaces). In this book such a pattern might match the sentence

```
"  I was one of the last to see Viatron alive.  "
```

or any other sentence containing "Viatron".

By constructing a pattern of the segment I wanted to see, eschewing arbitrary, irrelevant, and ephemeral locators like pages and lines and fixing my attention on essential features of form and content, I could move freely and efficiently through any sort of text I might want to edit.

As luck would have it, *The London Stage* Project did get funding for a Beehive. But even though I had the hardware, text-editing Nirvana was still some distance away. I had never programmed a computer, and as a flunker of college math, I knew I'd make a mess of it if I tried. I sent a call for help over the grapevine of computing humanists and soon got word of the availability of Reid Watts, just about to graduate from the University of Kansas with a major in math, physics, and computer science. He was recommended as a "gem for the sort of post you're thinking of" by one of his teachers, a computing linguist whom I knew and very much admired. He told me to act fast because "it may be a long time before you find another such candidate." I offered Reid the job right away, and he took it.

He was indeed a gem. He was very thin and very well-organized. He locked his bicycle to the building every morning at eight, went to his desk and wrote a list of tasks for that day, executed those tasks, unlocked his bicycle every night at five, and went home to dinner with his charming wife, Debbie. He had gone to high school in Zürich, Switzerland, where his father was a theologian in the Baptist Seminary, and he and Reid used to sail around in a little boat on Lake Zürich. He had broken his legs several times as a member of his school's ski team — I imagine he was a fierce competitor — and despite some quarrels with the school authorities, he had absorbed the kind of education in which names like Rousseau and Kepler rest easily and ideas come easily in any language, including those used by computers.

He'd gotten into programming by working summers for IBM Zürich, where his boss was the famous Nicolaus Wirth, than whose writings on programming technique none have been more influential or abstruse. As a result of all this, Reid was a very philosophical programmer. He would look at you quizzically at times and ask searching questions out of the blue, like, "Does the program process the data, or does the data process the program?"

On the day of his arrival in October 1973, I outlined my idea for a text editor to Reid. The next day he appeared in my office with a piece of paper containing his plans for implementing what he called "SITAR." "What is SITAR?" I asked. "System for Interactive Text-editing, Analysis, and Retrieval. S-I-T-A-R. Isn't that what you wanted?" So it was, and so it is.

Because PDP-11s were then stingy in their allotment of memory, the system we arrived at consisted of a set of independent programs called into action by commands, all administered by another program, which Reid called the **front end**, whose task was to interpret and define the operator's wishes and call up the right module for the job. The top line of the video screen was reserved for writing these commands. Reid arranged it so that the front end would ask for any extra information it needed to execute a command — a file name or a pattern — if the operator hadn't given it on the command line.

Thus EDIT plus a filename and pattern, would supply the screen with revisable text, MORE would bring up the next page, SKIP would eliminate everything in a text prior to the piece of text on the screen, CHOP would strike out everything after it, REPLACE would substitute one string of characters for another every time it occurred, COPY would duplicate a file, CREATE would set up a new file, DELETE would wipe out an unwanted file, PRINT would type out a file, breaking it into lines and pages, and STOP would finish up SITAR, freeing the computer for other work. SITAR would accept a short form of any command, consisting of just the first two letters.

Because *The London Stage* Project required an information retrieval system capable of finding anything in its 8,026 pages, we also specified SHOW, which would find and display a pattern without allowing any editing, and FIND, which would copy all occurrences of a pattern into a separate file, counting how many. To increase the usefulness of these commands, we made it possible to use special generic characters in search patterns, typed with the CONTROL key. Thus CONTROL/X stood for any printable character; CONTROL/L stood for any Letter; CONTROL/N stood for any Number. For example, to FIND all entries in a mailing list from the given section of a state, one could follow the first three numbers of the Zip Code with two CONTROL/Ns, meaning "any Number." Thus, in my mailing list, where an asterisk delimits the beginning and end of every address,

```
"x... 549NN...x"
```

will retrieve all addresses in the Appleton area of Wisconsin.

In less than four months, Reid got SITAR up and running on Lawrence's PDP-11/45. Now, seven years later, Nick was converting Reid's creation to Microsoft BASIC. Nick was a different kind of programmer with a different sort of job. He did make lists of tasks but not for the day, and he didn't work from eight to five; in fact, he seemed not to regard the clock as pertinent. As deadlines approached, the intensity of his work tended to increase. He could easily drop programming and pursue other interests—astronomy, friends, his girl, a book. He had a good store of youthful optimism, too. He was afraid that the conversion of SITAR would be too small a job to earn him the wages he was depending on. I told him not to worry, that I needed a formatter that would produce proportional spacing on the 737, and he could keep on adding features to that all summer if need be. But, although I wrote up minimum specifications for such a formatter, I had had recent warning that days are as grass, and I doubted that he would get that far.

Reid's SITAR was an elegant, economical, clear, and meaningful structure, and it was beautifully annotated with those marginalia that programmers call **remarks**, but Nick's project was messier than the one I'd assigned Reid. Instead of designing a system to fit the clear and distinct capabilities and constraints of RSTS and BASIC-PLUS, Nick had to chisel, bend, squeeze, and stretch an already existing program to fit CDOS and Microsoft BASIC. It is really easier to write a book in a given language than to translate accurately one that has been written in another. The reason is that the second language so often lacks a word for a concept found in the first. It goes without saying that approximate translations will not work on computers.

I still have Nick's first list:

1. Change function definitions that go with LEFT, RIGHT, MID (minor). FNC$ and FNI$ are compatible. All references are compatible. No! See 9.
2. All OPEN statements must be changed, to indicate Random or Sequential. CLOSE statements are compatible.
3. Integer constants don't need the percent sign. Integer variables do.
4. DIM 1, etc statements are illegal. Try to do it with FIELD statement.
5. All arrays must be dimensioned.
6. All REMark exclamation points must be changed to apostrophes.
7. Cannot OPEN or KILL an OPENed file.

8. All DEC system calls must be deleted. No replacement yet found.
9. Remove all user-defined function calls within user-defined function calls. Easiest to not use FNC$.
10. Take "RECORD" out of GET and PUT statements.
11. All literal single or double quotes must be referred to by their ASCII codes.

Those 2,727 lines of code obviously needed a great deal of work, but in our first week at The Lake, we had encountered nothing but setbacks. I began to fear that unless things settled down considerably, I would have no SITAR to take to England in September. Unexpected interruptions and delays were, in the very nature of things, bound to continue. Only a few days more than seven weeks remained before Nick must return to classes in Arizona, and seven weeks go fast, especially in the summer. We would finish the birthdays with mine next week. But in the last week of July came the reunion with my cousins. And the yearly renewing of ties with our summer friends, though a joy and a delight, would entail a lot of parties. In the sixth week, all work would stop while we packed up and moved operations to Appleton. Since these were only the distractions I knew of, seven weeks would be little enough to convert SITAR. Therefore, I announced to the family that we were in a state of total emergency.

Week Two

The second of Nick's eight weeks began on Monday, July 7th, my birthday. I wanted a new BASLIB from Lifeboat and a repaired printer from Centronics. For the family, in view of the fact that only a few weeks earlier it had been doubtful that I would have another birthday, the occasion had become a unusually significant. They planned a day, which they formally announced by a poster done in red marking pen in the form of a PERT flow chart (Program Evaluation Review Technique) that assessed the time spent on breakfast, wound-dressing, walk, lunch, fixing water pump, swim race, cocktails, surprise, and dinner. I was asked what I most wanted to do on my birthday, and "Go see *The Empire Strikes Back*" popped instantly into my head. The PERT chart was duly adjusted to fit the movie in.

The surprise was "Three Score Years in the Life of BRS II," from which I discovered that, from my children's point of view, my peccadilloes were more interesting than my achievements, and certainly funnier. The movie required a convoy of cars to a shopping mall on the closest freeway. Dick Best and crew from the camp next door went along, he in greasy shirt and jeans from working on his water pump, and he sat next to Aunt Janet, who'd primped for my birthday party and looked like a socialite from Grosse Pointe. All told, there were fourteen viewers from The Lake, and all declared the film to be almost as good as *Star Wars*. Nick said it was better the second time.

On Tuesday Nick went off to visit friends until Saturday, on the premise that work on SITAR would be fruitless without a BASLIB he could trust. At least he could drop off the printer at the Walk-In Center in Woburn on his way.

Meanwhile, I began to harass Lifeboat and the Walk-In Center with phone calls which they easily took in stride. The Walk-In Center reported an unusually busy week. Lifeboat's order clerk promised to look up my order and call back. By Wednesday, she was able to tell me that updates take two weeks. I protested that that this was not an update but a replacement of faulty merchandise. She said that made no difference.

Without frequent printed copies of his programs, a programmer has difficulty tracking down the source of the inevitable errors in them, he makes so many changes in the course of his daily work. I wanted if possible to have a printer for Nick when he returned on Saturday. Knowing that on Friday everything would get postponed until Monday, I made one of my desperation Thursday calls to the Walk-in Center. They told me to call Monday, that they had such a backlog of repairs that they were going to work on them Saturday and Sunday. To pass away the time, Devon and I spent the rest of the week writing a *User's Guide to Camp*, using Cromemco SCREEN, which we found easy to learn but a bit finicky. With two families having seven grown children who might visit The Lake at any time of year, some standard operating procedures were becoming necessary. Since these procedures have to alter with time and circumstances, the power to publish new editions easily by computer is a blessing. But for SITAR, week two was almost a total loss.

Over the weekend, Nick had no course but to use the flawed compiler, hoping against hope that the flaws would not affect the facilities he was using. He now confronted the **pointers**. Because of SITAR's modular design, pointers are a big problem for it, and Microsoft BASIC didn't have good tools for handling them.

Pointers arise because of computers' insensitivity to meaning. Although computers can identify a word, because every word is a set of numbers, they don't recognize it as having a meaningful place in a meaningful context the way you and I do. "Slings and arrows," we say. "That's in the 'To be or not to be' speech in *Hamlet*: 'Whether to suffer the slings and arrows of outrageous fortune.'" In the first place, the computer has to match every 17-character string in *Hamlet*, starting at the beginning, to see if it equals the numbers for "slings and arrows," and then it could only tell you (having counted) that the phrase starts at, say, the 27,429th character and ends at the 27,445th. These numbers "point to" "slings and arrows"; they are its "pointers." But in practice, it's more complicated. The computer would have predivided *Hamlet* into **blocks** of arbitrary length (not acts and scenes) and located the pointers as the 37th and 53rd bytes of block 107 of the file named "HAMLET." The situation is even worse if "slings and arrows" spans two blocks.

When SITAR finds a string that matches a pattern, it has to store the pointers somewhere until it's ready to do something with the string. Then, if we have **record I/O** (block Input/Output), which thank goodness both our BASICs do, the next time SITAR wants the pattern, perhaps to put it in another file, instead of searching all over again, it looks up the pointers and goes right to the block and byte address in the file, using arbitrary numbers instead of locating it in the story line as a human reader would do.

Another great contributor of pointers is SITAR's "hole." Any editing system has the big problem of allowing for the fact that a file may grow in the process of revision. Reid's solution was to put a "hole" in the file that traveled along as the computer searched for the pattern. When the computer arrived at the pattern string, there would be a hole beside it into which the user could write as much text as the hole had room for. Since Reid couldn't decide in advance how big the hole for insertions should be, he arranged that SITAR would ask its user, when he first entered a file, to decide how many lines he wanted to insert (and if the answer was less than ten percent of the file, he gave him ten percent anyhow).

Deletion was less of a problem. It simply increased the size of the hole. To allow for cases in which the hit string spanned two blocks, Reid invented what he called a "fill block," whose functioning I do not understand and will not try to explain. Needless to say, it too gave rise to pointers.

Since the easiest way to move the hole was to keep it always at the beginning of the file and move bypassed text to its end block by block, the true beginning and end of the text got lost in the middle of the file, or would have if Reid hadn't made SITAR continually correct the beginning-end pointers every time it moved a block. More pointers.

If SITAR had been all one program, storing pointers would have been simple. The program would have reserved a place in computer memory for keeping them, and there they would have stayed until the program finished its work. But, on account of the PDP-11's shortage of memory, SITAR had been broken into modules, one for each command (and three for EDIT and FIND). Every time the front end had to call a new module, DEC's RSTS cleared memory and loaded the new module. When the new module went to work on any file, it had to know that file's current pointers. So every time a module left a file, SITAR had to store the pointers where they could stay—in an ancillary disk file.

Reid actually had to establish three safe-keeping files: a temporary one in which the tripartite modules (EDIT and FIND) kept a file's pointers while they switched around among their submodules; a permanent one in which SITAR put a text file's pointers when it stopped processing it; and a permanent one for standard information that all modules used in common.

I now proudly present SITAR's official list of pointers exactly as set down in Reid's excellent documentation:

H: points to the block at the head of the file.

T: points to the block at the tail of the file.

P1: points to the block on the left side of the hole.

P2: points to the block on the right side of the hole.

P3: points to the end of the file.

P4: points to the block in which the last hit began.

P5: points to the character at which the last hit began.

P6: points to the block in which the last hit ended.

P7: points to the character at which the last hit ended.

I1: stores the number of characters in the fill block.

P9: tells system which disk block to deliver next.

Creating and maintaining the pointer files by means of Microsoft BASIC was one of Nick's big headaches, because, to use my translating metaphor, Microsoft BASIC didn't have words for the way BASIC-PLUS did it. BASIC-PLUS had **virtual arrays**, thus described because RSTS put them on a disk but treated them virtually as if they resided in computer memory. Arrays are tables in which computers look up numbers that they need to know, as we use trigonometric tables. Using virtual arrays, all Reid had to do was write "Let P2 = 6", and it was six, even though P2 was some bytes somewhere on a disk. To store pointers in Microsoft BASIC, Nick had to create regular disk files, obeying all of the protocols that disk files entail, and load them into Z-2D memory whenever a SITAR module needed to look at or change them. Handling SITAR's pointers in Microsoft BASIC required a lot of extra, tricky programming code.

Week Three

On Monday morning of the third week, having over the weekend experienced questionable results in his efforts to store the pointers, Nick was reluctant to waste any more time with an equivocal BASLIB. Furthermore, he now came squarely up against one of those things they never tell you, or one of those things that everybody else knows but we had to find out. We had not realized that on my computer system it would take five minutes to compile a SITAR module.

Even the best programmers rely a great deal on trial and error. When it takes five minutes to test a hypothesis, a programmer wastes an awful lot of time waiting for results. If, thanks to thin documentation and the unavailability of experienced advice, you must do an unusual amount of experimentation, as Nick had to, you may spend most of your time waiting for results.

Therefore, on that Monday morning, Nick thought it best to visit friends on Cape Cod while I arranged for an emergency shipment of the Microsoft BASIC **interpreter** with Lifeboat Associates. Though a program that is interpreted to the machine one line at a time runs more slowly than a program compiled in advance, it runs right away; and if there's a bug, it aborts right away, giving the programmer a fast result, if not the result he wanted.

But Lifeboat would not send the interpreter until they had received a signed nondisclosure agreement from me promising not to sell or give away any copies. So I ordered by mail, enclosing an extra nondisclosure agreement that had been sent with the compiler, giving my MasterCharge number, marking the order URGENT in prominent places, and requesting that they send it by Express Mail to the post office in the city of Lawrence, Massachusetts, our nearest Express Mail depot, ten miles away. With luck I might have the interpreter by the end of the week when Nick returned.

That done, I turned my attention to the printer. A call to Woburn ascertained that it was ready for me to walk in and pick up. By now Devon thought she was strong enough to face Chicago again, and we took her to the plane in Boston, picking up the printer in Woburn on the way. When I plugged it in on my return to The Lake, I fully expected it not to work. But it wonderfully did work. The trouble, written on the repair slip, had been "Head on wrong side of switch. No charge." Studying the slip, I realized with chagrin that I had been the culprit again. That day two months ago when I had fixed the skewed platen and smelled electronic smoke, I must have reassembled the printer with the printing head on the wrong side of the switch lever that stops the carriage when it returns. Thus trapped, the carriage couldn't even start across, let alone return. If I hadn't been so stupidly daunted by my ignorance of printers, I could easily have fixed it myself.

On Thursday of this week, Nick returned to further experiments with the pointers, using the equivocal compiler that took ages to compile. Frequent calls to the post office earned us no news of the Microsoft interpreter's arrival. That was the beginning and ending of the third week.

Week Four

At the beginning of the fourth week, the post office still had no interpreter. Inquiring at Lifeboat for the reason why, I soon found myself talking with a sympathetic person who identified herself as Betsy Green. After a thorough investigation she was able to tell me that they had no record anywhere of having received any such order as I described. In a state of consternation, I pleaded with Betsy to please, for the sake of my urgent programming project, expedite the posthaste delivery of a new order. She said she would be happy to do so but regretted that her hands were tied until she had my signature on a nondisclosure agreement. It happened that I still had another. We agreed that I would send it to her personally by Express Mail today, that it would arrive tomorrow, Tuesday, that she would immediately express the disks to me, and that I'd have them Wednesday.

There would be no interpreter, then, until Wednesday. In the interim Nick took the opportunity to visit his girl Debbie at Dartmouth's summer session. I gave him the urgent order to express to Betsy Green on his way.

On Wednesday morning, hoping to hear that all was well, I called Betsy at Lifeboat. All was not well. Not only had she not sent the disk, but she had not even received my nondisclosure agreement. Since Nick was away anyhow, I decided to give Lifeboat another day. Meanwhile, I received notice in the mail from Lifeboat Associates telling me why my first order, sent two weeks ago, could not be filled. My MasterCharge number was wrong. On checking, I found that I had indeed missed one digit of the sixteen. My opinion of this self-styled "lifeboat" now began to sink. Why hadn't Betsy Green been able to trace this order when I called last week? And since I had clearly marked it "URGENT," why hadn't they called me at once when they discovered that wrong number? Far from saving my life, they were watching me drown!

Casting about for some way to expedite the work while my programmer was away, I decided to print directories of all our disks and make a catalogue of all our files. I had seven directories to make of seven disks. Everything went well until I got to the fourth. When I commanded "DIR", the red light on disk A went on and just stayed on. The Z-2D was dead. It would not even reboot. When I RESET and hit RETURN, the red light simply went on and stayed on. Something was wrong with the computer. The hair on the back of my head began to prickle.

I calmed myself down and began to study the matter. When I put a disk in drive A, there was a funny rattle inside. I took out the disk and peered into the slot. I could see the steel wheel that turned the disk, but nothing suspicious. But when I compared the dim views inside both drives, I could see that a little white plastic windmill about an inch and a quarter in diameter, with its fans curled inward like the petals of a wilting daisy, was missing from drive A.

Now, what was I going to do? Drive A was broken. I didn't think we could operate without two drives. My SITAR project was in bad trouble. It would take a week or two to get it fixed in Boston, if I could find a place; a month if I had to ship it to Cromemco. The windmill's function was to hold the disk against the steel wheel, and drive A's windmill was gone—somewhere out of sight but apparently the cause of the rattle.

Kay, arriving on the scene, could see my distress. "You look awful," she said. "Disk drive's broken," I said. "Then why don't you fix it?" There is a myth in our family that when they were little, the children thought I could fix even a burnt-out light bulb. But I knew nothing of disk drives. I was ready to start calling numbers in the yellow pages. I knew only that disk drives were extremely delicate. The manual warned against warping them by screwing them too tightly to their mountings. The alignment of the heads was so critical that it had to be done with an oscilloscope and a special disk.

But then I took heart. Remembering how simple the printer's problem had been, I reasoned that if the drive was broken anyhow, what matter if I broke it some more? If there were any chance that I could fix it myself, I should, to avoid further delay, take that chance. If I finally did need professional help, the technician could just as well repair whatever further damage I might do. Using a flashlight, I could discern the windmill lying at the bottom of the disk enclosure. With my fingers I was just able to wiggle it out. It was worse than I thought. Not only had it fallen off its hub, but two of its eight petals had been bent so that they now hung limply. I tested one of them too much, and it fell off. Since these petals were curved inwards in such a way that they gripped the disk and held it up against the drive wheel, more or less in the manner of a clutch, they were obviously important. I was in dire straits unless this clutch would work with only six of its petals in commission.

It appeared that the manufacturer had attached the windmill by melting some of its plastic over the circumference of the hub. How could I get any sort of melting tool into that slot? I didn't dare disassemble the drive for fear of spoiling its delicate alignment.

Maybe I could glue it onto the hub. There was no torque on this windmill; it simply spun freely around while the drive wheel pressed the disk against it. It needed only enough adhesion to keep it from falling off when the clutch was released and the disk removed. I decided to use rubber cement, the glue you can undo. It was truly surgeon's work, but with one finger pushed through the front slot of the drive and another through a hole in the bottom, I succeeded in positioning the windmill over its hub and pushing it on. Thus repaired, the drive worked as well as ever, and I promised myself to be more gentle in mounting disks ever after.

The next morning I awoke to Thursday in America, the day on which something drastic has to be done if you want action this week. When I got her on the phone, Betsy Green reported that she had my order in hand now and would send it out right away. But after I hung up, I had the feeling that she'd hesitated about getting it to me this week. When I expressed my worries to Kay, she cut right to the core of the matter at once, as she always does, saying, "All of this fuss with Lifeboat is not worth it. You ought to get someone in New York to go to their office and get the disk for you."

Precisely, I agreed, but who? There was Cousin Hannah, the writer, and there was my college roommate, the lawyer, but we couldn't see ourselves asking them to go and get some floppy disks. Benny's girl Vicki, a student at Columbia, would have been a likely candidate, but she'd gone home to California. But how about Vicki's roommate? We had to get the number from Benny in Berkeley, but we couldn't find him in until eleven PM, too late to call her. Early next morning I made my strange request to Vicki's roommate, JoAnne Donnelly, who didn't know me at all but who was not only willing but happy to run the errand.

By noon she had called to report that the BASIC interpreter was on its way via Express Mail to the post office in Lawrence. I asked her what kind of a place Lifeboat was. "Oh," she said, "I guess it's just an ordinary kind of New York office, but they've just moved, and it seemed a bit confused."

That afternoon Nick came back from Dartmouth, unhappy to report that Debbie had broken off with him but consoled by the fact that they were still close friends. Later on the cousins arrived. Jack and Bunny came from Florida, where Jack, an engineer like my father and his, ran a combination feed store, garden store, and tack shop and Bunny taught children with hearing and speech difficulties. Ross and Pat came from Phoenix, Arizona, where Ross was in the business of fabricating steel. Pat is a native Arizonan who always drives a pickup truck and who has overcome enough physical afflictions to kill a weaker person five times over. Joyce (Jack's twin) and Donald Duncan had come from Milton, Massachusetts, where Don taught math at the Academy and Joyce did Academy accounts and helped H & R Block do income taxes. Cousin Richard, the biggest Schneider in both body and soul and once a first-rate electronic engineer, couldn't come. He lay stricken with Parkinson's disease in Massachusetts, where his big-hearted landlady, Thelma, had become his nurse. Richard was something of a legend at The Lake because he had swum around the island, almost a day's journey, and because, when we were boys, he'd picked up the local bully and dumped him the lake like a sack of potatoes.

This excellent society of relations can cause delicious feasts to appear and housework to disappear without any apparent expenditure of effort, and they make the hours whiz by in animated discussions, gales of laughter, feats of skill and strength, and shows of talent. During sunset drinks on my father's screen porch, we were surprised by the skirling of a bagpipe filling the cove with powerful emotion. It was Donald, The Duncan, of course, saluting the day's end with his ancestral instrument as he paced slowly back and forth on the dock, barely visible through the trees. After dinner Jack got out his guitar and rendered us a part of his large repertoire of old songs and folk tunes: "Boll Weevil," "Starving to Death on My Government Claim," "Blood on the Saddle," "Blue-Tail Fly," an exact imitation of Tex Ritter's "Rye Whiskey," including the hiccups, and "Old Shep," the saddest song ever sung.

On Saturday morning, a phone call revealed that JoAnne Donnelly's interpreter had indeed reached the post office, and it was added to the list of things to get on that day's excursion for provisions.

Meanwhile, the men, being engineers by heredity, education, occupation, or association, needed an engineering job. I had been plagued in recent years by rotting wooden doorsteps, and I had determined to put a stop to them by replacing them all with flat boulders. When I pointed out the enormous rock I had chosen for the front doorstep, fifty yards away and over a hill, they chortled with glee. They brought to the task not only brawn but brains. The principal tools were a block and tackle, ropes, round firewood logs, some poles, a crowbar, and a pickaxe. With these, we applied all the mechanical advantages: the inclined plane, the wedge, the lever, and the pulley. It was beautiful to watch that one-ton boulder inch back and forth up that hill and down into its proper niche, just as if it had had a will of its own, while the cousins and I mostly stood around and talked about the next move. This project consumed much of the day, and Thelma and Frank, her brother, who had joined us for the day, found our antics most entertaining.

During the afternoon the shopping expedition returned with the interpreter disks. I thought I should copy them right away, so as to have a backup in case of damage to the original. But I could not copy the Betsy/JoAnne disks. I could not even get a directory of them. They were unreadable. That evening I listened with mixed feelings as Don played "Amazing Grace" on his bagpipe to the setting sun. Thus ended the fourth week.

Week Five

The fifth week began with me on the telephone talking to Gary Sawyer at Lifeboat. He fired a set of questions at me. "Yes," I answered, "it was a Cromemco computer"; "Yes, it was set up for double-sided disks"; "Yes, I had specified Cromemco Z-2D on my order"; and "Yes, it was operating under CDOS." "Well," he said, "we have had some problems with Cromemco because they keep changing things. Maybe it's your operating system." He sounded as if it might be my fault. "All I know," I threatened, "is that your ad in *BYTE* says that Microsoft BASIC will run on a Cromemco Z-2D." I then made a speech in my King Lear voice, which came quite naturally under the circumstances, emphasizing my pressing need, the shortness of time, my imminent departure for England, and Lifeboat's recalcitrance to date.

"All right," said Gary, when he was sure I was done. "Here's what you do: You send me back our interpreter disks. And also send me two disks of your own that you have initialized with CDOS. Put a file of some sort on one disk. That way we can find out what the problem is. We'll put the programs on your own disks to be sure they're compatible." I supposed that all this meant I got no interpreter until some time next week. "Oh, no," said Gary, "if you get those disks to me tomorrow, I should get the replacements back to you before the end of this week, maybe Wednesday." I begged another courier to the post office from the assembled family and did as directed.

This day the cousins took off for Joyce and Don's cottage in Maine; they would be back with lobsters on Friday. Kay and I had been much impressed by Cousin Jack's Datsun, and, discovering that we had a Datsun agency in nearby Nashua, we went over there to see if we could find a good one to take to England. I was happy to make the trip because the Centronics factory was over there too and I might be able to pick up the parts I had ordered for the 220-volt conversion. Thus, on our way to the Datsun dealer, we called at the factory. The receptionist's blank look clearly told me that what I was trying to do had never been tried before, but she plugged me in to Sales, who plugged me into Tech Support, who plugged me into Service, who put me on hold for five minutes and then reported that yes, there was an order, but no, it wasn't ready yet. We did, however, find a Datsun station wagon that day at a very good price, and we bought it.

On Wednesday, I thought it wise to check Gary Sawyer's progress, in case there was anything I should be doing on my end. He averred that they were working on it and expected a result soon. Today? "Probably." On Thursday, last chance to save this week, Gary was always "on another line" when I called, and no amount of holding would suffice to reach him. It was already after four in the afternoon when I finally cornered him, and he had not sent the software. I had gotten mad in advance, predicting this outcome, and the words I'd been thinking now flew out at Gary. "If you can't get this done, I have to take it to someone at Lifeboat who can. I want to speak to your president, if you have a president in this fouled-up outfit."

"We do have a president," Gary shot back, I thought defensively, and for a long second had nothing else to say. Then he said, "Please wait a minute." I sensed that he put the phone down on his desk and walked away. Not long after, he picked up the phone again and said, "Here's someone who can help you." A new voice came over the wire: "This is Bob Halsall. What seems to be the trouble?"

I poured out my woes, same as before. In response, Bob said, "Uh huh, here's what you do: send me at once two disks initialized by your computer, with a file of some sort on one of them. As soon as I get them, I will make some tests, find out what's wrong, and send you good copies of the software. You will have them on Saturday morning." This was the voice of a Caesar or at least a General Washington.

Now I was getting somewhere. I thanked him effusively, stumbling over my words in tail-wagging gratitude. "I'm sorry you had to get to me," he replied sympathetically. "Hey, where are you anyhow?" I told him where. "Hey," he said, "I'll be flying almost over you Friday afternoon. Going to my place in Vermont. I could drop off the disks. You have an airfield near-by?" I didn't think so, nearer than Manchester. Bob said he'd look into it.

It was now 4:50. Bob had to have those disks in New York tomorrow morning. The deadline for Express Mail was 5:30. Could I make the ten miles into downtown Lawrence in that time? Kay was willing to try. I copied the required magnetic information onto the disk; we jumped in the car, wound our way impatiently through New Hampshire, sped over the freeway, dropped down into Lawrence, slid up to the post office, ran in, and breathlessly asked the man at the window if we could still send Express Mail. "Maybe," he said, with some amusement. "We'll see what we can do." It was 5:35.

Friday, the cousins arrived with Maine lobsters, and all except Pat and me, the walking wounded, dashed off to Massachusetts to visit their their stricken brother Richard.

Nick drove off to the Boston Airport to pick up my brother Dave and his wife Ann, who came first to join the reunion and second to take up residence for their month at The Lake: Dave, a career diplomat, taking a well-deserved month's leave from duties as ambassador to a Third-World country and equally deserving Ann, the hardworking and adept director of America's social presence there. It was the year of the Iranian hostages, and we were glad to have Dave and Ann safe home, at least for a while.

Pat and I whiled away the afternoon with SCREEN, writing a proclamation to be read that evening in honor of Joyce and Don's twenty-fifth anniversary. Pat was delighted to see our ideas taking shape on the screen, the new ones slipping easily into their proper places and the better continually replacing the worse until we had the best we could do.

I called Bob Halsall. He had the disks ready to send, and everything was under control.

That evening, with Dave and Ann adding lustre to the occasion, together with authentic Maine lobsters boiled exactly right by Maine cooks, we celebrated Joyce and Don's anniversary. Indomitable Jack had a poem to go with Pat's and my proclamation, the bagpipe bleated gleefully, the anniversary presents were enthusiastically appreciated, and the guitar twanged accompaniment as we sang "I've Been Working on the Railroad," "Going to the Hamburg Fair," and other songs our fathers taught us. Don recited his poem of the boy orator who forgot his lines and patched together a string of hilariously juxtaposed famous quotations. Some of it came out like this:

> When freedom from her mountain height cried, "Twinkle,
> little star,"
> Shoot if you must this old gray head, King Henry of
> Navarre!
> Roll on, thou deep and dark blue castled crag of Drachenfels,
> My name is Norval, on the Grampian Hills, ring out, wild
> bells!

> If you're waking, call me early, to be or not to be,
> The curfew must not ring tonight! Oh, woodman spare that
> tree!
> Charge, Chester, charge! On, Stanley, on! and let who will
> be clever!
> The boy stood on the burning deck, but I go on forever!

On Saturday Nick went off to visit a friend at Harvard, and I called the post office to see if they had anything from Lifeboat. They didn't and said to call later.

About eleven o'clock I got a phone call from Federal Express at Manchester: "We have a Courier Pak for you. Our driver wants to know how to get to your house from your post office." "Which way is he coming from?" I asked. "Don't know which way he's pointed. That's where he's at now. He just radioed for us to get directions." I told them how: south one mile, turn right, go one mile, big rock at the bend, take the right fork, wind through the woods, over the bridge, up the hill, watch for the sign, wind down and around to the brown camp at the lake.

A little later Manchester called again. "He's at the rock. What's he do now?" I told them again, and in two minutes, there he was in his big red, white, and blue truck, a symbol of American high-speed high-tech, bouncing into the retreat my father chose to get away from telephones. "Sign here," he said, as if he navigated the back woods every day.

I ran up the stairs with the disks, put the one containing the interpreter on drive B, and asked for a directory. I got one, showing that all was as it should be. Now to copy the interpreter to a disk of my own. If I couldn't copy it, I couldn't interpret with it either. Under XFER, disk drive B executed one, two, three, four, five thunks. All seemed well. Then there was a series of grating sounds, and this message dropped onto my screen:

```
Read error, Drive B, Cylinder 05, Surface 00, Sector 03, Status 08
Continue (C), Retry (R), Ignore (I), Cancel (CONTROL/C).
```

I pondered the error message. Why did CDOS offer Retry, Ignore, and Continue, as well as cancel, if it weren't sometimes desirable to go ahead in spite of errors? I decided to see what happened if I tried "Continue". What happened was that drive B kept on going for several more thunks and then reported the same error on a higher cylinder number. To make short of the matter, by continuing I managed to copy the whole file with only five more error messages. On finishing, XFER reported, "24K BYTES READ"—exactly the right length.

I copied the interpreter eight more times but never did better than five errors. Apparently there were a dozen bad spots on the disk. XFER could get past some of them successfully some of the time and others never without an error. I stopped trying when errors began to multiply on cylinders 5 and 9. It was clear that the disk was getting worse and worse.

I couldn't get through BASLIB at all. But it was the interpreter we really needed.

In the midst of this jousting with error, I was interrupted by a most unexpected phone call. It was nobody but Bob Halsall himself, calling from his house in Vermont, wanting to know how I was doing. I was thunderstruck. No one at Lifeboat had ever before called me, although many had promised to, and here was Bob calling when he hadn't even promised to. I had to tell him that things were going badly, five errors in the interpreter and unable to copy BASLIB at all.

This news did not dampen Bob's spirits one bit. "Do any of those copies load?" he said. "How do I load?" I asked. "Put it in drive A and write 'MBASIC'. I'll hold." I did as he said and after thirty seconds of disk activity saw this:

```
BASIC-80 Rev.  5.1
[CP/M version]
Copyright 1977, 78, 79 (C) by Microsoft
Created:  14 Jan 80
26581 Bytes free
Ok
```

When I reported this to Bob, he said, "Try FILES. That uses disk I/O and everything." I wrote "FILES" and immediately got a directory of the whole disk. Hearing this, Bob said, "You're all right. You're in business. It works."

I was about to thank him and hang up when it struck me that Bob might now consider the matter of the interpreter settled. "You're not going to leave us with errors, are you?" I said. Of course he wasn't, and, having done this well, he was sure he could solve the problem on Monday. I should send him immediately one more disk, this time containing a program as well as a data file.

Week Six

On Sunday, Brother Dave, who, in the course of his career in South Asia, had been a regular Sunday sailboat racer in such places as Karachi, Poonah, and New Delhi, sailed our 45-year-old Snipe against stiff competition and in two races came in fifth and sixth out of ten starters. This was good news—in a way—because I'd been coming in last so consistently that I had concluded that we needed a new boat. Now I was forced to admit once more that we just needed a better sailor.

When Nick got home from Harvard that day, he was happy that perhaps he at last had an interpreter to work with but unable to do much work with it, being occupied with entertaining Debbie, now a friend instead of a girlfriend, who had come down on a two-day visit from the Dartmouth summer session. The rest of week six was devoted to packing up, going back to Appleton, and resettling there.

In six weeks, Nick had ironed out the syntactical divergencies of BASIC-PLUS, and he had written but not debugged the routines for storing and retrieving the pointers. He was confident that if the interpreter worked, he'd have SITAR working in short order, but I, having missed almost every deadline I'd ever set during fifteen years of computing, now began to despair of taking SITAR with me to London.

Week Seven

We were back in Appleton. I had gained ten pounds, I was steady on my pins, I had a healthy tan, but I still tired easily. Thanking our stars for the Science Hall dolly, the wheelchair ramp, and the elevator, Nick and I pushed and pulled the great black box and its paraphernalia up to my office on the fourth floor of Main Hall, which now became the site of frantic computing for the sixteen days and nights left of Nick's eight-week summer.

Main Hall, built in 1853 out of nearby Fox River stones with Amos Lawrence's Massachusetts textile money and having four two-story Ionic columns to hold up its front porch and a cupola on top in rude imitation of Harvard, is an unlikely residence for a computing machine, the more so because Main Hall houses humanistic study at Lawrence, and, except for a few computer terminals in the basement, is devoid of any machines more sophisticated than a Xerox copier. In fact, Main Hall is so unsympathetic to technology that when my literary-historical-philological colleagues visit my office they apparently do not see my highly visible computer. I deduce that they refrain from remarks on it for fear that a long lecture-demonstration may ensue which they do not want to hear, and of course they are absolutely right. They *would* get a lecture-demonstration, and they do *not* want to hear it.

With little more than two weeks left, I drastically reduced our goals. We would stop all work on SHOW and FIND, the information retrieval modules, on which Nick had spent too much time already. We could also get along without SKIP, CHOP, and REPLACE, which I could accomplish by transferring text to SCREEN.

If he had any extra time at all, I wanted him to write a rudimentary PRINT program that would justify the right-hand margin of text as it divided it into pages, paragraphs, and lines. Because it could move the carriage one fiftieth of an inch, the Centronics 737 could stretch a line to a specified right margin without putting perceptibly uneven spacing between words. Cromemco's formatter did the job crudely, by doubling a few spaces in a line, with disconcerting results.

Using the interpreter and confining himself to EDIT, Nick began to make real progress. He debugged the pointer-filing system and set to work on two other features of BASIC-PLUS SITAR for which Microsoft SITAR had no equivalent: handling the Beehive's batch send, and managing long strings.

In ordinary interactive operation, computer systems read characters from a terminal no faster than a human being can type. They are not designed to receive bursts of a thousand characters a second, the speed at which the Beehive could send them and which an efficient SITAR required. In fact, so foreign to conventional computing was SITAR's batch send that Reid had had to revise the RSTS operating system itself to get the original SITAR working, a daring and ticklish operation. But BASIC-PLUS did at least have a word for reading a stream of text from a terminal. Microsoft BASIC did not. So Nick had to make up a word for "read batch send" out of the bits and pieces available in CDOS and Microsoft BASIC.

CDOS did have a **system call**—128—that would read one character from the console each time it was issued, and that was all we knew about it. Nick's problem was to write a program that would issue this call as fast as the Beehive sent characters—a thousand per second. Nowhere in Microsoft or Cromemco manuals was there a hint of how to do it. Nick was looking at a black box whose laws of behavior he could deduce only by trial and error. He was in exactly the same position as a scientist looking at nature. To explain the behavior of nature, a scientist constructs a hypothesis and then devises an experiment that will say "yes" or "no" to that hypothesis and not "maybe."

The batch-send procedure consisted of three steps. The first was a result of the fact that, for some reason known only to its designers, the DM20 would not do its "page dump" unless told to do so by the computer. So, when the operator wanted to send a batch, he punched a SEND key that sent a special code to the computer, and the computer then replied with another special code that asked the DM20 for its page dump. Second, the computer read the batch, one character at a time, and third, it stored the batch in its memory. In week seven Nick would send a batch to the computer by some stratagem or other and look for it in memory. It would not be there. So he tested the following hypotheses:

Hypothesis one: Something was going wrong in the first step. To ascertain the truth of this possibility, Nick wrote a little program called CURSE, which was simply a rigorous exercise in processing special codes for both the terminal and the computer. They completed CURSE without making a mistake, proving that nothing was going wrong in step one of the batch send.

Hypothesis two: The batch was getting lost in memory. Perhaps there wasn't sufficient free space to receive the batch. Microsoft BASIC contained the word "FRE" which was supposed to free up unused memory. He put FRE into his screen-reading program, but it had no observable effect.

Hypothesis three: The interpreter couldn't read the batch as fast it was being sent. What *was* the interpreter's top speed? Who knows about these things? Where do you look up the answers? Nick slowed down the terminal's rate to about 14 characters per second, using special codes. But the interpreter still couldn't read the whole batch, even though the DM20 took more than two minutes to send it. Either the interpreter was too slow, or we needed another hypothesis.

The only way to speed up the computer would be to write the batch-send routine in assembly language, which would speak directly to the Z80 without the intermediary of an interpreter. Now we were truly in trouble, for Nick had never written a program in assembly language, though he had some dim idea of the way it was done. We had no Z80 programming manual. But Nick remembered seeing some examples of Z80 routines in our Cromemco manuals. Perhaps he could steal enough ideas from them to write a batch-send routine in Z80 mnemonics. But not before dozens of excruciating trials and errors did he at last find a combination that for some mysterious reason worked:

```
        ORG     0C000H
        ;PROGRAM TO READ SCREENFUL OF TEXT
        ;THIS ROUTINE TO BE INSERTED INTO SITAR
        LD      D,0
        INC     HL
        CALL    5
        CALL    5
GET:    CALL    5
        INC     HL
        LD      (HL),A
        CP      27
        JP      Z,STOP
        CP      13
        JP      Z,STOP
        CP      92
        JP      NZ,GET
        LD      (0C800H),HL
        LD      D,A
        JP      GET
STOP:   LD      A,D
        CP      92
        JP:     RET
        END
```

The left-hand column contains imperative verbs: LD means "load," INC means "increment," CP means "compare," JP means "jump." The right column contains whatever the verb needs to do its thing. For instance "LD D,0" means to put the number 0 in memory location D; and JP Z,STOP means to jump to the

STOP section of the program if the previous CP (comparison) produced zero (i.e., the numbers compared were equal). The statement CALL 5 causes the computer to accept one character from the terminal. Why three CALL 5s in a row? It simply wouldn't work with one or two. Thus Nick spelled things out to the computer.

The next step was to run these mnemonics through the assembler program supplied by Microsoft, which converted them to machine code, and splice the resultant set of zeroes and ones into SITAR. Because Microsoft's cryptic documentation assumed that Nick already knew what it pretended to explain, this splicing became another exasperating trial and error procedure.

Trying to catch a Beehive batch send with an assembly-language program kept Nick busy during most of week seven. When he got it working, Microsoft BASIC at last had a word for what to do with a batch from a DM20. It was PAGE, the name he gave to his assembled mnemonics.

I occupied myself with other worries. The promised replacements of the interpreter and BASLIB were still not forthcoming from Lifeboat. Kay and I were so busy getting our house in order for the year in London and Nick was getting along so well with the error-ridden software that I let that matter rest. Worse trouble threatened from another quarter. Computerlab had not received my DM20. We were still operating with Lawrence's terminal, but I couldn't take that to England. Alex checked his source and said, "It's on the way." That vagueness after so long a wait sent me into a tantrum in which I wrote him so rude a letter that Nick cautioned me against sending it. I decided to take his advice. After all, the main thing was not getting justice but getting the terminal.

Hardly had I simmered down than Angelo called, worrying about cash flow and wanting me to pay for the Z-2D. In response, I spoke as quietly as I could, through my teeth: "I will not pay anything whatsoever until I have everything I ordered. A computer without a terminal is not a computer." Thus passed away week seven.

Week Eight

It was now time for Kay and me to go to the Mayo Clinic, where I would undergo a set of blood tests and Dr. Perrault would decide whether I was fit to undertake a strenuous year abroad. Early Monday morning, we waited in his office to receive our instructions for the day. He soon swung in from the hall, wreathed in smiles, wearing his grey, yellow, and blue plaid suit set off by a well-coordinated tie, and very happy to see me looking so well. After a quick physical examination which confirmed my improved appearance, he checked off the blood tests he wanted me to take.

Just as I thought we were about to leave, Kay said, "Don't you think I ought to have a mammogram before I go to England? I haven't had one for a year." "Good idea," said Dr. Perrault, who knew that Kay's great-grandmother, grandmother, and mother had all suffered from breast cancer, and he checked off one mammogram for her. We were to report to his office at three that afternoon for the results of our tests, and then we would be free to drive home. So, after mammogram, blood tests, and lunch, we packed our bags and checked out of the hotel.

That afternoon at three, when he swung into his office, Dr. Perrault's smile was more reserved. He turned to me first and said, with his customary French inflections, "These test are fine, but I want to see the iron-binding that won't be done till tomorrow." Then he picked up Kay's X-ray, clipped it to the panel on his wall, flicked on the light behind it, and pointed with a pencil. "Can you see this?" he said; "Little spots right here?" We nodded but weren't sure. "This is the right breast. There may be some abnormal cells there, and I would advise a biopsy so we can be sure."

This biopsy would require surgery and two days of observation in the hospital. Dr. Perrault had already spoken to a specialist in such matters, a surgeon named Dr. Sylvester Sterioff. If we agreed, Dr. Sterioff would do the biopsy early on Wednesday morning. He would, of course, first want to do his own examination, and we had an appointment to see him tomorrow afternoon.

So, instead of driving to Appleton that afternoon, we unpacked our bags, re-registered at the hotel, and called all the children (except Benny, who was doing summer research in Peru). For many years we had been afraid that something like this would happen, but we had not expected it to happen just now, just when we were looking forward to a glorious year abroad. It was decided that Nick and Devon would fly to Rochester the next morning, but that Mackay should stick with her summer job at Oak Ridge National Laboratories.

Tuesday afternoon, basking in family solidarity, Nick, Devon, Kay, and I crammed ourselves into one of those consulting rooms made to accommodate one patient and one doctor. When Dr. Sterioff arrived, followed two steps behind by a resident, we noticed that he had sympathetic eyes, gentle hands, and a soft voice. There was nowhere for the the resident to sit. Dr. Sterioff reviewed the X-ray evidence with us, and then he carefully examined Kay. "Mrs. Schneider," he said compassionately, "we tentatively diagnose intraductal carcinoma of the right breast. We may be wrong. The good thing, however, is that when the abnormal cells reside within the duct, they have not yet begun to colonize." He allowed this to sink in.

"Now, what I propose to do is resect a piece of tissue about as big as this:"—he put the end of his left thumb between the thumb and forefinger of his right hand. Suddenly, he looked about in consternation. "They're taking notes!" he said to the resident.

Sure enough, Nick was jotting away on one of his yellow, legal-sized pads. "Don't worry," said Kay, laughing gaily; "we always take notes to be sure we understand everything."

"OK," said Dr. Sterioff, still somewhat uneasy; "if pathology does confirm our diagnosis and if none of the surrounding tissue indicates abnormality, it is entirely possible that we will have removed all the cancerous cells in your body. We will not know this for certain until Thursday, when we have the full report from pathology. Therefore I do not propose to proceed further than the biopsy tomorrow morning." He raised his expressive eyebrows as if to say, "oK?"

We checked each other's faces silently and then we all looked at Kay. "Well," she said, "if that's what you think is best, let's do it."

Next morning I waited in the hotel room for Dr. Sterioff's post-operative call. I expected it as early as nine, but it did not come until twenty-two minutes of ten. "She took the surgery very well, and she's out of anesthesia and back in her room. The preliminary pathological analysis does suggest intraductal carcinoma, but the good news is that there appears to be nothing in the surrounding tissue. But we won't know any of this for sure until we get the full report tomorrow." I thanked him for his good work. When I arrived in her room, Kay was groggy, limp, and restless, but happy that Dr. Sterioff was pleased with her.

Now we faced a long day of hope and doubt, like accused persons waiting for a jury's verdict. To pass the time, Kay addressed Christmas letter envelopes to be left with an Appleton neighbor for stuffing with holiday wishes from London when the day approached.

Thursday afternoon at two, Dr. Sterioff came to Kay's room with the verdict, and Nick, Devon, and I were there too. He arrived on the hour, towing his resident, and we stiffened ourselves. Pathology did confirm his diagnosis of intraductal carcinoma. It was almost certain, he told us, that her breast now contained no abnormal cells. Very probably the biopsy contained them all. However, no one could ever be sure. The family history had to be considered. "To be absolutely certain, Mrs. Schneider, you ought to have the breast removed. I would call it necessary rather than optional, but you should decide."

We looked at Kay. Perhaps one little tear started to come, but it didn't. "I think I should have it off; what do you think?" We thought so, too, hating the thought. "In that case, we'll do it tomorrow morning. I plan a modified radical mastectomy—lymph glands, but not so much muscle tissue. You will have a neat scar about five inches long where the right breast was."

"But will I be able to go to England on September 15th?" Kay asked, always planning. "I certainly believe you'll be ready to go by then. But after you get back, you should think seriously of having the other breast removed," he said regretfully. On Friday morning of the eighth week, not long after dawn, Dr. Sterioff gave Kay exactly the neat scar he said he would. It was my scar, too.

That was the eighth week. On Saturday Kay sent Nick home to work on the computer, and Devon and I stayed on to keep her company while she recuperated for another week. Nick thought that in the three days left to him he might just possibly finish the job.

Final Days

But he now confronted the worst problem of all, compensating for Microsoft BASIC's inadequate string functions—LEFT, which delivers a substring on the left side of a given string; RIGHT, which delivers a substring on the right side of a string; MID, which delivers a substring in the middle of a string; and INSTR, which locates a given substring in a string. There was nothing wrong with what these words meant—DEC's LEFT, RIGHT, MID, and INSTR *meant* exactly the same things—but there was a great deal wrong with how much of a string they could deal with. Microsoft BASIC's attention span was much too short to study SITAR's long strings. It could not deal with a string more than 256 characters long, less than four lines of text.

It had been evident to Nick from the start that this limitation would mean trouble, but he did not know how much trouble until the final weeks of the onslaught. At first, he had tried to deal with each string-handling problem as it arose in the several SITAR modules, but after patching up a few trouble spots, he realized he was repeating himself. The obvious solution was to write each function once and for all, and use the new functions every time they were needed. He called these new functions BUFSUBS, meaning "buffer subroutines." Nick now strove to complete his BUFSUBS in these last three days, while his mother recuperated from her surgery about 200 miles away with Devon and me in attendance.

A **buffer** is a space reserved in memory as a temporary storage or work space. Since memory is always limited and the work is usually unlimited, computers divide the work into a sequence of bufferfuls and process these one at a time, like a man at a desk working through a pile of papers. In order to display a screenful of text that matches a user's pattern, SITAR needs a work buffer at least as big as the screen—1,920 characters. But Microsoft BASIC could span only 256 characters. It was as if Nick had a map on which he could find the distance between Boston and Providence with no trouble, but in order to get the distance between Boston and Washington, he had to patch together three overlapping maps and add the Boston–Providence distance to the Providence–New York distance and then add the New York–Washington distance to that. Thus Nick grappled with the BUFSUBS.

A **subroutine** is a piece of a program that does a particular job that has to be done frequently, the way a carpenter might resort to his nail-hammering routine during the course of building a house. In BASIC, a program calls upon a subroutine by saying "GOSUB n", in which "n" is the number of the line where the routine begins. When the subroutine finishes its work, the program continues where it left off, the way a carpenter would return to the next step of building a house.

To indicate the nature and scope of Nick's achievement, I quote his LEFT BUFSUB:

```
9200 REM  xxxxxxxxxxxxxxxxxxxxxxxxxxxxxxxxxxxxxxxxxxxxxxxxxxxxxxxxxxxxxxx
9205 REM   LEFT STRING
9210 IF GETSTR=1 GOTO 9225
9215 HP=FNMODU(HP+LP-1,MAXBUF): TP=FNMODU(HP+NC,MAXBUF)'RESET HEAD & TAIL
9220 LENBUF=NC: GOTO 9275
9225 IF NC>LENBUF THEN NC=LENBUF
9230 IF NC>R THEN PRINT "CAN ONLY HAVE";R: NC=R
9235 LP1=FNMODU(HP+LP-1,MAXBUF): HC=FNMODU(LP1,R)
9240 FBUF=FNMIN(NC,R-HC+1): FBL=FNBLK(LP1,R)
9245 GET$=MID$(BUF$(FBL),HC,FBUF)
9250 SBUF=NC-FBUF
9255 IF SBUF=0 GOTO 9275
9260 SBL=FBL+1: IF SBL>NBL THEN SBL=1
9265 GET$=GET$+LEFT$(BUF$(SBL),SBUF)
9275 RETURN
```

All this is Nick's translation into Microsoft BASIC of the single word LEFT in DEC's BASIC-PLUS. He has actually done most of it in his own words—FNMODU, SBL, GET$, and the like—which he explains to Microsoft in the modules that use the BUFSUBS. In fact, Microsoft supplies little more than the IFs and the equal signs. The great irony of all this extra work is that I had myself to blame for it, having insisted on Microsoft BASIC to begin with, innocently assuming that LEFT meant LEFT and RIGHT meant RIGHT in any language.

The evening before he flew to Tucson, Nick called us in Rochester to say goodbye. He would take Sociable with him, our old mother cat and a great favorite of his, so that she would have a good home while we lived in London. As for SITAR, he said, "I'm sorry, Dad. We came awfully close. I even got it mostly working, but it still has some bad bugs. I just ran out of time."

I had been prepared for this but had never lost hope. Somehow, I wasn't as badly disappointed as I had thought I would be. As Devon and I and Kay sat together in Rochester, three survivors of three family catastrophes, somehow Gary Sawyer with his bland assurances and Bob Halsall with his private airplane didn't seem very important after all.

CHAPTER VI

THAR SHE BLOWS!

NICK HAD no objection to spending Christmas in London with us and would be happy to finish SITAR at that time. Kay and I, nursing our scars, were all the more determined to live intensely in England. We could have agreed with W. B. Yeats when he wrote,

> An aged man is but a paltry thing,
> A tattered coat upon a stick, unless
> Soul clap its hands and sing, and louder sing
> For every tatter in its mortal dress,
> Nor is there singing school but studying
> Monuments of its own magnificence.

Appleton, Wisconsin, is a marvelous place to raise children, but having spent three sabbaticals in England, we had come to depend on the Old World for spiritual sustenance. This might have been why, only one week after undergoing major surgery, Kay could miraculously find strength to cram all the planning, arranging, winding up, and packing for which we had reserved the month of May into the two little weeks that remained before we left.

And she did not take any short cuts. Thanks to her acute economic foresight, we always travel heavily. We never rent, holiday, or fly at retail rates, and we systematically avoid the cost of cooking, housekeeping, driving, ticketing, shipping, and other tourist services by doing for our ourselves. Finally, to avoid buying anything, we take everything. Kay's plug-in frying pan provides instant room service at no extra cost; her cans of hash, stew, spaghetti sauce, boxes of pasta, cans of bacon and butter provide the ingredients; in-cup heating coils enable in-room tea, coffee, and soup. Her haircutting kit eliminates my need (such as it is) for a barber. We always get the limit of duty-free cigarettes and whiskey, the cigarettes for cheap tipping and the whiskey to avoid buying drinks in any bar or dining room. A wife of Scottish origin is worth her weight in gold.

Kay has never been able to find a cheap flat in London, but she always does find a quaint, old place with quaint, old electricity and plumbing, and considerable Old World charm. Packing to make economic use of such a place is no easy task. For instance, one must not forget the 220- to 120-volt transformers that enable us to use our own razor, hair-clipper, electric blankets, radio, coffee pot, hair dryer, and sewing machine. Nor the fins, masks, and snorkels in case we bring off a Mediterranean holiday. Nor the guidebook collection, Scrabble, playing cards, chess, office supplies, clothes for England, Scotland, and Wales, and just in case, Spain, Portugal, Corfu, and the Alps. Gelusil for me, face cream for Kay, umbrellas, aspirin, walking shoes, the sewing kit, Spanish lessons on Berlitz tapes. Getting the Datsun to Hoboken on the day it must embark without driving it there ourselves and getting it from Southampton to London on the day it debarked while we were still in Appleton took a great deal of managing.

As I reviewed my present position, I saw that a number of things would have to fall into place before I left, and whether they would or not would be touch and go. I didn't worry so much about forgetting to take something I would need for conducting my classes and whatever research and writing I might do. London's resources would take care of such omissions. But fitting out the computer was a more risky business.

After some hesitation, I decided I would not make the change to 220-volt, 50-cycle operation until I got there, because I wanted to be able to use my computer up until the last minute. As Signal Corps radar technician, Heathkit builder, and chronic tinkerer, I felt I could accomplish that conversion independently if I had the wiring diagrams and the components.

I had sent away for the Beehive manual in week seven but didn't have it yet. And in week one, I'd ordered from Centronics the ribbon drive motor and power transformer for the printer but didn't have them yet. I did have the Z-2D manual, and it contained the necessary diagram. Drive A had broken petals on its clutch wheel. It probably wouldn't last the year, and I ought to replace it. Lifeboat still hadn't supplied error-free disks of Microsoft BASIC. What if my own equipment was at fault after all? If so, I might have to send out my disk drives for professional repair. I still didn't have the terminal I had ordered from Computerlab and couldn't take Lawrence's DM20 to England. I had almost a full box of paper, but I would probably need more printer ribbons. Did I have all the PDP-11 files I would need? Many urgent matters were pending. Could I settle them all before I left?

If I had written a diary of this ultimate fortnight, here is probably how it would have gone:

Saturday: 30th of August. Returned to Appleton from Rochester. Called the children: Mackay, finished with summer job at Oak Ridge, packing up at Earlham for term of study with Lawrence in London. Ben working hard at Berkeley. Devon thinking of going to Denver to make a new start. Nick had to have Sociable put away. Cat still purring, but vet diagnosed breast cancer and peritonitis! In her case terminal. Had brought up thirty litters and our four children.

Sunday: Church. After lunch over to office to check mail. Centronics stuff came, but ribbon drive motor is wrong one, clearly marked "120v, 60 hertz."

Monday: Labor Day. At office, made 2 backup copies of working Microsoft disks. Printed directories of all other disks, taking stock. Also got directory of PDP-11 files. Decided I would need to transfer mailing list and draft of Restoration comedy article from PDP-11.

Tuesday: Called Lifeboat, asked for Bob Halsall: busy on another line. Held five minutes and gave up. Called Alex and Angelo: had no news of Beehive, would call supplier. Called Bob Halsall again: out of office. Got Gary Sawyer, says they are working on it. Called Centronics: correct part is on its way. Called Beehive: They couldn't find my maintenance manual order. Would rush new order. 4:30: bled one pint at blood bank.

Wednesday: Called Cromemco for advice on Lifeboat disks: Marcia said to try Lifeboat's disks on a dealer's drive to rule out my drives as source of trouble. Phoned Lifeboat: Gary says they will send replacement disks Federal Express Thursday, arrive Friday. Asked if I could speak to Bob: no, but "Bob has you very much on his mind." Angelo called: Beehive was in, where did I want it delivered? Told him Science Hall loading dock. Box showed it had left Salt Lake in June bound for an electronic jobber in Los Angeles, had left there in July and spent the rest of the summer on a Pacific Intermountain Express truck.

Thursday: Tried new Beehive: worked fine. Paid Alex and Angelo $5,664.90 for Beehive, Z-2D, and accessories. Called Tandon, maker of my disk drives. Plugged in to taciturn engineer, Frank Allen; reported broken petals; "What's your name and address, I'll send you new ones." After lunch, found note to call Janet at Centronics: wanted to know whether the part for which she was making out an order was in exchange for a part I was returning, and if so, what was the part number of that? "63669271−4002," I said. "Right," she said; "it should be 304200150−1002. Right?" "All I know is it should be 220 volts, 50 cycle," I said. Called Inmac computer supplies: ordered two ribbons for the 737 at $6.75 each.

Friday: Got Computerlab bill for $176, interest on unpaid bill for three months. Sent it back to Angelo with note to the effect that he had a lot of nerve and I refused to pay it. Kay called: Lifeboat disks had arrived at house, Federal Express. Cost her $27. After lunch tried them. Worse than ever. Unable to reach Bob Halsall, out of the office, but left message that merchandise was unacceptable.

Saturday: Worked on transferring mailing list and draft of article from PDP-11 to Z-2D. Made cable to connect Beehive to PDP-11 outlet. Wouldn't work. Spent all day trying to find mistake. Had "data in" and "data out" reversed, because couldn't figure out whether they meant in and out of computer or in and out of terminal.

Sunday: Couldn't transfer any files with computer center shut down. Packed books.

Monday: Unable to transfer mail list or article from computer center to my office via Nick's GETRSTS. Called Nick: said he had told me not to waste time on long-distance transmission. It would work only if I took the Z-2D to the computer center. Hauled computer and Beehive down to basement of Science Hall. Ran GETRSTS on Z-2D. Unplugged a terminal from PDP-11, uplugged Beehive from Z-2D, plugged PDP-11 into Z-2D. Using free terminal of PDP-11 transferred mail list to Z-2D with Peripheral Interchange Program (PIP). Same procedure for article. Hauled computer back up to office. Printer ribbons arrived from Inmac, UPS Blue.

Tuesday: No disks from Lifeboat and only one week left. Called Bob Halsall, got him: said disks shipped yesterday Federal Express. Asked him what he thought problem was. "I have no idea." Angered by this casual answer, decide to make sure it's Lifeboat's fault. Took their disks over to Computerlab, tried them on one of their Z-2Ds. Couldn't even get directories. Angelo still didn't have boxes, still at old store. Would get.

Wednesday: Spent morning writing a letter to Bob Halsall:

Dear Bob,

It's very sad that after three months, a hundred dollars' worth of phone calls, a personal messenger to your office (another $50), two 20-mile trips to the nearest Express Mail depot, four of my disks sent to you, three Federal Express shipments (one charged to me), endless amounts of time and family disruptions, and a dozen bitter disappointments that I still don't have the Microsoft interpreter and compiler running on my Cromemco Z-2D computer. Yesterday we could not read any of your disks on a brand new Z-2D at Computerlab, Neenah, Wisconsin.

The bitterest disappointment was being unable to provide tools for a programmer, under contract and paid for a summer's work. He couldn't even get one of my programs up and running before it was necessary for him to return to graduate school.

We have never received a shipment of source disks from you that our machine can read in its entirety: sometimes we can't even read the directory, sometimes we can read some of the files, but always we get errors in crucial pieces of the software. Trying to program when you don't know whether an error is your fault, the interpreter's, or the compiler's is maddening to say the least.

What bothers me the most is not your technical difficulties, but the continual runaround that Lifeboat has given me. For a typical example, when I called yesterday wondering why I hadn't received my software, you said you'd sent it out yesterday. When Federal Express reported nothing today, I called your shipping department for an airbill number so they could trace it. These people said nothing had been shipped. This episode illustrates the dishonesty of many computer companies—the image they put before the public is nothing but a big bluff. Their support people will tell you anything to get you off the telephone. Promises are made with no intention of following through. When the customer tries to get attention, they put him on hold until he gives up. If, by threatening to sue for false advertising (Lifeboat specifies Z-2D compatibility in *BYTE* magazine), the customer does get some attention, it's more promises, more disappointments.

Yes, you did finally send me copies by air express, often at your own expense, but only under continual pressure. But why were there so many failures? We see it all the time in computing. When people get in a jam, they start trying anything, hoping it will work, when what is required is a careful study of the problem and a methodical approach to its solution. Your inability to get to the bottom of this incompatibility smacks of sheer computer-room hacking at the most sophomoric level.

I have dealt with scores of computer companies since I began my first computer project in 1964. Many of them behave like you. Some exist only on paper, and the "President" answers the phone. Others are like Bell Telephone. When they tell you that they will install your phone on Tuesday morning, they install it on Tuesday morning. Above all, they tell you the truth: if you can't have it this week, they tell you so. The trouble with so many junior companies is that they can't say no. But telling a customer what he *can't* have is as important as telling what he can have. That way he can plan. That's why I like grownup companies. Centronics told me that they couldn't repair my printer until the weekend. Monday they delivered it in perfect working order. I didn't waste time during the previous week expecting to have a printer the next day. I spent most of last summer expecting to have an interpreter the next day, as promised. This last week has been the worst. On the basis of telephone conversations, I expected good software from you Monday, Tuesday, Wednesday, Thursday, Friday, and Saturday. And now we are into this week.

The really tragic thing about this matter is the crucial position you hold in the microcomputer business. It was the promise of interchangeable software that caused me to buy a CP/M computer in the first place. Lifeboat was a major part of the whole project. My goodness, nowadays you can publish software like a book: anybody in the country can read it. What a spur to creativity! What a godsend to the inexperienced user! What efficiency! What a saving of money and labor! We are back to the days of the Model-T when you could get all the parts from Sears Roebuck and rebuild your whole car. Nothing as exciting has happened in American industry since the standardization of nuts and bolts. American ingenuity let loose again!

And there you sit, holding all the cards. You are laughing all the way to the bank, no doubt; I note you commute to Vermont via your own airplane. You can make a fast buck, or you can shoulder a responsibility. Let's see more of the latter and less of the former. There's certainly room for plenty of competition in your field if you don't shape up.

On 15 September, I am transferring operations to London. If you ever do get around to producing good disks, please send them to me at 57 Great Ormond Street, London WC1N 3JA, and please send them air mail. Surface mail can take two months. But perhaps you have given up. In that case you owe me $675 for the interpreter and compiler. But that won't begin to cover my losses.

Yours sincerely,

BEN ROSS SCHNEIDER, JR.
Professor of English

Copies to: Mr. Gary Sawyer, Ms. Betsy Green, and President If Any, Lifeboat Associates; President, Cromemco Corporation; Editor, *BYTE Magazine*; President, Microsoft; President, Digital Research

Sent letter and copies. Correct ribbon drive motor arrived from Centronics.

Thursday: Maintenance Manual from Beehive came: has circuit diagram for power supply showing 220-volt wiring. Mackay arrived from Earlham, excited about London.

Friday: Received Lifeboat disks via Federal Express prepaid. Copied them without any errors at all. Called Computerlab: Angelo has boxes. 3 packing days left; Kay's strength waning, but Mackay pitched in and saved the day.

Saturday: Kay and I picked up computer boxes while doing errands in afternoon. Actually 2 nested boxes. Just able to tie them into open trunk of Dad's old Buick.

Sunday: Wrote Bob Halsall that delivery of interpreter and compiler was now complete, without further comment, copies to all recipients of former letter. Packed books and papers for London. At home, taped up Kay's cartons.

Monday: Packed Beehive and Z-2D in original boxes. Z-2D expands from 2½ cubic feet to 16 cubic feet. Air Wisconsin picked up Kay's cartons at our house this evening at 6:30. Mackay and I took my computer and book cartons to airport in Buick, Z-2D on roof. Total shipment: 29 boxes, almost a ton.

Tuesday: Drove to Chicago. No standbys available today. Slept at Devon's apartment.

Wednesday: 7 AM: secure standbys at O'Hare. Lunch at Art
   Institute, outdoors. Late PM, flew standby to London.
Thursday: Arrive in London at 11 AM their time. Met by col-
   league in our Datsun: he had had no trouble getting car at
   Southampton.

The flat, constructed in 1727, was as quaint, curious, and
charming as advance notice had proclaimed. The walls sloped
inward at a ten-degree angle and were covered on the outside
with slate, because we were really living in the roof. There was a
hill in the middle of the flat and the floors sagged from the walls.
There were two 18th-century clocks, one a grandfather, both
keeping good time. None of the furniture appeared to be less
than 200 years old, and some of it was clearly more than 300
years old. The Sheraton desk had six little drawers with ivory
knobs, seven cubbyholes, two slide-out shelves on the sides, and
a leather writing surface that pulled out and slanted up, all en-
closed by a roll-top and standing on thin legs with brass feet.
   The carpet in the hall was a bit loose, the bathtub water
heater groaned like an ocean liner's bass whistle, the faucets
leaked, the towel racks were loose, the doors that should be open
swung closed, the doors that should be shut swung open, the gas
stove went put-put, the windows rattled, the floors creaked, and
all the furniture slanted. But we thought it was perfect.
   It took two sixty-mile trips through heavy traffic to get our
29 boxes from Heathrow Airport, but we would not pay the
tribute in money and delay which a delivery service would have
exacted. When the first load arrived, we asked help in getting it
up the stairs from our landlords, The Society for the Protection of Ancient Buildings, whose offices occupied the first three
floors. Upon hearing that the Americans needed help with their
luggage, about five young ladies and gentlemen made themselves
available, looking very dubious. It was a hot day for London, and
soon they were sweating, which Britons don't allow for. When
they saw how much was packed into and onto the car, they grew
more dubious, and when they heard that this was only one of

two carloads, they positively disbelieved. "Wherever are they going to put it?" they said to each other, not caring if we heard.

But when this band of confirmed antiquarians, who disapproved in principle of any higher technology than pendulum clocks and wooden windmills, saw the huge box that held my Z-2D and discovered that it contained a computer, they exchanged looks that would have shriveled us had they been directed our way. But somehow they heaved it up to the flat. It was too wide for the staircase and had to be held above the banisters.

My main concern, of course, was whether the computer would work after being hurled through O'Hare, trundled all the way across Heathrow, carried through London traffic on top of a swaying Datsun, wrestled up four flights of narrrow stairs, and then converted to twice its accustomed voltage.

The circuit diagram of the Z-2D manual showed that I was to put the two primary windings of the transformer in series instead of in parallel; that is, end to end instead of side by side. By the law of transformers, this would nullify the effect of doubling the voltage. Very simple, but I now discovered that the diagram showed a transformer with taps into its windings numbered 1 through 6, whereas I possessed a transformer with taps numbered

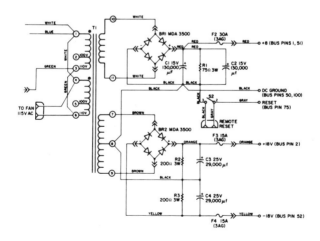

1 through 7. Which was the extra tap? The diagram showed colors, however, and I had no course but to believe them. On my transformer, the white and green leads from the power plug connected to 5 and 7; on the diagram, the white and green leads connected to 4 and 6. Taking my computer's life in my hands, I disobeyed the diagram, and soldered the 220-volt line to 5 and 7.

With trepidation I executed the manual's pretest procedure: 1) Pull all circuit boards out of the S-100 bus. Measure resistance between ground and the S-100 bus mounting rail. If zero, do not plug in. My volt-ohmeter said infinite. 2) Plug in computer. If red "on" light goes on and then off, fuse has blown, and there is trouble. The red light stayed on, and I sniffed nothing suspicious. 3) Check voltages on S-100 bus. All were as specified. 4) Unplug system, and plug in circuit boards. All seemed normal, but I wouldn't know for certain until I booted up with the terminal.

In the process of pretesting, I noticed something disturbing about the manual: it consisted of instructions for putting together a kit. I recalled that the reason my Z-2D hadn't been ready when I returned from Yucatán was that Angelo hadn't assembled it. Now I remembered that I had paid the catalogue price for a Z-2D "assembled and tested." I assumed that meant at the factory. I didn't know. But I did know that kits cost less than assembled and tested units. Anyhow, it worked, I had paid my money, and I had other pressing concerns.

Another anomaly jumped out when I went to work on the Beehive: the diagram of the 220-volt version had an extra circuit plugged in across the power line. It looked like some kind of a filter, with a coil in one side of the line and a capacitor across it. Could I get along without it? I had no course but to go ahead; anyhow it would probably affect the *quality* of the power and not the *quantity*. It was impossible to trace the wiring this time because the colored wires were all plugged into a switchboard with the wiring hidden under it. I would have to depend entirely on the color-coding again.

Proceeding blindly with the 220-volt diagram, I moved the red wire from 8 to 6, the blank pin from 5 to 4, the blue from 4 to 5, the other blank from 10 to 8, the brown from 9 to 10, the white from 6 to 9. I checked and rechecked. I took off the housing and switched internal switch 3 from "off" to "on," obeying the manual's dictum: "To avoid beat interference, the display rate should match the power line frequency." "On" synchronized it with 50 cycles. As I plugged the terminal in, I hoped that the line filter was optional. Perhaps it wasn't, because the picture I got was a good bit smaller than normal. "Steady," I said to myself and looked in the manual for a section on the video monitor. I was surprised to discover that I could have any one of four OEM models and that I was expected to be able to tell which kind I had. After much close analysis of the illustrations, I decided that my monitor had to be a Zenith D12. Then, deciphering cryptic instructions, I managed to enlarge the picture to normal size, using tiny controls on the monitor's circuit board.

I then turned my attention to the 737. This conversion turned out to be the simplest of all. Putting in the new transformer was merely a matter of substituting the brown, blue, red, yellow, and orange leads of the new transformer for the brown, blue, red, yellow, and orange leads of the old transformer. The main problem with the ribbon drive motor was mechanical. At first I thought I might need a special tool to get the split washer with the two little holes in it off the shaft of the old motor, but, after many tries, I did the job with a screwdriver and brute force. I couldn't get the leads of old motor out of its power connector, so I cut them off and forced the new leads down beside what was left of the old ones. The printer passed the sniff test, and I was eager to boot up the computer and know what my fate was to be.

I cabled the components all together, turned them on, pressed RESET, and hit RETURN three times. Shortly thereafter, though it seemed an age, the blessed words came down:

```
CDOS version 2.17
Cromemco Disk Operating System
Copyright (c) 1978, 1979
```

I then called for a printout of disk B's directory, and the printer worked too. My computer was with me in London. I had a cup of tea.

The setting was our bedroom. I couldn't really put the computer in the living room or the dining room because they were too public. The kitchen was small and busy, and Mackay had the other bedroom, which was also her study. The hall was narrow and dark. I moved the Georgian roll-top desk into the bedroom, opposite the foot of our bed and rolled up the top. There were about two feet between the desk and the bed, just room for a straight chair. The terminal went on the desk, and the computer sat on two solid suitcases to the left of it. Looking over the computer, I had a view through watery panes of a large block of public housing. Against the wall in front of me was an old print of red-coated hunters on long thin horses jumping a hedge and following long thin hounds.

I began my average day by rising at six, dressing, shaving, eating my oatmeal, and making my sandwich for lunch. I then tossed books and papers for the day's classes into my briefcase, schussed down the four flights of stairs to the street, backtracked through an alley into the cement garden of the public housing complex, noted again that they were all named for Wordsworthian places like Windermere, Ullswater, and Langdale, and burst suddenly onto a great river of London traffic, Theobald Road, a dense current of trucks, cars, motorcycles, bicycles, taxis, Rolls Royces, and various crossbreeds. Taking courage at a brief break in the avalanche of steel, I set one foot on the sacred zebra walk, and all this mighty river screeched to a halt. Holding my head high, I then hastened to the other side and joined a rapidly thickening stream of fellow-workers swarming toward the maw of the Holborn underground station. Just before I hit the ticket lines, I reached sideways for my *London Times*, held out for me with a "Roight, Sir," by the aged newsman at the entrance, who saw me coming. "Two shillins," he sometimes said, making a joke about bygone times which I eventually got.

Down the escalators I sank into the bowels of the city, as down a mine shaft, with blasts of dank warm air blowing hard against me, to my train's track and the billboards that never changed, selling beer, cigarettes, bras, movies, and retirement plans. Waiting, I studied the latest news of the Yorkshire Ripper, the Iranian hostages, and Arsenal, the resident soccer team. It was impossible to finish the newspaper even though I crossed several miles of city as my train drilled westward: Tottenham Court Road, Oxford Circus, Bond Street, Marble Arch, and Lancaster Gate were the stations at which I did not get off. Queensway brought me into action, to be lifted out of the pits with fifty others in an elevator operated by a large motherly black woman.

Now I tried to find as straight a line as possible through three blocks west and five blocks north, when hardly any blocks were quite square, and finally dropped gently into shady green Kensington Garden Square, on one side of which was an old house, now a hotel, where I taught my two classes with my sandwich in between. At about 4:30 I reversed the process in a decelerated condition, read the rest of my *Times*, and finally climbed one step at a time up to my flat, my loving wife, my dinner, and, if it wasn't to be a play, some Scrabble or some amazing BBC TV, and then early to bed and deep and dreamless sleep.

One morning a week, for the sake of my liver, I devoted to "venisection," British medicalese for "bloodletting." Shortly after arriving in London, I had gone to the nearest hospital and asked at the main desk where I could be bled. "We can't treat you here unless you're sick," they said. I decided I *was* sick, in a way, and they sent me to Hematology, where I soon told my story and presented documents to the head of the department. I had not been referred to him, and he had never seen me before, but he took me at face value. "I believe we can work you in." Thus the Hematology Department of University College Hospital of University College of London University became my official venisector.

London bus routes did not travel from my house to University College Hospital, and taxis were too expensive, so I walked the mile and a half to my weekly venisection and made the best of it. My path was rarely ever the same because the hospital lay on a diagonal and the streets were all at right angles to each other. I usually chose the most pleasant stroll through Russell Square, with its plashing waters, and streets that led me past Dillon's Bookstore. Once, in search of diagonals, I found a way to cross the University College campus by going up an alley into a back door of the main building. As I came up a flight of stairs into a spacious hallway, I saw a little old man sitting in a glass case and, after a start, knew with a shiver that it was the famous embalmed body of the founder, Jeremy Bentham, presiding forever over his institution. I was taken completely by surprise, having never paid an official visit to this curiosity, and very slowly rotting corpses were far from my mind. I did not often choose this path, my errand being chilly enough as it was.

Some unwritten and never-divulged protocol governed the selection of what "registrar" (British for resident or intern) would bleed me when I announced my need at the Hematology Desk. One chap was laconic and fast. Another talked about the theatre as he worked in the needle. One nervous young lady stabbed me five times in various arm veins without striking blood, gave up and called for help, found none, and, rather than send me away unbled, pulled eight syringes of blood out of my wrist to make up my pint. Another young lady, the head registrar, arranged a meeting of her crew on the telephone while waiting for me to fill the bag. When she got around to pulling out the needle, the bag was ready to burst, and, her mind being on weightier matters, she forgot to clamp the tube. The needle then became a hose that sprayed my blood all over the room, and she must have used a roll of paper towels wiping it up. Since she never lost her composure while all this was going on, I knew that she would go far in her profession. It always grieved Kay and me, especially Kay, who hates waste, that no use could be made of my blood. It was hemochromatic, it was diseased, and it had to be thrown away.

My walk home after bleeding was always a bit woozy. Once I hazily walked away from Dillon's with a load of guidebooks for a forthcoming trip and was arrested for shoplifting by the house detective. He wanted to know what I was doing with an expensive book on Turkey which I had not bought. I had some trouble persuading the manager that I was a true case of the absent-minded professor, and I even went so far as to tell him about the time I took the garbage to Cambridge University library and dumped my briefcase in the ash can. I told him that, while paying for my guidebooks, I had probably put them down on the Turkey volume and had then picked it up with my purchases when I left. Fortunately, my story fitted that of the clerk from whom I'd bought the guidebooks. The manager finally believed me. "But," he said, "you'd be surprised how many professors we catch red-handed."

My first brush with the English electronic establishment occurred when I tried to buy fractional fuses. During the course of rewiring my components for 220 volts, I realized that their main fuses were now all twice as big as they should be. If the watts remained constant and the volts doubled, the amps must be halved. Indeed, the rubric beside the fuse of my printer read, "115 VAC 1 Amp 230 VAC ½ Amp." I also realized that fuses in the low-voltage lines feeding my S-100 bus were much too big, having been installed at the factory on the assumption that I would use all twenty-one slots of the bus, not just four. A close study based on the actual power ratings of my boards showed that I needed to have fuses of several different fractional values, and I set out one day to acquire these at my nearest electrical shop. Only minimum fuses would guarantee maximum protection for my precious boards.

In England, almost every commercial street has an electrical shop full of gleaming white plugs and sockets of various sizes and shapes with massive shining brass contacts. Next to the butcher and the baker, England had now installed the electrical outfitter in place of the candlestick maker. My nearest outfitter was just a block away, along with my baker, my grocer, my butcher, my stationer, my hardwareman, my art dealer, my bank, and two of my six pubs. Walking in confidently, I stated my wants to a

suspicious elderly gentleman behind the counter: two each of ¼,
½, ¾, and 1½ ampere fuses. He looked as if he were going to
say, "These Americans!" but he said instead, thin-lipped, "The
closest yer going to get is one amp, and I may just have one of
those." He rummaged in a box. "Nope," he said. "Those are on
order."

I asked him where I could get fractional fuses. "Not in
England," he said. "We don't use them." His look seemed to
suggest that odd-sized fuses would be shoddy goods. I asked him
what one did if one's TV blew a fractional fuse. "Yer gets those
from the bloke wot sold you the set."

I refused to believe one witness, however, and hastened
over to Tottenham Court Road, past Southampton Row, the
British Museum, and Gower Street, certain of vindication. In my
previous years in London I had come to know Tottenham Court
Road as Electronic Avenue, but I soon discovered that things
had changed. It was now Hi-Fi Street. Healds' grand furniture
store no longer queened it over the broad half-mile, but strove
helplessly for notice against a score of here-today-and-gone-to-
morrow stores, all blasting the ears of passersby with high-decibel
rock. Their windows were so crowded with tape recorders, tone
arms, amplifiers, speakers, earphones, radios, tapes, and records
that all you saw was a myriad of red price tags with black prices
felt-penned on them, blooming on a black and chromium bank.
Inside, the shelves were similarly crowded with shouting wares,
and the floors, corners, and back rooms were littered with freshly
torn paper cartons and white styrofoam packing. Lines of knowing
lads and lasses were giving stout shirtsleeved men at cash registers great amounts of money and carrying away cartons of electronic bliss.

The stores all had "audio" or "electronic" in their names,
but when their loud merchandise blew a fuse, it seemed obvious
to me that its purchasers surely wouldn't get a replacement from
the man they bought it from, even if they could find him again. I
tried, anyhow. Sure enough, when I finally got to the head of
a cash-register line and shouted my needs, I was greeted by

an unbelieving grin. "Yer get those at an eletricoo shop," he shouted back.

Up and down the street I went. Some of these hi-fi stores even sold computers, and there was even a Heath computer store, but none of these knew anything about fuses, either. When I asked the Heath dealer what a person did when he blew a fuse, he said, "'E sends it in for service."

Finally, just as I was about to give up, having exhausted the whole concourse, I came upon a store on the north end of the Road whose windows were full of dusty old meters, transformers, circuit boards, gang switches, transmitters, power supplies, soldering guns, and such, just like the original rightly named Radio Shack I used to frequent in Scollay Square, Boston, as a teenage tinkerer. This one was in a cellar too and not much farther from a sex shop than the Radio Shack had been from the Old Howard burlesque theatre. The bald-headed man who ran this place knew just what I wanted and why I wanted it but feared he had exhausted his stock. His place was the last outpost of true electronics on Tottenham Court Road, but I could see that he was selling out. He did have two ¾ ampere fuses, enough to gainsay my first nay-sayer but not enough to satisfy my needs. He said that the Edgware Road was the place to go.

It was several months before I sampled the Edgware Road. It wasn't until I had been told about five more times that fractional fuses were un-British that I finally took the Green underground instead of the Red (District instead of Central) one afternoon on the way home from work and rattled over to Edgware Road. On debarking, I soon found myself in a subterranean warren of pedestrian walkways that centered in a mammoth cave. In the center of this cave was a shack of the sort where hot dogs are sold at a fair. In this shack were hundreds of little boxes neatly stacked on shelves, and the sign across the roof announced "A and G Electronics—Radios Repaired" in amateur lettering.

In the dim light I discerned the proprietor, a permanently smiling Hindu or Pakistani, fixing a very old radio under a weak light bulb. "Yis?" he asked, looking up suddenly. I hadn't even meant to ask, but he definitely wanted to know. "What iss it?"

Steeling myself for another denial, I gave it to him straight: "Two half-amp fuses, two quarter-amp fuses, and two one-and-a-half amp fuses." "One moment, pliss." He began looking in the little boxes. In about three minutes, he carefully placed six fuses on the counter in a row and asked for a fraction of a pound. I paid him, disbelieving, because I couldn't check the ratings in the dim light. But in the daylight of the Edgware Road, I saw that they were exactly right.

This part of Edgware Road looked suspiciously like Tottenham Court Road, though the hi-fi was less dense. But I was still curious to know where I might buy electronic parts if the need arose, and I continued my search for stores where I wouldn't be viewed as a threat to Church, State, and Cricket. So I tested several Edgware shops and was happy to discover that a request for fuses was considered perfectly normal. These stores also had those ranks of little boxes that signify an inventory of resistors, condensers, transistors, connectors, and the like, and a comforting amount of dust.

My vindication was not perfect, however, for these merchants were patently members of the Asiatic hordes. I never proved that I could buy an odd fuse from a True Briton, and I doubt that I could have.

In London I used my Z-2D mainly to expedite my classes. Thanks to its power of insertion and deletion, SCREEN proved to be an efficient medium for generating and maintaining my lists of assignments. By revising an old schedule I could save the work it would have taken me to retype the whole thing and have it typed again neatly by our secretary. Nothing in the schedule had to be permanent. When plays were announced that deserved to be fitted into my courses, I just put in the changes and published a new schedule. For instance, when we finally did get tickets for *Nicholas Nickleby*, it was no trouble to cancel *Wuthering Heights* and substitute a set of assignments for Dickens' novel, leading up to the great performance.

The Shakespeare schedule was even more affected by our fortunes at the theatres. The final schedule looked like this:

B R Schneider   ASSIGNMENTS FOR ENGLISH 33L   Fall 1980
Introduction to Shakespeare

Sep T 23   Background. The Dresser, Queens Theatre.
    Th 25 As You Like It, I and II
    S 27   Finish AYL. Rosencrantz and Guildenstern are Dead, Young Vic.

      T 30   Lear I, II.
Oct Th 2   Finish Lear

      T 7   Merchant of Venice I, II. MV, St George's Theatre.
      Th 9   Finish MV. Paper I due at 5 PM! the page vs. the stage.

      T 14   Macbeth I, II. Macbeth, St George's Theatre.
      Th 16   Finish Macbeth
      S 18   Workshop on Romeo and Juliet, Olivier, 10:30

      T 21   Midterm break
      Th 23   Midterm break
      S 25   Workshop on R and J, Olivier, 10:30

      T 28   Romeo and Juliet
      W 29   Lear, Young Vic
      Th 30   Finish Romeo and Juliet
Nov S 1   Hamlet I, II

      T 4   Finish Hamlet
      Th 6   Stratford, As You Like It, 7:30.
      F 7   Stratford, Hamlet, 7:30
      S 8   Stratford, Romeo and Juliet, 7:30

      T 11   1 Henry IV I, II
      Th 13   Finish I Hen IV. Old Vic, Merchant of Venice. Paper II due at 5 PM.

      T 18   Much Ado I, II
      Th 20   Finish Much Ado
      S 22   Old Vic, Macbeth
      S 23   Old Vic, Horatio's version, 7:30

      T 25   Measure for Measure I, II
      Th 27   Finish MM. Paper III due at 5 PM.

EXPLANATORY NOTE: The Dresser*: a play about staging King Lear.* Rosencrantz and Guildenstern*: a play about* Hamlet *as experienced by the two most minor characters. Young Vic: Small theatre devoted to good plays for young audiences. Old Vic: Original National Theatre, now under new management. St George's: theatre devoted to staging Shakespeare. Workshops: a noted Shakespeare scholar experiments with staging R and J, working with actors of National Theatre. Olivier: one stage of the new National Theatre. Stratford: Shakespeare theatre at Stratford on Avon. Horatio's version: lecture on* Hamlet *as seen by Horatio.*

My 737 could also take the place of a Xerox machine. The street value of a Xerox copy in London was about twenty cents in fall 1980. Although my printer took about five minutes to print a page, it could keep on printing for hours. Since my computer was costing me money just sitting there, it might as well be doing something useful. So the 737 became my free Xerox machine and duplicated hundreds of copies of course assignments, exams, and other handouts during the course of the year.

Although I found SCREEN a dozen times better than a typewriter, I still longed for SITAR. As I have said, SCREEN's modes of insertion and deletion are dormant. For instance, in order to execute an insertion, I first had to strike the 'i' key. I could not strike the 'i' key unless SCREEN was in the ready state. I couldn't get it to the ready state without getting it out of delete mode or whatever else I was doing by striking the ESCape key. When I struck the 'i' key, I had to wait a second or two while SCREEN freed up a line for the insertion. If I started inserting without waiting, I would type several characters into the void before SCREEN was ready to record my insertion. I would then have to backspace and insert the missing characters. If my insertion went beyond the end of the line, I must wait for SCREEN to free up another line. If I didn't, I would type more characters into the void. Then, when at last I had finished my insertion, if I wanted to make another insertion somewhere else on the page or delete something, I would first have to strike ESCape and wait for SCREEN to readjust the text to my insertion before I could reposition the cursor.

Another source of grief was the shifting meaning of the space bar in SCREEN's four editing modes. In the ready mode, striking the space bar moves the cursor to the right, not affecting the text over which it travels. In insert mode, the space bar behaves normally. In delete mode, the space bar erases as it moves forward and the backspace key restores text as it moves backward. Not until one strikes ESCape does the computer permanently discard text that the space bar has blotted out. In write-over mode, the space bar erases and so does the backspace key. If one makes a typing mistake and backspaces to fix it, one erases all the writing he has backspaced over and must do it again. To correct such a mistake without rewriting, one must ESCape from writeover, move the cursor to the error, and invoke insertion, deletion, or writeover again, sometimes two of these. In my hands SCREEN continually defeated itself. I don't know how many times I have inserted a 'd' instead of putting SCREEN in delete mode. Perhaps hundreds.

Lawrence's London program provides its students many opportunities for cultural enrichment. There are of course the theatres and the museums. But to encourage wider exploration of Britain and the Continent, we always have a free week in the middle of the term, which we make up for by crowding in extra classes before and after.

My wife's first name is actually Mackay. Dear Boo was a Mackay before she married. And daughter Mackay also bears the name of the clan. So in midterm break of 1980, while our students scrambled over Ireland, Wales, France, Italy, and Spain, we did something we had always wanted to do. We made a pilgrimage to the land of the Mackays. It turned out to be mile after mile of cold, wet, windy, reddish-brown, deserted moors and ponds, similar to arctic tundra, as far away from London as on the British island you can possibly get. Except for the cactus land of northern Mexico, it was the most uninhabitable land we had ever seen. By asking natives as we approached the northern coast of Scotland, we found the family seat in the village of Tongue, not far from John O'Groats. In the kirk of Tongue, the main pews were upholstered in Mackay plaid, and the kirkyard was full of Mackay bones, collected from all over northern Scotland for many an age. There was even a Mackay Mackay buried there.

Looking for a bed and breakfast, we came upon a house called Tongue Mains. A "mains," according to my old *Webster's Collegiate*, is the "home farm of a manor." Tongue Mains, whose mistress cordially took us in, did indeed lie at the gate of the manor of Tongue. Our landlady told us that the present laird [sic] of this manor was the Countess of Sutherland but that it was really the family seat of the Mackays, who had sold their birthright to the Sutherlands in the eighteenth century in order to raise an army. Our landlady, reasoning that a mother and daughter both named Mackay had a right at least to see their ancestral home, announced our presence over the phone to the Countess herself, and she without hesitation commanded us to appear at her door at eleven the next morning. At that hour, the Countess, smiling benignly, led us through spacious halls and the kitchen to a large stone room where she directed our eyes to the Mackay coat of arms, a dagger in hand with "Manu Forti" under it, carved over the fireplace just exactly as it is worked in silver on Dear Boo's brooch. After showing us the whole house and garden, she sent us on our way with a glass of true Scotch, neat, without ice. Although we hadn't even known that one existed, our pilgrimage had stumbled on its proper shrine.

Teaching Shakespeare against a background of live performances of his plays was a revealing experience for me. My job, essentially, is to help students appreciate literature that is above their heads, under the assumption that, since they pay me, it is not so far above mine. In London, the British actors and directors did most of my job for me. And they did it so well that never before had a class of mine gotten so close to the mind of Shakespeare. It comes as a pleasant surprise to Midwestern American students when they discover that a Shakespeare play is more than a sequence of flowery speeches, that people having certain feelings might actually use such words, that these people are responding to actual events, and that they are making their meanings crystal clear. The English of Shakespeare is rapidly becoming a foreign language, like King Alfred's and Chaucer's. But by paying close attention to the meaning of his words, skilled British actors can deliver the emotional and intellectual content of his lines almost as if they were speaking modern English. Even though most of my students had passed their eyes over *Macbeth* in high school and in my course, some of them probably *read* the play for the first time when they saw it on the London stage.

T. S. Eliot has said somewhere that he hates to see a great drama on the stage because it never comes up to the image of it that he holds in his mind. Actual performances may well seem pale to a major poet looking down from on high, but looking up from below, where most us are, a comparison between the expected and the actual can be enlightening. After seeing Michael Pennington as Hamlet at Stratford on Avon, a student asked, even before we could get into a classroom, why they had that bare light bulb hanging down above the stage. Later, many members of the class had answers, and some were good ones.

There was no way to explain that light bulb without explaining what that production, at least, thought Shakespeare had in mind. Besides the light bulb, the production scattered many other clues to its conception of Hamlet's problem, like the bare stage revealing the ropes and pulleys, the flats against the wall, and the bricks of the building; like the big trunk from which actors sometimes took props or costumes; and like Michael Pennington's overtly histrionic behavior, his waving a broadsword around when there was no one to fight, and his active stage-managing of the play within the play. All these clues together suggested that this production thought Hamlet was a self-dramatizer; indeed, that he saw himself as an actor in a play and therefore had difficulty in coming to grips with the real world.

As my class and I reviewed the text, we found much support for this interpretation: Hamlet's obvious overacting of his grief in act one, his decision to "put an antic disposition on"—that is, to act a madman's part—his enthusiasm for dramatizing his father's murder—"the play's the thing"—his overreaction in the scene where he accuses, judges, and condemns his mother, his insensitivity to Ophelia—"get thee to a nunnery"—and his callous reaction to his murder of Polonius—"I'll lug the guts into the other room"—all fruitless, unwise, and unkind acts that a man in close touch with reality would not indulge himself by doing. In such ways the performances taught Shakespeare's plays for me.

A bad performance worked just as well as a good one because it gave my students the pleasure of looking down from above.

Peter O'Toole's universally damned version of *Macbeth* made the hero such a preposterous, swaggering, bloodthirsty villain that the character became an object of laughter. Our discussion afterwards led to interesting questions about the nature of tragedy. Comparing two performances of the same play, as we could with the *Merchant of Venice* and *Macbeth*, inevitably brought us to the question of what Shakespeare had in mind. *Rosencrantz and Guildenstern Are Dead* and *The Dresser*, the one seeing *Hamlet* from the point of view of the two most minor characters and the other showing *King Lear* from backstage, also opened up new dimensions.

In the course of her work at Lawrence, Mackay became a devotee of word processing. She was better at SCREEN than I was, quite well managing to keep its peculiarities in mind as she worked. Her papers were clean and errorless, and, at least in one case, SCREEN helped her get a higher grade. When she got her final Art History paper done and run off on the 737, typically an hour before her deadline, it was obvious that although the parts were all there in good order, the transitions were missing. The main thread wasn't there, and it was hard to see the point of the parts. With SCREEN she patched in the transitions in the short time that remained and ran the paper off again. It got a memorable A.

The most magnificent theatrical experience of the term—*As You Like It* and *Hamlet* at Stratford were close seconds—was *Nicholas Nickleby*, which my Major British Writers class attended after a study of the novel. Forty-seven Top Actors playing 1,125 Characters! Forty-eight Lightning Scene Changes! Eight hours long and never a dull moment! All the excitement of a circus and buckets of tears besides! It was a fitting celebration of the advent of Christmas. The English say that Dickens invented the Spirit of Christmas. It is true. He summed it up in his *Christmas Carol* with Bob Cratchit carrying pitiful Tiny Tim, who bravely says, "God bless us every one." And now in the play based on his novel, he made the point again when the curtain came down with Nicholas Nickleby carrying the pitiful ghost of Smike in his arms while the cast softly sang, "God Rest Ye Merry, Gentlemen."

The Schneider Christmas took place far from the world of Tiny Tim and Smike. We spent it traveling in Spain, the six of us in our five-passenger Datsun station wagon, one person always taking a turn in the luggage space behind the back seat and the suitcases tied to the roof. Kay and I and Ben, who joined us in London, ferried the Datsun from Plymouth to Santander in 24 very rough hours. Mackay, who went to see friends on the continent first, joined us by train in Madrid. Nick and Devon flew straight to Madrid from the States, and all six of us arrived at the airport simultaneously.

Our trip had no settled plan except for the rendezvous in Madrid on the morning of December 19th. Kay had painstakingly worked that out with the far-flung children and the airlines. Each day, we decided what we would do next when we got up in the morning. Knowing next to nothing about Spain, we put ourselves in the hands of Michelin et Cie, the Green Guide for things to see, and the Red Guide for where to eat and stay. These guides rigorously grade every attraction and accommodation. If there are three stars beside an entry, it is worth a trip. For instance, referring to the Michelin guide to the United States, if you take a trip to Niagara Falls***, it will be worth it, wherever you start from. Two stars means that the attraction is worth a detour from the shortest path between three-star attractions. One star means that the attraction is worth a stop if your road takes you past it. A spectacular view is decorated by a set of rays, red if exceptionally so. In the Red Guide, especially nice lodgings earn a rocking chair after their names, red if exceptionally so.

This is the route we ultimately took, guided by Michelin: Santander*–Picos de Europa***–León**–Salamanca***–Madrid Airport (Mackay, Nick, Devon join the party)–Toledo***–Córdoba***–Carmona–Ronda**–Granada***–Madrid*** (lose Nick and Ben to Paris, Mackay to Earlham)–Burgos**–Santander*–London***.

In Picos de Europa, we saw picturesque villages tucked into the sides of snow-capped mountains amid bright green pastures so steep you could fall out of them. It was a miniature Switzerland. Blocked by snow on the pass we had chosen, we undid thirty hard miles and detoured to Salamanca via Oviedo, spending a night in León, with its hulking cathedral and medieval city walls. A sign had warned us against taking that pass without chains, but we translated it on the way back, not on the way up. We had wondered indeed why we were all alone up there.

We were especially fond of Salamanca, whose old university had become a symbol of academic freedom. Of course it was packed full of great art and architecture, as a three-star city is obliged to be. But there was more to it. Maybe it was the omnipresence of roistering bands of university students, who might have burst into "Gaudeamus Igitur" at a moment's notice, or the civilizing effect of the finest *plaza mayor* in Spain, a spacious colonnaded neoclassical square, or the huge Christmas tree in the center around which madly singing teenagers continually danced in counter-revolving rings, definitely keeping the downtown from dying, or maybe it was the University English Department's version of *The Second Shepherd's Play*, in which the hilarious hosannas of the clowning angels, played by professors, stopped the show.

After gathering in the rest of the family at the Madrid airport, we went to Toledo. We found it very tightly packed, as if trying to keep itself in El Greco's view; our Datsun, just as tightly packed, could barely squeak through its main arteries. We missed the best El Greco museum because our day was the day it closed, but were consoled by the famous El Grecos in the cathedral and the omnipresent *tapas* (hot snacks). Córdoba demonstrated how to convert a mosque into an extraordinary cathedral without sacrificing any arabesques.

Christmas drew us to Carmona, a town without a single star. As the day approached, Kay began to look for a nice place in which to spend it. She chose Carmona because, according to the Michelin Red Guide, there sat El Parador Nacional Alcázar del Rey don Pedro (King Pedro's Fort National Halting-Place) with a red rocking chair, a red eye-dazzler, and a red "elemento particularmente agradable," to wit: "conjunto de estilo mudéjar" (con-

Left to right: Benny, Kay, Devon, me, Mackay, Nick

structed in the Spanish-Moorish style). Red symbols are very scarce in Michelin's Spain, but everything at Don Pedro's Fort was truly red. Michelin couldn't tell us that there would be a stirring midnight mass inspired by a large youth choir which sang medieval carols and "The Little Drummer Boy" with equal gusto, that some of the cuter members of this choir would pick up Nick and Ben and take them to their gang's Christmas party, where they would be declared *amigos* for life, and that on Christmas afternoon the citizens would be testing young bulls in the local *corrida*. So Carmona became our own little Spanish town forever, and in our memories, at least, it has one large silver star.

Ronda had earned its stars by being perched on a cliff, inventing the art of bullfighting, and inspiring the poet Rilke. It also contained a most pleasant surprise, the Hotel Residencia Polo, where they had so lovingly coordinated walls, doors, furniture, linens, drapes, tiles, and towels in white and blue as to make us feel we lived in a work of art, and not without unlimited hot water and plenty of central heat. It befell us because it was an anomaly in Michelin terms: a "comfortable" hotel at our usual "plain but decent" price.

The Alhambra of Granada is indeed worth a trip from wherever you are. The legendary beggar must have induced a great deal of charity with his famous lament: "Give alms, woman! For I am in Granada, and I am blind." But when we got back to Madrid***, we could spare that great city only one full day. We did manage to see Flamenco dancing, make a rapid survey of the paintings in the Prado, and eat the best *tapas* in Spain. We also saw a stunning production of *Macbeth*, of which Kay and I understood but one line, "Mañana y mañana y mañana." Although they seemed to have lost the knack of it in London, they really did know how to do this play in Spain. They set the witch scenes in Goya's black period, with some of his horrors of war interspersed; the main character was the best actor in the country; and they invented an omnipresent comic servant, whose obscene clowning (as the Porter) shifts to puzzlement and misery while he (as Seyton) watches his idol disintegrate. In the end, the victorious lords celebrate the restoration of justice and decency with the enthronement of the True Prince (undeniably Juan Carlos), just barely managing not to step on Macbeth's severed head, which lies on the floor, signifying *nada*.

The crusty bread of Lerma, well-known north of Madrid but unknown to Michelin, is worth a detour, if not a journey. In Burgos we found two tombs of El Cid, whose epic I had been trying to decipher, the original one in a monastery and the present one in the big brute of a cathedral, much more his style.

We got back to London on the third day of 1981. That evening Nick and Ben arrived by train and ferry from Paris. I think they had gone to Paris from Madrid partly to avoid 24 hours on the Santander-Plymouth ferry, on which Devon and I were indeed miserable, but not Kay, who likes big waves. Our *boulevardier* had managed a date with the French girl he had met in a restaurant in Salamanca, and both he and Nick had had a good time with Ben's French friends dating back to his year of study abroad while in college.

Nick feared that in the two weeks remaining, he might run out of work on SITAR. I reminded him that when he got it working on the interpreter, he still had to compile it and that I still needed a formatter that would right-justify proportional spacing on the 737. He still faced the old problem of persuading the computer to accept a stream of text from the terminal. Last summer he had gotten to the point where it would accept everything but the first few characters of a batch send. He thought the breakthrough was close at hand, but he spent most of the time left trying to reach it. The process ultimately consisted of trying every likely combination of three parameters, each of which had numerous possible settings, in hopes of accidentally striking the right one. He had no documentary help from Microsoft, Cromemco, or Beehive, who were perfectly silent on enabling a batch send, and even the hunch that these parameters might be crucial was based on trial and error. It might have been several other things altogether.

This part of the project was the hardest for me because all my previous computer projects had been cliffhangers. If they finished at all in the time allowed, it was always at the last possible moment, and always then because just when I thought the system was ready to go, an unexpected snag cropped up. It was hard, too, because it isn't easy to keep a young programmer at work in London. Nick had to look up his school friends from our sabbatical in '71–'72, which entailed many late nights and a great deal of daytime sleeping, and he had to take in shows like *Educating Rita* (who educates the prof) and *The Accidental Death of an Anarchist* (a most hilarious and satisfying attack on the establishment), along with the rest of London's youth. There were also the plays we wanted him to see and the friends we wanted him to meet. Thus, while Nick was confidently expecting to win his game of SITAR roulette at the next spin of the wheel and never winning, I watched the sand pour through the hourglass.

The three floating parameters were these: the baud rate, the placement of the baud rate change, and the "sleep."

The baud rate: The computer normally communicated with the terminal at 9600 baud, meaning 9600 bits per second. It was apparent to Nick that the higher the speed, the more characters got lost in transmission. Our equipment was also capable of operating at 1800, 1200, 300, and 150 baud. But anything slower than 1200 was too slow for a usable SITAR. Nick's best strategy, on the face of it, was to try to get it working at 150 baud and then, once he understood the problem, see how far he could raise the rate of transmission. In order to find out, he had to put instructions for changing the rate from 9600 to an acceptable lower rate into SITAR itself.

The placement of the baud rate change: The second variable was where to put the instructions for a reduced rate. Nick tried them at the beginning of the program, just before the batch send, and at various spots in between. Each instruction consisted of two steps, one to change the computer and the other to change the terminal. He could switch the terminal first, or the computer first. Which way should it be?

The sleep: SLEEP is a statement in some BASICs which causes the computer to take a break for a specified time. Microsoft BASIC didn't have a SLEEP. The need for SLEEP arose because we were missing only the first few characters of a transmission from the terminal. Perhaps it took a few microseconds for a baud rate change to take effect. Perhaps the terminal and the computer needed time to let their instructions sink in. If the system needed time to adjust, how could Nick make the program wait, and how long would it have to wait?

Nick struck upon a way to make Microsoft BASIC sleep by sending the program into a meaningless **loop** and getting it out again, like a man exercising on a stationary bicycle, getting nowhere, and quitting after his meter reads so many miles. Here is the BASIC formula for a meaningless loop: "FOR I = 1 TO 11; NEXT I". "I" is just any old variable in an equation, like "X" or "Y"; programmers always like to use "I" and "J" for any old variable. This statement causes a program to do the same thing (in this case, nothing) eleven times and then go on to the next operation. A meaningless loop, then, would put the program to sleep for a while, but how many loops would enable a rate change to take effect?

Trying to find the right combination of these three parameters sent Nick into a loop of his own in which he changed a variable, ran the program, and changed a variable again. Sometimes he got transmission but lost characters; sometimes the computer got hung up and had to be rebooted, sometimes the program went on but nothing happened to the text on the screen. It could be that the baud rate was too fast, that the sleep was too short, or that one of the parties to the transmission was not synchronized to the other. It was hard to figure out which error caused which effect. Nick guessed and spun the wheel, again and again.

As the days went by one by one without a breakthrough, the Z-2D seized upon the opportunity to rivet attention on itself. Every so often, not in the midst of programming activity but perhaps while waiting idly for us to finish lunch, it went dumb. When we asked it to do something, it wasn't there. The only way to bring it alive was to reboot and start over again. I checked plugs and sockets and interconnecting cables, even went so far as to take out all the circuit boards and plug them in again, thinking that there were 400 contacts on them and that it only took one bad one to spoil all. But these shifts availed not. There was now a strong possibility that the computer would fail irretrievably before Nick found his answer.

But, as the final days approached, disaster struck from another quarter. The disk on which Nick was debugging SITAR began to report errors. The harder we tried to run SITAR, the more "read errors" we got, until it was useless to try any more. This disk contained all of the work Nick had done since we had returned from Spain. Without it, he would have to retrace his steps, starting over with last summer's final version. How would he ever remember all the changes he had made?

I was already in a bad mood. My class in Restoration Drama was giving me trouble. The night before, only half of them had turned up at a performance of Wycherley's *Plain Dealer*, as rare and exciting an event as an eclipse of the sun, perhaps even as rare as Halley's comet. And now this. Sabotaged by the Z-2D. It wasn't fair, it wasn't one of the things I had or could have planned for, it was unacceptable, it was treason. I pulled out the disk and looked at it. Sure enough, it had a shiny, scraped, out-side track.

I threw the disk with all my might across the room. I kicked the waste basket as hard as I could and slammed the door of the room so hard it shook the house. Nick rose up from his seat at the computer, panic in his eyes. "Dad," he almost screamed, "it's only a machine. How can you get mad at a machine?" He was right, but it wasn't the machine that made me lose my tem-per; it was something that now appeared to be even less under my control—my miserable fate.

Thus chastened by my son, I tried to see what I could sal-vage from the wreckage. It could be that the disk had been worn out by dust particles under the heads, or it could be that the drive had gone bad. Very fortunately, although some of the files were irretrievable and inoperable, the precious SITAR files could be copied onto a new disk. All was not lost. The drive worked. We had escaped intact.

The last days passed inexorably without noticeable progress, and on Nick's last evening but one I came home tired, damp, out of breath from climbing four flights of stairs, after a long hard day at the office, having been jostled in streaming crowds and deafened by underground trains. As I came in the door, Nick's voice came down the hall: "Dad, come here."

I dragged myself into the bed-computer room and flung my raincoat and briefcase on the bed. "Try SITAR," he said. I did. I called up a file, it splashed on the screen, I changed a few words. I pressed the SEND key and waited. After a bit, the screen went blank, the red lights on my disks turned on, and the disks rattled busily. I called for the same screenful again. The disks rattled some more and splashed the text on the screen. It was all there, with the changes in place. "Nick, you've done it," I said and shook his hand. "I think so," he said, giving an extra shake, "but try everything." Everything worked. Maybe we called him Nick because he never finished until the nick of time. Come to think of it, he was born overdue. Kay's diary for this day, January 15th, 1981, contains the brief notation, "Nick has been a great help to Ben with his 'beloved' computer."

Actually I was elated and disappointed at the same time but tried not to let the disappointment show. Yes, my long quest was over. The burnt-out printer interface, the inadequacies of Microsoft BASIC, Alex and Angelo, my biopsy, the cancelled wedding, Lifeboat Associates, Kay's surgery, the transatlantic shift, 12 pints of blood down the drain, delay, misfortune, false hope, frustration. All this dwindled away to nothing. Nick had brought SITAR into being.

But it was not the SITAR I had expected. It was very slow. The SITAR of Reid Watts, mounted on a PDP-11 in BASIC-PLUS, had slid through text with neglible delays. But an age transpired between screenfuls of text moved by Microsoft BASIC on a Z-2D. "This is absolutely terrific," I said to Nick, forcing a broad grin. "Just wait until we get it compiled."

CHAPTER VII

MY BEAMISH BOY

WE STILL do not know the best settings of the three parameters
that enabled SITAR to read a batch send. Nor do we know exactly why they worked. We only know what values worked. Here
is what worked as it appears in CRT on line 1036:

```
1036 PRINT CHR$(155)+"72" : OUT 0,136 : FOR I = 1 TO 333 : NEXT I
```

The baud rate that worked was 1200. The place where Nick
put it is two lines before the program sets up the computer to
receive the stream of text from the terminal. The order of the
baud rate changes is terminal first (PRINT CHR$(155) + "72")
and computer second (OUT 0,136). The sleep is 333 loops (three
hundred probably would have worked, but Nick's fancy preferred

a loopy-looking number). These parameters may not have been the optimal ones, but they worked, and Nick's time was up, for tomorrow he would fly away.

On the 16th of January we saw him out the door with his backpack. In half a day he would be back in Tucson with his telescopes, and my sights would shift to July, when he'd join us again and compile SITAR. Then it would run, according to Microsoft advertisements, at least three times faster. That, I thought, ought to be fast enough.

Meanwhile, I spent the second term teaching courses in Restoration Drama and in Literary Analysis, the course our department offers beginners. Restoration Drama was assisted by live performances of Wycherley's *Plain Dealer* (1677), Vanbrugh's *Relapse* (1696), his *Provoked Wife* (1697), and Sheridan's *Rivals* (1775—a throwback to the Restoration). Only in London can you see four plays from this period in three months. I worked into Literary Analysis the Young Vic's inventive performance of Shaw's *Pygmalion* (the source of *My Fair Lady*), in which an actor playing Shaw himself delivered the author's preface and postscript and, putting on an apron, also doubled, beard and all, as Henry Higgins's commonsensical housekeeper. I also had each member of the class do a paper on a play of his or her own choice, comparing the text to the stage version. I received papers on Ratigan's *Browning Version*, Hellman's *Watch on the Rhine*, Brecht's *Life of Galileo*, Priestley's *Dangerous Corner*, and Pomerance's *Elephant Man*, the play about the famous freak and medical curiosity. It was chosen by almost half of my class.

This was the winter term of my discontent. Restoration Drama, which is really more distant from Middle American youth than Shakespeare is, couldn't seem to compete with London's more immediate excitements. Nor did close analysis of poems and stories, a process similar to explaining jokes, amuse a clientele much of which was present because there were only eight courses to take in London. Getting the students to talk about these things was like pulling teeth, a complaint often heard in the halls of academe; I wasn't accustomed to performing the operation every day. I thought it was my weekly loss of blood that made me so tired, but probably it was these classes.

Bugs now began to turn up in SITAR as I used it to work on a new chapter for a tentative second edition of a book I had written about *The London Stage* Project, called *Travels In Computerland*. New ships take a shakedown cruise to allow errors in construction to crop up before they take on passengers; my software was having its shakedown. Programs must include instructions for what to do if their users make mistakes. If the "error recovery procedures" aren't sufficient, programs will do undesirable things. There is no easy way to foresee what "error conditions" are possible. The readiest way is just to let them happen. On the 31st of January I wrote Nick the following letter.

> Dear Nick,
>
> You will be happy to know that SLOW SITAR, as we shall have to call it, is 1,000 times better than fast SCREEN. The reason is that SITAR (actually the Beehive) is fast where it's important, making changes in the text, and SCREEN is fast where it's not important, supplying the screen. I have just finished rewriting 20 pages of my update chapter for *Travels*, and it was simply marvelous not to have to think about executing every little insert, delete, and writeover. I don't see how I could have done it in three days without SITAR.
>
> And so I am eternally grateful to you for putting me in business again. But there are a few things that could stand attention that I am sure you are dying to hear about.
>
> 1. Unrecognizable command causes drop out of SITAR to "Ok" [the Microsoft interpreter's "ready" sign], causing loss of last screen revisions when SITAR is run again. This error should send us back to the command line state.
> 2. If you happen to misspell SYSTEM [to get out of SITAR and back to CDOS], the interpreter goes back into SITAR, with mystifying results. Where in the STOP module would you put the SYSTEM command, so as to idiot-proof this place?
> 3. STOP leaves the terminal at 1200 baud. What do I change to get back to 9600 baud?
> 4. Failure to give a file name in caps causes files full of garbage, and SITAR gets confused unless they are deleted.

It sure would be a help if SITAR would accept file names in lowercase.

5. It would be nice if we could delete a whole screenful by putting the backslash [end of text code] at the beginning of the first line. If I do this, CRT [the screen-handling routine] goes into a loop, sending the screen forever with a beep every time it starts over again. If you keep at least one character on the screen, CRT stays in business. The only way to get out of this loop is to reboot the computer, confusing SITAR.

6. SHOW refuses to budge after sending a screenful. It is therefore unusable, but I don't really need it a lot.

I concluded by hoping that Nick would soon send me fixes for these bugs in the form of programming code that I could patch in. Slow SITAR was indeed slow. I have just now (February 1983) entered a time capsule and whisked myself back two years to the SITAR of February 1981. I produced this eerie state simply by putting on a disk of SITAR dating back to that time. The effect was similar to that of listening to the voice of a deceased friend on a recording. Here is my time study of bygone SITAR:

Bring up computer:	19 seconds
Bring up SITAR:	1 minute, 8 seconds
Bring up file for editing:	1 minute, 10 seconds
Bring up next screenful:	1 minute, 52 seconds
Search through 5 pages:	3 minutes, 28 seconds

One minute is only a 1,440th of a day, but it is an age when there is work to do. To imagine what it is like, suppose that a house painter, whenever his brush ran dry, had to wait a minute or two before he could dip it in his paint can. For a writer with ideas in his head, such a delay is even more intolerable. SITAR was slow because it was always moving program modules or text on and off the disks out of and into memory. It was slow because it took 18 seconds to read the screen and then 26 more to adjust the file to the changes. I pined for the compilation of SITAR.

But what I wrote to Nick was true; in spite of these frustrating delays, slow SITAR was still a better tool than SCREEN. Thanks to the Beehive's instantaneous editing keys, I could make dozens of changes between batch sends without interference from sluggish software. But I developed a whole new set of work habits. While waiting for SITAR to digest a screen, I found little jobs to do, like shaving, making a cup of tea, or setting my desk in order. My desk was never neater.

One day, while working on my chapter, I had a terrible fright. I had gone to boil water for a cup of tea. During my absence, the Z-2D went to sleep, as had been its wont for some months now. It wouldn't boot up again, so I took out all the circuit boards and put them in again. But it would not wake up, whatever I did. I had promised to submit the chapter in February. The month was running out. There were Cromemco dealers in London, but the British, with their cheerful habit of muddling through, tolerate longer downtimes than we do, whether they interrupt power plants, railways, telephones, or computers. I foresaw months of downtime for my Z-2D while a dealer waited for technicians to get back from holidays or a part to arrive from the States, the dealer having sent his request by sea mail (which takes at least a month) and then discovering that he had ordered the wrong part.

I absolutely had to fix the thing myself. I took all the boards out again, but this time I pressed all of the chips on each board into their sockets, sometimes hearing a gratifying click that perhaps signified a bad contact. But loose chips were not the trouble. Once more I pulled out the boards.

As I pulled out the memory board, I felt something loose under my fingers—a hair, a string, a wire? It was a wire. Sure enough, when I inspected the board, I saw that a very thin pale green wire about two and a half inches long was loose on one end. Apparently Cromemco had made a last-minute revision that hadn't held.

I concluded that I had found the trouble, but I was at a loss about what to do. An arc with the radius of that wire would touch 16 possible contact points, but only one of them was cor-

rect. I'd never be able to decipher the circuit diagram, and the chances were that the revision wouldn't appear there anyhow. I regressed to the instinctive level of a "screwdriver mechanic." As a screwdriver mechanic, I immediately saw that the wire wanted to connect to one particular solder point. If I let it alone, it lay that way. Using a magnifying glass, I then saw on that point what looked like a crystal or two of solder flux and a roughness probably caused by the melting of solder. So I soldered the loose end of the wire to that point. Was it the right point? Only God and Cromemco would know, and Cromemco had probably forgotten. All I know is that after that my Z-2D worked, and that it hasn't gone to sleep since.

In due course Nick sent me programming code to take care of the error conditions in slow SITAR whose causes he could decipher from the printouts. There must have been more to some of them than he thought. But he did give me a good fix for the one that was giving me the most trouble, SITAR's refusal to accept file names in lowercase. The fix went thus:

```
11160 FOR I = 1 TO LEN(G$)
11165 CHAR = ASC(FNM$%(F$,I,1))
11170 IF CHAR < 96 THEN 11180
11175 MID (G$,I,1) = CHR$(CHAR-32)
11180 NEXT I
```

I couldn't understand what these lines meant, but I found I could copy them into the program, heeding useful warnings from the interpreter if I left out one side of a parenthesis. Apparently Nick's fix loops through the file name subtracting 32 from each letter *if* it is lowercase. Curious as to why the magic number was 32, I consulted the table of characters in my Beehive manual and found that each capital is conveniently 32 digits lower than its corresponding small letter. Nick's loop simply spelled out any small letters in big letters for our illiterate software.

About this time I had to do something about my printer. For several months now, it had been erratic about spacing between lines. The problem had gotten progressively worse, and now it seemed as if the slightest drag on the paper would cause the printer to give up spacing altogether and type in place. It wasn't hard to get at the spacing mechanism—I just had to remove the five screws holding down the cover—and then I immediately found the trouble. It was only a loose set screw on the spacing motor's drive pulley, the happiest kind of trouble for a screw-driver mechanic. But this set screw did not call for a screwdriver; it called for a hexagonal wrench so small that I couldn't find one in any local hardware store. So I tried smearing epoxy glue all over the axle and setting the screw with a very sharp-pointed knife. It shouldn't have worked, but it did.

Between winter and spring terms, we went to the north coast of Cornwall. The experience was so powerful that when I recollected it in tranquility on our return, I wrote the following spontaneous overflow in the form of a general letter for Kay to slip into her correspondence.

Dear Friends and Relations,
    Between terms we had two weeks in which to do as we pleased. Now that I think of it, we were roughly in the same boat as Wordsworth, starting off to be a poet about 200 years ago (substituting "we" for "I"):

> Free as a bird to settle where we will.
> What dwelling place shall receive us? in what vale
> Shall be our harbor? Underneath what grove
> Shall we take up our home? And what clear stream

Shall with its murmur lull us into rest?
The earth is all before us. . . .

Thanks to colleagues who communicate at Christmas, we
knew of an institution that fixes up and rents antique houses in
lovely places so that they won't become victims of progress.
Although prospective renters are advised to reserve at least a
year in advance, Kay knew by intuition that a perfect place
would be vacant just then, and she called and it was. Dwelling
place? Mill House #1. Vale? Coombe Valley, North Cornwall.
Grove? Stowe Wood. Stream? Duck Creek, outside the back
door. It was so much better than anything we could have imagined, and we were so suddenly there and back again, that we're
still in a daze.

We didn't walk from London as Wordsworth did, but we
went down via Salisbury Plain as he did, and wound up and
down and around the Quantock Hills where he and Coleridge
designed the Romantic Movement and wrote most of their best
work: Racedown, where Wordsworth and his sister Dorothy
"lived on air and cabbages"; Alfoxden House, where dumb
answers to dumb questions gave rise to Wordsworth's dumbest
poetry; Nether Stowey, where Coleridge's house faces a pub
called The First and Last, being on the edge of the village, not
of eternity; then off to Coombe on the highroad down which
Coleridge (accompanied by Wordsworth) walked when thinking
up *The Ancient Mariner* and down which a Person from Porlock
came to interrupt the composition of "Kubla Khan."

What we found at Coombe would have been enough to
generate another Romantic Movement, if we'd been Wordsworth and Coleridge and they hadn't done it already. Outside
the kitchen door is a cobblestone courtyard where we can sit at
an old oaken table with pretty little birds or loll in a deck chair.
The sea, which we can hear and see from the kitchen door, is
about a mile away, at the end of the valley, in a notch between
green hills rising on either side in gull-wing curves, only where
the gull's head would be is the white surf. The setting sun
drops into that notch. At the edge of the kitchen courtyard runs
the murmuring stream "that lulls us to our rest." Looking
inland, about three miles away at the top of the valley we see
the Gothic tower of Kilkhampton Church.

We dwell in a thatched house full of old furniture and old
pictures. There is a good collection of old books dealing with
these parts. We can light a big fire in the walk-in fireplace and
curl up with *A History of the Parish and Church of Kilkhampton*
by the Reverend Roderick Dew with an introduction by Bishop

of Truro (2nd edition; London: Gardner, Denton and Co.,
Ltd., 1928). The first thing we see when we open our eyes in
the morning is the perfect curve of a green hill cutting across a
bright blue sky in the middle of the white frame of a twelve-
paned double window. We get up and find out what's over the
hills, walk along a 400-foot cliff above a crashing sea, far above
the birds, in the bright sun. Watch the waves, no two the same.
Get hungry. Eat the best lamb chops ever known. So many
total surprises, and all of them pleasant. A true vacation.

Back in London, it was time for English Romantic Poets
(Blake, Wordsworth, Coleridge, Byron, Shelley, and Keats) and
Major British Writers I (Chaucer, Shakespeare, Donne, Milton,
and Swift). I wanted my students of Chaucer's *Canterbury Tales*
to become acquainted with "the medieval mind" and the way it
liked to categorize everything and file it in a neat little box, as in
the Parson's catalogue of sins, where flattery is the fifth type of
swearing, which is the first of the six types of anger, which is the
third deadly sin, all of which are branches of pride, which is the
first deadly sin and the root of all evil, recognition of which leads
to confession, which is the second part of penitence, which is the
road to Jerusalem the Celestial. Chaucer likewise categorizes his
pilgrims. I thought I should take my class to Westminster Abbey
to show them how Gothic cathedrals, with their arrays of stained-
glass windows, statues of saints, and carvings in wood and stone,
make an equally exhaustive catalogue of all there is.

We caught the bus to Westminster instead of going to class
one day and pushed through London traffic to the Abbey, only
to be told by a regretful cleric that no visitors were allowed that
afternoon because there was to be a private ceremony. I hastily
made up a lecture on the outside of the cathedral, which I had
never really looked at before. It had a great number of very
satisfactory gargoyles, flying buttresses, and spaces divided into
spaces divided into spaces, enough to make my point about the
medieval mind. To fill up the rest of the hour, I took them to
the lawn just west of Parliament on the Thames, where I pointed
out that the Victorian idea of the medieval mind, as illustrated in
the neo-Gothic building and ancillary statues, put more emphasis

on the Holy Grail than on the Seven Deadly Sins. Then, sitting on the lawn, I had them pronouce their Chaucer lesson in middle English. I thought it was a pedagogical fiasco, but I gathered later that those students looked back on Chaucer at Westminster as a moment of high romance. That, they felt, is what foreign study is all about.

What better place and time to study English Romantics than England in the spring! It was a happy coincidence that the professor of art history had many of my students looking at Blake's heroic paintings and engravings at the Tate Gallery just when we took up Blake in my course. In the spring break, many of them crisscrossed the English Lake District, where Wordsworth's soul had "fair seedtime." I had hoped some of them would visit the Quantock Hills, which, after our last trip, I had decided was the true birthplace of English Romanticism. If they must go to the Lake District, I hoped they would try to locate sites mentioned in Wordsworth's poems. I hoped some adventurous ones would perhaps find Greenhead Ghyll, where Wordsworth's Michael sat beside his unfinished sheepfold "and never lifted up a single stone," so great was his grief for the loss of his son Luke. Perhaps some might even get as far as the Vale of Chamounix, on the slopes of Mont Blanc, where Wordsworth, Coleridge, and Shelley experienced cataclysmic revelations.

I promised to give special consideration to any papers that treated the site of a Romantic poem, but my hopes were unrealistic. The grand scope of my students' excursions allowed too little time for locating places like Greenhead Ghyll.

One weekend, towards the end of April, Kay and I drove to Cambridge to survey the scene of the first year of our marriage and enjoy a thirty-first reunion with Liz and Tony Potts. In 1949, Tony, then an undergraduate, had magnanimously taken on the responsibility for introducing Kay and me to the rites and privileges of Cambridge, where I was then a Research Student. He was joyfully assisted by Liz Rushbrook Williams, then his fiancée and now his wife. Cambridge hadn't changed much, except for the traffic patterns. The librarian of St. John's College, who'd shown me precious unpublished college records of Wordsworth's performance (poor) as an undergraduate for use in my doctoral dissertation, could still greet me by name after all those years. Nor had Tony and Liz lost the zest for life they had shown us when we long ago poled our punt to a green spot on the banks of the Cam and picnicked among the swans or when we danced all night at the May Ball. But while the four of us retraced old times, I wondered how I could work in a visit to St. Neots.

St. Neots had no Michelin stars, but for me it was worth a detour because it was the home of Cromart, Ltd., headquarters of Cromemco, U.K. For some months I'd been hoping to visit Cromart, partly out of curiosity and partly because the September–October issue of *I/O News*, "The Official Publication of the International Association of Cromemco Users," had announced "huge floppy disk storage" by means of a new 16FDC disk controller board. I did need more disk storage, because my text files were continually overflowing the limits of my disks. Lack of space also cut into Nick's programming efficiency. The announcement had made clear that if I replaced my 4FDC disk controller with the new 16FDC, I could store twice as much information on my disks: they would have **double-density**.

I also hoped, for the sake of SITAR, that if the drive packed text twice as tight, it would move it twice as fast. The announcement didn't say. Nor did it tell me whether my present drives would work with a double-density controller. Nor did it tell me whether the double-density controller could handle single-density files, of which I now possessed a bundle. Nor did it tell me whether I would need a new version of CDOS. Therefore, just before going to Spain, I had written Cromemco asking all these questions. By return mail I got a reply, but no answers. Instead, Cromemco's user service told me that my dealer would be happy to help me and that my dealer in the U.K. was Cromart, Ltd., 12 Huntingdon Road, St. Neots, Cambridgeshire.

And that was why, after our excellent reunion with the Pottses, Kay and I found ourselves in St. Neots, looking for 12 Huntington Road. When we finally found it, the address housed an architect. I assumed that Cromemco or I had made a mistake, but Kay said, "Why don't you ask the architect if he knows where Cromart is?" I was ready to give up. "Just ask," she said; "it will only take a minute." So I did. The architect knew all about Cromart. It had moved out on the perimeter of the town, closer to the nearest freeway exit. Following his directions we soon found it, housed in a glorified warehouse.

Inside the door were the inevitable potted plants, the smashing receptionist, and the form to fill out, stating my business. The receptionist vanished with my form, and a young man in a gray pin-striped suit soon appeared, smiling politely, and said, "Yes, the 16FDC will work on your present system; it is transparent. But we are a consulting firm. You should talk to one of the Cromemco dealers in London." The price? "About 400 pounds, I should think." With that, he disappeared, as if that were all there was to it. The word **transparent** lingered after him. If it meant that my drives, operating system, and files would not "see" the difference between single and double-density, that one word did indeed answer all my questions. Except whether double-density would give me double speed. But I persuaded myself that I needed the extra space anyway.

Four hundred pounds was then almost a thousand dollars, about twice the price quoted in *I/O News*. Therefore, on my return to London, I wrote Nick to buy me a 16FDC at one of the computer stores in Tucson or Phoenix and bring it with him in July. It did occur to me that perhaps I might be asking him to smuggle, but I thought the British markup was outrageous and told Nick to plead ignorance if held up by H. M. Customs and Excise. After all, I didn't know whether a 16FDC was dutiable or not.

When spring break arrived and our students dispersed all over Europe, Kay and I went off to a cottage overlooking the cathedral in the small Welsh town of St. David's, perched on the tip of Pembrokeshire, as far west as you could go in Britain, barring Lands End, Cornwall. The people around us spoke Welsh to each other, but to us English with a musical lilt. The cathe-

dral, whose floor was a perceptibly inclined plane, dated back to
the days of St. Patrick, the beach lay on a trade route for commerce in stone axe-heads between Britain and Ireland, and the
landscape was peppered with menhirs, megaliths, stone circles,
cromlechs, and other vestiges of the Stone Age.

A cromlech

On this ancient trade route, we drove along the Presely
Hills, the spine of the peninsula, worn down to outcroppings of
huge igneous boulders as old as the earth, piled up like giant
cromlechs. Among these we felt the presence of monstrous earth
gods and imagined unspeakable rites, for some of these boulders,
called bluestones, had once had so much totemic power that they
were dragged, or dragged and floated, all the way to Stonehenge,
120 miles away.

We had been told not to miss the old square Methodist
chapels. In such a chapel in one small village, we remarked on
the exceptionally good acoustics. "Oh, yes," the sexton nodded
gravely, "that's because they have buried a horse's head under

each corner. It's very good for the singing." At the bookstore just outside the main gate of the cathedral, we bought the *Mabinogian*, a storehouse of Celtic myth and legend, and read about Bran the Blessed, a thinly disguised god of fertility. As long as Bran's severed head stayed buried in London, it would preserve the land from plague, but some fools, of course, dug it up. As we walked the cliffs of the wild seacoast and clambered over the prodigious hilltops, we felt four thousand years of civilization melt away.

One day shortly after our return from St. David's, Kay, who is always planning the next adventure while engaged in the last, announced that Clytha Castle, near the English/Welsh border, was reserved for us for a week in July, and, for the week after that, there being no vacancies in Coombe Valley, she had arranged for an apartment at Houndapit, a converted barn on the bluff above Coombe. Clytha was described as a "folly," a mock Gothic structure, reproduced in the 18th century mainly to improve the view from a manor house. This one, however, had a modern kitchen next to its keep, three bedrooms, and two baths. After Houndapit, she hoped we could find a nice house on a Greek island before we went back to Appleton.

Upon hearing this news, my mind turned inevitably to SITAR and its compilation and to Nick, who must do the compiling. "Kay," I said, "I don't think Nick will be able to finish his programming for me before we go to the castle. There won't be enough time. Nick may need as much as a month before he gets it all cleaned up." "Very well, then," she said, "we will have to take the computer with us. If you have to program, you can program in Wales and Cornwall." I hoped we wouldn't have to.

The crowning moment of this term was our pilgrimage to Stratford on the weekend of the 22nd of May, on which we were accompanied by some twenty students. On Friday afternoon we saw Michael Pennington as Hamlet, Kay and I for the second time. On Saturday afternoon we saw *As You Like It*. It was even better the second time and just perfect for the month of May. For the interlude before the evening performance of *The Mer-*

chant of Venice, new that spring, Kay put together a picnic for us all in the green glade beside the River Avon between the theatre and the old church in which Shakespeare is buried. A Stratford butcher gladly baked her a big turkey, a vintner chilled a half-dozen bottles of white wine, a greengrocer supplied the makings of a large salad, and a baker took a half-dozen loaves of bread out of the oven. Kay contributed the coordination, the paper plates, the knives, forks, and spoons, and a large pot of her special curried mayonnaise. It rained some gentle rain, and the sun burst through.

After the picnic came the *Merchant of Venice*. It was the least ambiguous of the three versions I saw that year. The stage was round and bare except for props. Shylock was skinny, and he sat on a high stool counting coins on a high desk like the one we see in illustrations of Scrooge's counting house. Portia sat in a big chair huddled in a great robe, which she shed little by little from one act to the next, as a butterfly sheds a cocoon, until she emerged in all her glory at the end.

On June first I graded my last exam and could now concentrate entirely on SITAR. Let joy be unconfined, the season said, but I was more of Hamlet's opinion, that this world was weary, stale, flat, and unprofitable. The weeds possessed it merely. As I surveyed the forthcoming summer, I saw burdocks and brambles rising up to choke SITAR. Nick would not arrive in London until the 30th of June. After ten days in London, we would move operations to Clytha Castle for a week and then to Houndapit for another week. That left one week in London before we went to Crete, where Kay had just found a spectacular place for us to end our year abroad. Although that gave us four weeks for SITAR, much time would be wasted in dismantling, packing, and setting up households. The computer, the terminal, and the printer were three hostages to fortune, three myriads of delicate circuitry just waiting to be dropped, jarred, jolted by erratic electricity, clogged with dust, or shaken to pieces by bumpy roads; there were countless connections ready to open, wires to short, and transistors to drop out—millions of chances for something to go wrong.

When Nick called with the news that he was going to climb Scottish mountains with an astronomer friend from the 4th to the 13th of July, I saw the project's chances of completion dwindle to something like one in one hundred.

Nick reported that he could not find a Cromemco dealer in Tucson but, since he was stopping to visit friends in Boston on his way to London, he had ordered a 16FDC from a dealer in nearby Wellesley. Her name was Leslie, and she was prepared to ship it to me direct if her order from Cromemco didn't arrive in time. But shipping was one sure way to get involved with Customs and Excise, and it might well nullify the saving I hoped to make by purchasing the controller in the States. Therefore I wrote Nick a letter instructing him to stop Leslie from shipping it direct. I also listed the programming jobs I expected him to complete while in England and reminded him who was paying his passage.

During the month of June, I distracted myself by spending the days at the Public Record Office on Chancery Lane, turning over a hundred pounds of papers siezed by Prime Minister William Pitt's spies when he stamped out English political societies in 1795 for sympathizing with the French Revolution. It would be some consolation if I found William Wordsworth's name among the membership lists or signers of resolutions. In his long poem on the growth of his mind, he had declared himself "an active partisan" of the Revolution, but no external evidence justifying such strong terms had ever been found.

On his arrival at Heathrow on the 30th of June, after hugs from me and kisses from his Mom, seeing the question on my face and knowing what it was, Nick said, "It didn't come in time, Dad. Leslie will hold it for instructions." We wouldn't be compiling in double-density, then. Turning our attention to SITAR, we again scratched any further work on the FIND modules so as to concentrate all effort on the editing sequence. Soon, much to our surprise, in only four days and just before he left for Scotland, Nick successfully compiled that sequence of modules. Light flashed at the end of the tunnel. But . . .

We were **I/O bound**. As SITAR labored to bring up one screen of text, deposit that, and bring up another, ages transpired. It was only about ten percent faster. It was I/O bound because it spent most of its time waiting for Input and Output from the disks. We knew that because now the red light signifying disk activity was on all the time, except for the screen-digesting period. Before compilation, the light had frequently gone off while the computer worked by itself. Since now the computer polished off its compiled instructions with lightning speed, nothing but our slow disks and the 1200-baud batch send blocked the way to fast SITAR. It was bad enough that every edited screenful necessitated a rearrangement of the disk file. Worse still was the fact that every module of SITAR had to be loaded from disk into memory each time it was used. To EDIT a passage in a file, SITAR loaded the "front end" to interpret the command, which in turn loaded ED for further command processing, which in turn loaded SEARCH to find the passage desired, which in turn loaded CRT to put the passage on the screen and take it back after editing. To put another passage up for editing meant reinitiating the whole sequence.

As I have explained in Chapter V, SITAR was broken up into small modules because the PDP-11 system for which Reid Watts designed it limited the amount of memory available to each sharer of its time. Since PDP-11 disks were very fast, the time spent loading modules was negligible. But loading a module from 5¼-inch single-density disks took twenty to thirty seconds, and loading three of them almost a minute and a half. "I was afraid of this," Nick said. But I hadn't been. When I had ordered the Microsoft compiler more than a year ago, I had placed complete faith in it, and there it had rested until this day.

Nobody ever tells you these things. The ads may tell you that floppy disks are many times faster than punched paper tape or cassettes, but not that they are many times slower than big hard disks on macrocomputers. Cromemco's catalogue does not specify the speed of its floppy disks. Tandon, the maker of my drives, specifies "Seek Time, 5 microseconds track to track," and "Transfer Rate, 125/250K bits/sec." Five millionths of a second sounds fast enough for anybody, and 250,000 bits per second is 16 pages of data per second. Obviously, these figures have little to do with reality as I now knew it. When you have been accustomed to waiting 5 or 10 seconds for the next screenful of text to appear and you have to wait a minute and a half, *then* you know how slow floppy disks are—after a year's work getting ready to find out.

"One thing I can do," said Nick, "is rewrite the batch send to take advantage of the compiler." That would be some help, because the batch send took more than a minute of computer time. But we didn't know how much help. With dampened spirits we ate dinner. Afterwards I said to Nick, "If we're wasting so much time loading modules, why don't we merge them and load them all at once and be done with it?" "I was thinking of that," he said, "but 64K won't be enough for them all. We can consolidate some of them, anyhow."

I suppose that the seven days between Nick's departure to Scotland and his arrival at Clytha Castle were the worst I'd spent since the days following that ill-fated biopsy a year earlier. I now stared failure in the face for the first time, not just setbacks of schedule from Lifeboat's recalcitrance or Nick's running out of time but an insurmountable stone wall with a sign on it saying, "You can't do this at all. You never should have tried." I was a Robinson Crusoe who had carved out a boat too big to launch. I was a fool, or, as the father of my childhood friend used to say, I was "a fool and a sucker which is worse." We would take the computer to Clytha Castle, Nick would try a few things, they wouldn't do enough good, and that would be the end of it.

I tried to persuade myself that while there were still things to try, there was hope, and moreover that until those things had failed, I had no business desponding. I filled up the long week vainly searching for Wordsworth's name in the confiscated documents. Now, as I scanned the most likely dates, it began to be evident that I wasn't going to find him. I should have foreseen this outcome, too, because it was apparent that a dozen people had sifted those papers before me.

Clytha Castle stands on a long rolling hill, most of it pasture dotted with sheep, and overlooks a large gray stone manor house about a mile and a half away on the other side of a winding road. About ten miles beyond rises a range of purple mountains, looking like giant weatherbeaten boulders. Above, across, and behind scud heroic gray and white clouds against a light-blue sky. The castle, or mock-castle, presents to the view of the manor house a square keep about fifty feet tall, joined by a crenelated curtain wall to a round tower of the same size. In the keep, a grand bedroom sits on top of the living room; both have huge fireplaces and twenty-foot ceilings. You wouldn't need a battering ram or a traitor inside to take this castle, because it has only two walls. Reaching back from the keep is the other curtain wall, terminating in another round tower. In this tower is a round bedroom fifty feet in diameter and thirty feet high, completely dwarfing the emperor-sized bed, which has a Napoleonic bedcurtain made of gold cloth—the kind that drops from a medallion twenty feet above the bed. Kay and I slept in this bed. There is nothing else to the castle but a kitchen and dining room beside the keep, with a bedroom and bath on top of them. Between our bedroom and the keep was a passageway about fifty feet long. On the window sill of a tall Gothic window in this passageway, I ensconced the Z-2D.

Into this castle put the following people: Kay and me, Aunt Janet and Nephew Chris; Daughter Mackay, just graduated from Earlham, and her Cambridge University friend John Pryor; Nick and his mountain-climbing friend John Spencer; Rachel Gibbs, wife of a London physician, a friend dating back to 1965 when our boys went to the same school in London; Lady Pollock, her daughter Jill, and her grandaughter Rosie, aged one year. Her husband George and I had skied for Cambridge against Oxford in 1949, when, during the annual Joint University Alpine Holiday, it developed that I was 1) eligible for the team as a Research Student at St. John's College and 2) good enough to make an English ski team that year. I disgraced the U.S.A., and Oxford won. It wasn't until 1965, on our second English sojourn, that I discovered that I had been skiing with the son of a baronet—not just George, but Sir George.

Not all these people were present at the same time, but their comings and goings were all crowded into the week at Clytha, along with a seven-mile hike along Offa's Dike to the ruins of Tintern Abbey, near where Wordsworth "felt a presence that disturbed [him] with the joy of elevated thoughts"; excursions to White and Raglan Castles, ruined but real; an evening of Welsh dancing; a bushwhacking exploration of a prehistoric hill fort; daily hikes in the hills around us; and three big meals a day. Against this backdrop Nick programmed, and I struggled to keep him at it. I believe our guests saw me as the ogre of the castle. Indeed, Kay's diary for this period remarks, "I wish the computer had never been invented."

At the Clytha site, Nick and I struggled with our logistics problem. How many merged modules could our computer compile? Nick knew that the compiler did not load all of a program into memory at once, but he didn't know how much memory it would need as it proceeded bit by bit. Microsoft documentation gave no hint. There was nothing for it but to compile more and more modules until Microsoft BASIC said, "Out of memory." Then we would know what the limit was.

I hoped that we could compile the whole editing cycle as one program. Reid Watts had designed this cycle so that, once you entered it, you could keep on editing without going back to the front end. It would be nice if we could include the front end too, but that would be frosting on the cake.

Merging these modules was, typically, harder than we had expected. They had been written to work independently. A variable might have one name in one module and another in the next, as you might call your female parent "Mother" in one sentence, "Mom," in another, and "she" in the next. For instance, strings B2$ and C1$, though they were identical, had no connection to each other that a computer could conceive of. Nick had to change both to GET$, and then comb the modules to be sure that he had renamed every one. To miss even one mention would produce a SITAR that, if it ran at all, ran crazily. There was also the problem of OPEN and CLOSE. It was fatal to close an already closed file or to open an already open one. But each module originally opened every file it wanted to use and closed it before leaving the module. When Nick merged the modules, much of this opening and closing could be dispensed with, but we were pestered with "File already open at line 1026" messages until he found and eliminated all of the redundancies and omissions.

There were other redundancies. Each module began with a long set of definitions and parameter settings. Once per module was enough, and economy was of the essence. And **GOTO**s and **GOSUB**s were a mess. If a programmer wants to use over again a routine he's already written, he tells the program to GOTO the line number where it starts or GO to the line number where a special SUBroutine begins. After a GOTO, the program keeps on going from where it is. After a GOSUB, it performs the subroutine and then returns to where it was before it went. A SITAR module might have a score of GOTOs, but when Nick merged modules, lines were renumbered, and GOTOs got lost. So, too, he had to use new addresses for his SUBroutines. There were also **CHAIN**s to ferret out and convert to GOTOs. When one module of the original SITAR shifted operations to another, it CHAINed to the next module, and Microsoft loaded and ran the new one. Once merged, a module was already loaded and had to be found by a GOTO. If Nick had any more time after he succeeded in harmonizing the merged modules, we wanted to try a higher baud rate for the batch send, and we hoped he'd have time to patch the batch send routine into the compiled version of CRT to take advantage of the compiler's greater efficiency. And there were still some bugs left over from his January session.

In the chaos of Clytha, Nick kept his nose to the terminal. It was not long before light again penetrated the tunnel. In his previous experience of compiling one module at a time, the compiled module was always bigger than the uncompiled source. But when he compiled merged modules, the compiled version was smaller than the source. That being the case, there was now a chance that we could merge everything and still have enough memory left to run it all at once. For the first time, something they never tell you had worked in our favor.

Nick soon found that he could compile the whole editing cycle. But when he attempted to add the front end, the compiler smugly announced "Out of Memory." The irony was that, if we could have compiled it all, we could have run it all, but we couldn't compile it all because the compiling process itself needed too much work space. It was as if the piano would go through the door, but you had to move it in a crate, and the crate wouldn't go through.

On Wednesday morning of Clytha week, I heard Nick cursing in his narrow stone passageway. "Can't read the damn disk," he shouted, and the words reverberated in the keep. It was the disk that held the results of all his merging, and he hadn't yet made a backup of it. If it had gone bad, he'd lost three days' work. Nick went off to take John Spencer to the train, leaving me to ponder, "What next?" Remembering that one or two disk errors hadn't prevented me from retrieving SITAR in January, I decided to try copying at least the merged programs. I gave the commands, and holding my breath, I watched the disks light up and listened to the thunk-thunking of the drives. An age passed without a read error, and then another age, and finally XFER said

```
36 blocks transferred to A:ED.BAS
```

That saved the merged modules. I was able to save the precious front end, too. When Nick came back from the train station, I happily announced the news. "Good," he snarled. He was still disgusted with the disk drives.

He had now reached the point of patching in the batch send, and he wanted to know where the Z80 book was. In London I had found a book that told how to program a Z80 in assembly language. We searched all likely places, but as I feared, I had forgotten it. I was ready to drive to the city of Cardiff, 60 crooked miles away, and look for a computer store. Nick was about ready to send me. Finally, he said, "Let's see what I can do without it. If I get stuck, then you can go." Thank heaven he did not get stuck, because I'd have driven to London for it if need be, and that trip would have wasted a whole day.

At about this time we switched operations to the north coast of Cornwall. Houndapit, near Coombe Valley, had been a stone barn for several centuries, and now it was a brand new holiday apartment complex with a bright orange, yellow, chrome, and porcelain interior that suggested Howard Johnson's. Nevertheless, its fields had not yet given way to parking lots and fast food establishments. Out the window was a broad expanse of mildly curved pasture declining gently toward the high cliffs that demarcate the Bristol Channel. On this pasture lived a score of sheep and a dozen cows. The Z-2D commanded a view of the pasture, the sheep, and the cows; or the view commanded it, for sometimes a curious cow would gaze steadfastly through the window at Nick computing. Aside from the cows, there were fewer distractions at Houndapit. One day a sheep rolled over on its back and wouldn't get up, causing great consternation among the tourists. Kay feared that it might have gotten sick on some of the mouldy bread she had put out for the animals. After several hours, some men came with a truck to cart the sheep off, but when they went to load it, it gambolled away. We took trips to Tintagel, said to be King Arthur's castle, and to Bodmin Moor, one of the great waste places of the world, where ancient men had raised many stone questions. Nick didn't go to Bodmin, but he and Chris did climb a 50-foot rock, worrying their mothers no end.

I don't suppose that since Mackay was born, I had ever felt so much like an expectant father as I did during that week at Houndapit while Nick labored over the batch send patch and over new and old bugs in merged SITAR. It was now only a matter of time before we would find out what kind of a thing would come to birth. Nick never despaired, but Microsoft SITAR was not born at Houndapit.

I had made up my mind that we would not take the computer to Crete and have it disrupt another family adventure. I knew that if we failed in the few days left to us in London, Kay would propose taking it to Crete, in its three outrageous boxes. We both dreaded this eventuality, though neither of us said a word about it. But I knew I couldn't put us through any more split holidays.

> Hearts with one purpose alone
> Through summer and winter seem
> Enchanted to a stone
> To trouble the living stream.
> —W. B. Yeats

We had four days left. Kay reported to her diary, "Nick and Ben are working very hard on SITAR." On the third day Microsoft SITAR was born. It was a healthy, happy, bouncing, fast program, faster than I had ever dared to hope. It could be done, and Nick had done it.

On the island of Crete Nick and I danced the *sirtaki* in the tavernas with Mackay, Janet, Chris, Kay, and our Cretan hosts. In my mind's eye I could see Anthony Quinn and Alan Bates dancing on the beach in the movie of *Zorba the Greek*. But we were not celebrating the collapse of a foolhardy scheme. Nick had lifted the stone from the living stream and hurled it out of sight.

CHAPTER VIII

SEQUEL:
EXIT AHAB, TANGLED
IN HIS HARPOON LINE

Alice: But "glory"
doesn't mean "a nice
knock-down argument."
Humpty Dumpty: "When
I use a word, it means
just what I choose it to
mean."

THAT WAS the year we implemented SITAR, and that is the tale
I set out to tell you. But life and computing cannot be confined
to the boundaries of a tale, and some loose ends remain to be
tied. What about the 16FDC? Did I ever get a formatter for my
printer? Did the Z-2D and I live happily ever after? Did Kay and
I escape our maladies unscathed? Did Devon find a new life?
Did Mackay find a job after graduating from college? Is Nick
making progress toward Mars? Did Ben find a career in South

America? It is now two years since we danced the *sirtaki*, and I now know some answers to these questions.

On our return to London from Crete, we packed up everything and flew back to Appleton with six more cartons than we had brought. The extra cartons consisted mainly, I believe, of presents for friends and relations and two treasures acquired from our landlords, the Society for the Preservation of Ancient Buildings: our flat's grandfather clock, which I had given Kay for her birthday, and an old portrait on the wall of which we had grown fond.

Before settling down, we drove to the Mayo Clinic to have Kay's other breast removed, just as a precaution. The operation went smoothly, and there was no cancer whatever in the breast. Since then Kay has had three checkups, and, as Dr. Sterioff had predicted, she harbors no malignancy. As for me, blood tests on my return proved that University College Hospital had drained all the iron from my body. We have spent the last two winter terms at Akumal in the Yucatán, where I, on sabbatical, have been writing this book on my Z-2D and Kay has made friends with most of the fishes in the lagoon and a great many of the local Mayas, Mexicanos, and gringos.

Not long after her return from the family Christmas in Spain, Devon left Chicago to start a new life in Denver, where she got a job conducting public meetings about a proposed rapid transit system. Concurrently, she and Tom, who'd been her sweetheart in the sixth grade, renewed their old ties. Now they are married and living in Vancouver, where Tom teaches labor relations at the University of British Columbia.

Ben's mission in South America has lost a good deal of its simplicity: his impulse to help South America has in the course of graduate work shifted to a desire to understand it. He used to think that the only hope for South America would be for the United States to get out of her affairs, but he recently confided to me that judicious intervention might work better. And his once-clear mission has undergone another complication. In the pursuit of his Ph.D., he also began to pursue a bright and beautiful girl named Kathe, also working on a Ph.D. in Political Science at

Berkeley. But they specialize on different countries, and his dissertation takes him to Rio de Janiero, whereas hers takes her to Frankfurt. Facing a year on different continents, they decided to get married. In September 1983, at The Lake, they did so. They hope that by staggering their periods of research they may be able to spend a good part of their early married life together.

Not long after finishing SITAR, Nick chose the the ionic plasma spawned by the plumes coming out of the volcanoes on Jupiter's moon Io as the topic for his dissertation in planetary science at the University of Arizona. To the data collected by space probes, he added his own spectroscopic observations from a telescope on Mt. Hopkins. As for his expedition to Mars, it appears that Nick is making some progress in that direction. He is one of the prime movers of a project to design and build as a candidate for the next Mars probe a revolutionary rover that crawls over bad terrain by deflating and inflating sections of its tires. He and a team of fellow graduate students and professors have built a pilot version out of plastic bags, vacuum-cleaner parts, and pipe organ valves that works beautifully on sidewalks and in rooms full of furniture. NASA has funded the construction of a full-fledged rover for tryout on the Mars-like desert of Arizona as the machine that the backup probe will carry. So there is a good chance that, even if Nick doesn't soon get to Mars, at least his rover will.

Mackay has found not just a job but a calling. After our holiday on Crete, she went to Munich to seek her fortune as a translator of chemistry from German to English or the other way, hoping to make the most of her two majors at Earlham. But she couldn't get a work permit on this basis. Undaunted, she stayed on as a student of German, supporting herself as an *au pair* girl and private tutor in English. But after six months, she decided to be a nurse. She then joined Devon in Denver and went to work as a nurse's aide in the University of Colorado Hospital. At first she thought she didn't like full-time work, a common experience of recent college graduates, but she soon settled into it and shifted her sights to a career in midwifery. Since the most practical route to that specialty is to become a registered nurse first, she is now in training at The Northwestern University School of Nursing in Chicago, and we are happy to have at least one child in our vicinity.

Malfunctions

My computer system has not lived happily ever after but, like all created things, has had its ups and downs. In the process of writing this book, I have come to the conclusion that the printer and the disk drives are the components most likely to break down. Just after I got back to Appleton from London, the 737 began to type erratically. At first I was missing occasional descenders, especially on my 'g's. As a screwdriver mechanic, I wanted very much to oil the little hammers that made the dots, but, since the 737 manual didn't include the hammers in its oiling instructions, I thought I had better not. I tried exercising the hammers vigorously by printing a file consisting entirely of letters having descenders. This strategy seemed at first to help, but after a while the printer began to get worse. Now it was missing dots in all letters on the first inch of a line. I decided to take the head mechanism apart and see what that might lead to. Just taking something apart and putting it together again will sometimes fix it, whether you find anything wrong or not.

As I began to dismantle the printer, a little brown wheel that spun around as the printhead advanced caught my attention. It was the size of a quarter, and beside it was a curious metal arm reaching out to its circumference. The arm had a set screw that adjusted the gap between it and the wheel. The set screw was loose. I tightened it. The printer got worse.

It was time to call Technical Support at the factory. They told me to call my nearest Walk-In Service Center in Chicago. The Walk-In Center told me that it must be the printhead and that if I sent them the printer, they would install a new one for $200. Service men don't repair components any more. They just replace them.

What I needed was technical advice, not price quotations. Perhaps the adjustment of the little brown wheel had to be very precise. If so, I had no idea how to set it. I decided to see how far I could get with Tech Support at the factory if I refused to be shunted off to my nearest Walk-In Center. This time I told the man who answered, "The Walk-In Center doesn't know anything about it, and besides, they're two hundred miles away." This approach succeeded in bringing an engineer to the phone. He thought it could be a logic chip, or a cable, or any number of things. And the adjustment of the little brown wheel? "Oh, you mean the **Hall effect sensor**. That has to be exactly five hundredths of an inch. It fires the hammers as they pass over the paper." This Hall effect sounded important enough to be causing all my trouble. But no. After I'd borrowed a spark-plug gauge and set the gap exactly, my printer still missed as many dots as ever.

If it was a chip, as the engineer had suggested, I'd have to pass. I could never diagnose a bad chip. But what about a cable? There was a flat ribbon cable from the printhead to the circuit board; it must be driving the hammers. To test this hypothesis, I set the printer to work and wiggled the cable. I found out that if I pressed down on the end nearest the printhead, I got all my dots. Of course! The reason I was missing dots at the beginnings of lines was that here the cable was stretched the most. It was a very stiff cable. No wonder some of the wires had broken; they had been bent and unbent by thousands of carriage returns. I ordered a new cable from my Walk-In Center immediately, it came the next day, and it fixed the printer. The new cable was exactly the same inflexible kind, but at least when it went bad, I knew what to do. By avoiding the Walk-In Center, I saved $194 and two weeks of downtime.

My disk drives continued to ruin disks from time to time, and they cost me a considerable amount of text. Then one day I read in Cromemco's *I/O News* in a column called "Tec Tips" something that changed all that. The columnist was Richard Quinn, to whom I wish every blessing that God can grant. In this particular column, Richard observed that early Z-2Ds had been shipped with their cooling fans blowing *out* of the cabinet. This was not the best way to mount the fan, because there is no way to filter the air that comes into the cabinet to replace the exhausted air. If one reversed the fan so that it pumped air *into* the cabinet, one could filter the air as it came in. My Z-2D did indeed have a backwards fan, and I immediately did as Richard advised. I haven't had a disk fail since, and my disks, heretofore after a month of use worn shiny around their circumferences by the heads riding their surfaces, now never show the slightest sign of wear. Dust, drawn into my drives by a mismounted fan had done all the damage.

When my system got to be about two years old, my disks became unreadable for another reason. They showed no wear, but one drive couldn't read a disk made on the other. That symptom must mean that the heads of one or the other drive were off track. Since the unreadable disks had recently been made on drive B, I suspected it. But disk repair requires skilled technicians working with costly instruments. Tandon, the manufacturer of my OEM drives, estimated a two-month turnaround for "refurbishing" a drive ($90), and they wouldn't do anything less than refurbishing. My solution was to buy a new drive, first because I needed a drive right away and second because I thought that the way things were going, I should have a spare. I did not buy the new drive from Angelo because he charged more than Cromemco, nor did I buy it from Cromemco, who charged more than a Tandon distributor in Milwaukee. He sold me a drive for $300, $200 less than Angelo's price. Nor did I have the old ones repaired by Cromemco, who asked $50 more per refurbishment than Tandon.

Corporate Stupidity

In the spring of 1982, it being clear that Nick was now too busy with his telescopes to write a formatter for me, I made a stab at finding a ready-made one for my Centronics 737 printer. I called Centronics in New Hampshire, asked for Tech Support, and was told that I should call a certain number and leave a message on a recorder stating my needs. I did so, and in a few days a man called to report that he didn't know of any formatters for CP/M or CDOS but suggested that I call four software houses that he knew had written 737 formatters for other systems, giving me their phone numbers. So I did. One of these numbers had been discontinued, and the other three houses were dedicated to Apple or Radio Shack software.

Last summer, still not willing to believe that no one had written a CP/M formatter for the 737, I wrote an angry letter to the president of Centronics. I got his name from an annual report, which also showed that he was losing money hand over fist. I explained to him that I wasn't surprised at their lack of success in the micro market because of the way they treated their users. I complained of their nearly inaccessible Tech Support, their inadequate Walk-In Centers, and, of course, the lack of a CP/M formatter for the 737. "A company whose products won't run on CP/M, the absolutely universal operating system for microcomputers, must have a very strong death wish," I said.

I never heard from the president, but in a few months I got a letter from a "Tech Support Specialist," who had "checked" but had "not found any software compatible with the Cromemco and the 737." The reason he gave was that "the Cromemco is a serious computer and they do not get involved with word processing." I thought of the various meanings that sentence could have, all of them ludicrous, and wrote another letter to the president, to which I did not receive an answer.

Recently, a letter from Microdome Corporation of Denville, New Jersey, dropped out of the blue. It announced the availability of an "External Textformatting Interface" for the 737, an aggregation of chips and printed circuitry which plugged into the cable between the printer and the computer. It sounded like a great idea, and I ordered an interface immediately. But instead of an interface, I got a letter telling me that Microdome had no more interfaces in stock. When I called later to find out why, a very nice man with a German accent told me that he was sorry, that they had only a few left when they sent out the circular, and that none were left when my letter arrived. Furthermore, he did not think that they would ever make any more because Centronics printers were no longer in demand. Cheaper machines had taken over the market. He also told me that Centronics knew all about the Microdome interface. The company newsletter had even printed an account of it several years back.

Customization

SITAR, the program, remains pretty much the same as when Nick merged and compiled it. There have been, however, some radical changes in my system as a whole.

On my arrival in Appleton, the 16FDC was waiting for me. Leslie, following my instructions, had shipped it to one of my friends, who had held it for my return. But the new disk controller turned out to be less "transparent" than the man in the pinstripe suit had so easily assured me. All seemed to be well when I plugged it into my S-100 bus and initialized a disk. CDOS, as I expected, asked whether I wanted "Single Density (S) or Double Density (D)." When I answered "D" for "Double," I thought I had made the conversion. But although the initialization program appeared to work perfectly, the files I transferred to the disk were unreadable. After trying two brand new disks with no better results, I suddenly recalled that there were also questions about single and double density in CDOSGEN, but regenerating my system and answering the appropriate question with "D" was to no avail either. I then gave up and called Cromemco.

"Oh," they said, "what version of the operating system do you have?" I didn't know, offhand. "Well, you can't run double density unless you have version 2.36 of CDOS." I knew I didn't have that. The best way get version 2.36, they told me, would be to join "SUDS" (Software Update Service) for $95. Then I would get updates of SCREEN and FORMAT, which needed version 2.36 of CDOS and therefore included it. It sounded roundabout, but it was a lot cheaper than buying 2.36 outright. I asked him to transfer me to the proper person and joined SUDS immediately by MasterCharge. In less than a week I had version 2.36.

Double density *was* twice as fast as single density, and 16FDC SITAR was twice as fast as Houndapit SITAR. That's how I found out whether double density meant double speed. It's difficult to understand why Cromemco did not loudly advertise such a big selling point.

More speed was still to come. While in the throes of failing disk drives, I discovered a way to operate SITAR without any disks at all. An advertisement in *Infoworld*, the weekly newspaper of microcomputing, riveted my eyes. It was for SemiDisk, "three to thirty times faster than floppies." It wasn't a disk at all; it was a memory board that you plugged into your S-100 bus, and then, with a little program (included), you fooled your operating system into thinking it was another disk drive. The SemiDisk would work on any CP/M machine. If I had such a device, I would no longer wear out disks and drives, and SITAR would make another quantum jump in speed, perhaps enabling me to write with altogether negligible interruption by disk I/O, which still hampered my efficiency.

I knew that CDOS could handle software made for CP/M because it could handle Microsoft BASIC, which was made to run on CP/M. But would the little SemiDisk program that fooled CP/M fool CDOS? The answer, I found out from SemiDisk Corporation, was, "No." But the door was still open if a "CP/M for Cromemco," which I had seen advertised in *I/O News*, could handle SITAR. CP/M for Cromemco cost $235 and the Semi-Disk cost $2,000. The best course for me was not to buy the SemiDisk until I was sure that SITAR, now working on CDOS, would also work on CP/M.

I had CP/M for Cromemco up and running on the day it arrived. But the upgrade was by no means transparent. My first unforeseen difficulty arose when I attempted to convert my CDOS disks to CP/M disks. The "Implementation Notes" did have instructions for the conversion, but these instructions did not work for me. They told me simply to transfer all my CDOS files from double-sided disks to single-sided disks using CDOS; then, using CP/M, to transfer them all to blank double-sided disks. In short, a double-sided disk would not transfer, but a single-sided one would. When I got nowhere with CDOS's XFER and CP/M's equivalent, PIP, I tried PIPX and CONVERT5, also included with CP/M for Cromemco.

During several days, I tried all possible combinations and options of these utilities but got no farther. Finally, when I stopped spinning the roulette wheel and called the software house that had sold me CP/M, the man who answered proceeded slowly and carefully: "First you put your file on a single-sided, single-density disk on CDOS—oK?—and then you transfer it to a double-density, double-sided disk on CP/M—oK?" "Did you say single-*density*?" I asked. "O . . . K. I said *single-density*." That was the problem— I was trying to do it with a single-sided, *double-density* disk. I swear to you that nowhere in version 5 of those "Implementation Notes," dated 03/01/81, does the term "single-density" occur.

A far greater difficulty arose when I tried to run SITAR. It came up beautifully and filled the screen with text, but when I tried to send the screen to the computer, the system went dead and could be revived only by a reboot. It was the batch send again. Now ensued the most exasperating programming session in the history of SITAR, much exacerbated because it was conducted over the telephone, with the computer in Wisconsin and the programmer in Arizona. Time after time, Nick would dictate a chunk of assembly code to me, usually an attempt to discover the function of one or another Z80 code, and then hang up. I would then write the routine, run it, and call back with the results, usually negative. He would then scratch his head and give me something else. Sometimes I found him at his office, sometimes at home, and sometimes at the telescope on Mt. Hopkins, sleeping off a night of observations. Most of the exasperation occurred at my end as I wrestled with unfamiliar programming tools, using CP/M's cryptic instructions which assumed that I already knew what they were explaining to me.

It soon became apparent that our problem was a **system call**. When an assembly-language routine needs help from an operating system, it makes a system call. Under CDOS, the batch send routine called upon CDOS to accept a character of text arriving at its door by issuing system call 128. CP/M had no such thing as system call 128, and so it picked up its toys and went home. It would not accept a character arriving from the screen unless it heard call 6. Call 6 did not work the same as call 128, so Nick had to rewrite the whole batch send for the third time. Our futile sessions took place every day for two weeks. Finally, just after I had given up trying to do it over the phone and had hired a local student genius to do it for me, Nick called and said, "Dad, I think I'm getting close. Try this." I did, and it worked the first time. When I called back with the news, Nick was very much surprised because he had thought the routine was incomplete. It had only been a test of a minor bit of code.

I was now ready to present my case for a SemiDisk to Kay: I would retire next year. In my retirement I would do lots of writing. The SemiDisk would increase my efficiency. "Well," she said with a sigh, "it's a lot of money, but if you really think it will help. . . . "

I had the device in my office in less than three days. I plugged it into my S-100 bus, and SITAR's speed increased by a quantum leap. It could search a file as fast as Cromemco SCREEN, as fast as a Z80 could carry it, faster even than a PDP-11.

Another drawback of the Z-2D for my purposes was its enormous size, especially when packed, and its weight. After hauling it to The Lake, to England and back, and then to Yucatán, I saw that I had to pare it down, at least for traveling. On its first trip to Yucatán, the Z-2D went to Guatemala City by itself instead of to Mérida with us. When it finally got back to Mérida, it was impounded by customs. I telephoned Brother Dave in Washington and asked him to send the Marines, but he advised diplomacy; we laid the case before the American Consul, and she expeditiously bypassed the lower echelons of the Mexican bureaucracy and freed my computer. The reason it had gone to Guatemala City in the first place was that its 4′×4′ carton was too big to fit in the plane's regular luggage compartment.

In an attempt to avoid future mishaps of this sort, I again had recourse to the ads in *Infoworld*. Integrand Corporation had been heralding "MAINFRAMES from $200" ever since I had first subscribed. They meant that they could sell me an empty cabinet containing an S-100 motherboard with a built-in power supply and a place for my disk drives. On further inquiry, I found out that I could get from them a ten-slot mainframe with mounting facilities for two drives and a 120/220 volt transformer for around $400. It would be half as big and heavy as my 21-slot Cromemco mainframe, and even with my SemiDisk, I still needed only five slots. It was a deal.

This conversion was fairly transparent. The only tricky part was carrying out the photocopied instruction:

ATTENTION

MOTHERBOARD HAS PINS 53, 20 & 70 CONNECTED TO GROUND PER IEEE S-100 BUS DEFINITION

Confirm your cards don't use these lines BEFORE PLUGGING THEM INTO THE CARD CAGE!!!!

You may release the above bus lines by CAREFULLY

cutting the ground lands from pins 20, 53 & 70 with a sharp Xacto knife.

The ground lands are attached every other

connector on the solder side of the motherboard

The tricks were ascertaining that my cards were indeed nonstandard, dismantling the bus, finding pins 53, 20, and 70, cutting through the solder of the printed circuit with a razor blade everywhere the pins were grounded, and not cutting anything else. Apparently I did these things properly, because my new enclosure works perfectly. Best of all, it fits a $2' \times 2'$ carton that easily goes into a baggage compartment and no longer requires the intervention of the American Consulate.

When my Z-2D switched to CP/M, it underwent a personality change. Under the control of CDOS, it had been pedantic, inconsiderate, eager to help, and not much good at words; under CP/M, it was cryptic, rude, eager to cause pain, and just barely literate. However, CP/M worked faster when you got to know it.

What is the meaning of the CP/M command "PIP B:TEXT = A:TEXT"? If a man on the street were to see it chalked on the sidewalk, he might wonder what the hero of *Great Expectations* is doing in an algebraic equation. If he recognizes it as a computer command and looks it up in the CP/M manual, he will find **PIP** defined as "Peripheral Interchange Program." A program for interchanging peripherals? If he knows what a peripheral is, he may think PIP is used for switching video terminals, printers, and disk drives around. Only an old DEC hand would guess what it really is, a program for moving files from one place to another, although this is only the main thing PIP is used for on DEC computers and far from the only thing.

Now, let him turn his attention to the rest of the statement, "B:TEXT = A:TEXT". Let us suppose that he knows, somehow or other, that TEXT is a file to be moved. He is now free to wonder what an equal sign has to do with moving anything. Once it is explained to him that the second file is a copy of the first and therefore equal to it in some sense, he still has to deal with the colons. These, as everyone knows, designate that A and B are disk drives.

With this knowledge, now let him tell us which is the original and which is the copy: "B:TEXT = A:TEXT". Will he not assume that the original comes first? Wrong again. Everyone knows that, in programming code, the last is always the first. Otherwise, how could "$n = n + 1$" make any sense? And everyone knows that "$n = n + 1$" is the way all programs increment variables. If our man in the street should now dare to ask by what logic a number can possibly "equal" that same number plus one, the computing establishment will shout him down: "The question," as Humpty Dumpty said on a similar occasion, "is who is to be master, that's all."

But I have never been able to master such perverse usage, and I have made so many false starts and costly mistakes because of it that I have taken steps to avoid CP/M commands altogether in my conversations with my computer. Curiously enough, CP/M itself provides the means by which we can dispense with it. It has a program called **SUBMIT**, which, properly used, will translate plain English into CP/M gobbledygook. The program is a sort of front end designed to execute a batch of commands, one at a time, without stopping until the last is done. The batch must have the extension SUB, or SUBMIT can't find it. For example, if I command "SUBMIT STUFF", SUBMIT looks on my main disk for a batch of commands contained in a file called STUFF.SUB, and then it runs them, one at a time.

Because so many commands act upon entities (files, disk drives, and so forth) which may vary with the job to be done, this front end will substitute specific values for variables when it is run, just as a lunch menu may include the variable "beverage", for which we substitute the value "coffee", "tea", or "milk" when we submit our order. If I command "SUBMIT STUFF DUCK", SUBMIT will run the batch, substituting the word DUCK wherever the batch of commands contains a hitherto unspecified element. If I desire, the batch may contain several unknowns, just as a menu may list vegetable, salad, and dessert as well as beverage.

To summarize in the words of the manual:

> The SUBMIT command allows CP/M commands to be batched together for automatic processing. The ufn given in the SUBMIT command must be the filename of a file which exists on the currently logged disk, with an assumed file type of "SUB." The SUB file contains CP/M prototype commands, with possible parameter substitution ...

I can illustrate the way in which CP/M's SUBMIT utility can be used to defeat CP/M by explaining the operation of my command MOVE, which moves a file from one disk to another by means of PIP. Essentially, to move a file called TEXT from a disk on drive A to a disk on drive B, I command "MOVE TEXT FROM A TO B". Actually, I must invoke the program SUBMIT first. Since "SUBMIT MOVE TEXT FROM A TO B" is the kind of gobbledygook I am trying to avoid, I have changed the name of my SUBMIT program to a meaningless "@". If I write "@ MOVE TEXT FROM A TO B", I can see better what I mean. SUBMIT sees this statement as a command to execute the contents of MOVE.SUB, using the words that follow as a numbered list of items to substitute in MOVE.SUB: (1) TEXT, (2) FROM, (3) A, (4) TO, and (5) B. In the file named MOVE.SUB, I have secreted the CP/M command "PIP $5:$1=$3:$1", in which the dollar signs precede items to be looked for in MOVE.SUB's list. SUBMIT (disguised as @) looks at the statement in MOVE.SUB and, by substituting the items in the list for their numbers in the formula, perverts the whole statement to impeccable CP/M: "PIP B:TEXT=A:TEXT". CP/M has no use for items (2) FROM and (4) TO, which I use only so as to write plain English.

Programmers will say, "Why waste words?" My answer is that they make what I am doing clear to me, they are short, familiar words in a sentence I would naturally use for the purpose, and I therefore never make any mistakes. Well ... hardly ever. I ask them in return, "How often do you make mistakes with PIP? How much time do you waste typing '=' and ':'? How often do you get the spacing wrong? How often do you send the file the wrong way? Do you always get a PIP statement right the first time?" I might also ask one particular programmer, Gary Kildall, why he didn't write CP/M in plain English to begin with. There is no reason in the world for his not doing so.

By means of SUBMIT, I have devised a dozen plain English commands for the tasks I regularly perform, and my computer's personality now pleases me immensely. And why shouldn't it? It is my own. It is my personal computer.

CHAPTER IX

THE MASTHEAD: AN OVERVIEW

And I only am escaped alone to tell thee.

IN THIS chapter, I try to see the story I have told from the perspective of a disengaged bystander, less like the Captain Ahab of *Moby Dick* and more like its Ishmael, looking down from above at the tiny mortals on the ship's deck and the great ocean which surrounds it. No longer suffering the slings and arrows of outrageous fortune, disentangled and free, I will make some attempt to understand the computer culture with which I have necessarily become intimate. As I write, I reside at the mouth of

Yalku Lagoon in the resort settlement of Akumal, in the state of Quintana Roo, on the east coast of the Yucatán Peninsula, in Mexico. At this great geographical and cultural distance from the scenes of my endeavor, I hope that I can be dispassionate, though objectivity is not one of my strong points.

Yalku Lagoon is a narrow inlet about half a mile long, where underground freshwater streams mingle with the salt sea. *Terra firma*, under water or above, is made entirely of coral, still growing or dead millions of years ago. On land, this base supports a tropical jungle and, near the shore, groves of coconut palms. I live in Casa Christensen, on a point of land where Yalku meets the sea. In front of the house are some small limestone islands, which the endlessly pounding surf has shaped into giant mushrooms by hollowing out their foundations. The noise of the breaking waves was at first deafening, but I am now used to it. The texture of the limestone wherever the waves wash it has to be seen to be believed. Imagine a concrete sponge in which all the parts that jut out are sharp as broken glass, and you can approximate this texture. The seafront in the bright sun is always arrestingly beautiful: the white surf smashing the rocks, the bright green jungle across the lagoon, the scattered palms silhouetted against the sky, the big rollers sweeping into the lagoon, and the ocean in four shades of blue—sky blue, turquoise, dark blue, and almost black. Sunrises and sunsets seem like special shows put on for us.

From the road behind, the house looks like an enchanted palace in which Morgan le Fay might live. It is a dizzying sculpture of colonnade and swooping curves, some of them holding trees and shrubs in their arms. The center is dominated by a steep conical thatched roof that covers about half of the house. The garden wall is twelve feet high and topped by a Mayan molding that represents the boundary between earth and sky. The large rectangular columns of the porch and its walls are faced with small limestone bricks. Four Mayan masons sat for a year in front of the house, hacking these bricks out of solid rock. Each course of bricks has a different thickness.

Inside, the architect has created a mighty maze, but not without a plan. All the masonry is white. Every part of the house spins off like a planet from the sunken circular living room under the conical thatch. The cone is supported by a pentagonal fretwork, and the floor of the room, which is fifty feet in diameter, lies sixty feet under the apex of the cone. This room is partly circumscribed by a cement couch, well cushioned, which eccentrically surrounds a huge round coffee table made of polished black timbers. Behind this couch, and concentric with it, lie about four feet of interior jungle containing some fairly big trees and lots of giant plants, some of them large specimens of North American house plants. Reaching up through the interior jungle, nine pillars, faced with Mayan bricks, support the cone. The room is lighted by French doors opening out onto the foreshore. Underneath the thatch's long overhang is a terrace which commands the mouth of Yalku. The round dining table, also of polished black timber, sits on an interior terrace on the level of the kitchen, to which it is an easy walk. The kitchen is familiarly square on the outsides, but the long counter which separates it from the main room is an arc of no known circle.

The bedrooms are reached by a stroll through the library behind the interior jungle. This room centers on a large octagonal glass-topped table used as a museum case for sea shells, the castoff shells of lobsters and crabs, and coral specimens. From here, a passageway spins off toward the two downstairs bedrooms, and a snail-curved staircase swoops up to a spacious free-form hall with a view of the sea and, through the interior jungle, the living room. One side opens into the master bedroom. Leaving the master bedroom to take a shower, you step down into an oval bathtub made entirely of small yellow tiles with handpainted red birds on them. Before you can properly register all this, you see that you are standing naked in an an oval window, watching the white surf.

Every room, including the kitchen, has a partially shaded terrace, except for the library. The windows of the house are six feet square and, with their black trim, frame pictures of the sea, the jungle, and the lagoon. They seem like large color photographs hanging on the white walls. The floors are made of hexagonal red tiles. The walls are decorated with limestone reproductions of ancient Mayan bas-reliefs on hand-hewn bases of black wood. Heavy hand-hewn black wooden timbers form lintels wherever necessary. Santos and Silvia, their little girl Jenny, and their baby Rosario live in quarters beside the kitchen, and the whole family takes care of the fairy palace.

The reader can well imagine that, during the whole two winters we occupied Casa Christensen, we awoke with a shock every morning to find out where we were. It was possible for us to live there only because Casa Christensen was not, at this stage in Akumal's development, a truly rentable property overseen by a local manager who could furnish full services for carefree living. When we ran out of gas, water, electricity, or sheets, we shifted for ourselves. Bottled gas, drinking water, laundry, electrical supplies, generator parts (if any), and water pumps were 60 miles away in Cancun. But the continual repair jobs and the trips to Cancun were only minor irritants in such surroundings.

When not expediting water, gas, and electricity, I worked at the keyboard of my Z-2D, comfortably ensconced in the upstairs hall. When my eyes tired, I rested them on the moving picture of rock and surf outside the window over my my left shoulder, or swayed reflectively in the convenient hammock.

While I worked on my keyboard, Janet and Kay cooked, read books about birds, fishes, tropical trees, and Mayas, painted what they saw above and below the water, and snorkeled. But mainly they snorkeled. They estimate that they snorkeled several miles a day. Their daily reports included sightings of parrotfish, midnight parrotfish, batfish, frogfish, queen angels, French angels, blue tangs, sergeant majors, squid, barracuda, wrass, turtles, groupers, permits, stingrays, four-eyed butterflies, lobsters, queen triggerfish, moray eels, octopuses, a boa constrictor, and a shark, all swimming around in an exotic underseascape of caves and corals.

Last winter, I decided I wanted a record of maintenance at Casa Christensen and instituted a log book. Here is the month of January:

January 1: No power from Akumal generator; put new spark plug in house generator—runs much better.

2: Doug Christensen supervises Ernesto and Aurelio in house-to-house trouble-shooting of Akumal power system.

3: Good power all day.

4: No power. In the middle of the night, Ernesto spirits away his Akumal generator. Implementation of federal power begins. While they are revising the local power system, there will be no electricity for at least a month.

5: Butane registers zero. Gas pressure very low. Santos disassembles house generator motor; removes carbon. Runs better.

6: Get brake fluid for VW bus in Cancun.

7: Gasoline for generator low. Take tanks to Tulum for more gas. One winding of generator quits at night; put both house circuits on other winding.

8: Take electrical end of generator apart; reattach broken lead from winding to socket. Commutators dirty; sand them clean; split house circuits again.

9: Debug generator starter. Battery poles needed scraping. Refastened haywire hot lead; not much help. No butane; no help on this from Isidro. Santos and friend haul big butane tank to roof. Have to borrow correct regulator from Vincente at Casa Short. New tank gives low gas pressure; stove OK, but hot water tanks take ages to recover. Santos says Isidro promised to supply butane 4 days ago.

10: Mackay arrives Cancun with replacement for broken 737 printer: Epson MX-80. Much explaining to customs, flashing of documents on computer, etc. Get 10 gallons of gas.

11: Work all day wiring up Epson. Cable doesn't work; find open at pin on one end. But printer will print only in italics.

12: Try to implement bigger gas tank for generator by siphoning from 5-gallon container; very tricky getting air bubbles out of line. Use tubing that Nick gave me for Christmas. Ruben tears over in his clunker to tell us butane truck is at hotel. Santos and I go to hotel and lead driver out here to fill our main tank.

13: Generator carburetor that Al Devereux replaced in December cracked in two pieces. On Bob Chaney's advice try to find man to weld it in Cancun. Took all day. Finally found a maestro on Avenue Uxmal near Carretera Mérida who could tackle aluminum-antimony alloy: mañana a diez.

14: Carburetor done at noon. Maestro also named Ruben. Bob Chaney says he did good work. Cost 1,000 pesos ($6.00); gave him $2 more for gratitude. Install it immediately on return; works fine.

15: I think vibration of air filter assembly is shaking carburetor to pieces. Dispense with heavy metal cover. Air bubbles in gas keep breaking siphon suction. Rig bottom feed tank from 5 gallon oil bucket and butane fittings. Much better.

16–17: Chichén Itzá with Mackay. Stayed at Valladolid.

18: Generator shaking itself to pieces trying to start water pump. Pump can't get up enough speed to kick out starting condenser. Not enough current. Could be bad electrical line or inefficient generator. Try new pump condenser; no help. Disassemble pump motor. Cleaned condenser contacts, cleaned rotor, reassembled, being careful of bearing alignment. Seems to run better, but have to use more throttle to get pump going. Generator's governor assembly has fallen off and gotten lost. Rig rubber band as governor spring. Gives more throttle for increased load. At night one circuit of house starts blinking again.

19: Haul generator to back porch, take off electrical end; wiring OK. Problem is worn-out contact in generator's output socket. Solution: use other socket.

20: Kay and Mackay get 10 gallons of gas for generator in Tulum. Last 10 gallons lasted 6 days, and we use few lights at night.

21: Mackay leaves. Rented car quits at airport. K & J get replacement; it stalls all the time; Budget garage fixes it.

22: Saturday. Ruben fixes gas leak on roof (bad solder joint). Forced 1,000 pesos on him. Pump can't get up speed. Ruben says bad line through house. Must run directly from pump to generator; has cable, will lend. After installing Ruben's cable, Santos says, "No funciona."

23: Sunday. Out of water in roof tank. Uncouple pump and try turning shaft. "Soave," says Santos, so we try starting it again. With extra throttle, it works. But before tank is filled, generator fails: other side of carburetor cracked. Spent rest of day making a brace for the carburetor, rigging shutoff valve in gas line, cleaning air filter, etc.

24: Cancun by 8 AM, Maestro Ruben promises welded carburetor at 2 PM, delivers at 4. Back home at 6. Santos and I can't get carburetor to work; prime it; always dies after about 1 min. Another waterless candlelit night.

25: Santos & family go on three-week vacation. Take carburetor apart, compare to old one. Little piston valve not hitched to float. Hitched it, generator works, pumps tank, but still shakes carburetor loose from its mountings. Have to tighten mounting bolts every hour or so.

26: Pump capacitor kicking in and out. Finally get it going. Try to rig braces so that carburetor doesn't shake so much.

27: Unable to start pump; capacitor crashing in and out until breaker opens. Ruben stops by to see how we are doing. Says voltage OK but pump is bad. Buy new one in Cancun, Ruben installs at 6 PM, repairs Isidro's bad solder joints, revises pipes. Virtuoso exhibition. Forced 2,000 pesos on him, six-pack of beer. Still unable to start pump. Ruben says it needs to run on 220, will change it over at 7 AM tomorrow.

28: Ruben sets pump to 220; goes like a dream. At night one house circuit flickering; plug at generator is vibrating loose from socket.

29: Make solid foundation for generator to prevent its drifting around, causing plugs to slip out. Get gasoline in Tulum.

30: Stopped using plugs altogether; use bare tangs instead.

31: Tangs still creep out of socket. Carburetor bolts still work loose. Federal power only half done. Predict it will take another month.

As I swing in my hammock and watch the undulation of the waves, I think about electricity. Trying to run my computer on a generator powered by gasoline brought home to me how blindly we take electricity for granted in the United States. I knew from hard experience that we cannot take computing power for granted, but now I knew from even harder experience that we can't even take electrical power for granted either. And computers are so thoroughly embedded in our lives that if, for lack of electricity, all the computers in the United States went down tomorrow, chaos would reign. The whole fabric of computing is supported by a fallible system of electrical transmission.

Mexico has still not mastered the technology that it takes to distribute continuous electrical power. When federal power finally came to Akumal, it shut down randomly from week to week for four-hour maintenance periods. Whenever it was rainy and damp, the voltage dropped to 100. At that voltage, the Beehive went blank, but the Z-2D still went on. One evening, while we were staying in a hotel next to the ruins at Uxmal, our waiter Manuel took us to the neighboring town of Muna for the fiesta. Muna was pitch dark. We were out of gasoline, and there was no electricity to run the pumps at the filling station. Manuel got a friend to siphon a few gallons out of his truck. Inside a great hall, 400 people waited for the lights to go on, the amplifier to hum, the band to play, and the dance to begin. A few waiters were selling beer by flashlight. After an hour in the dark, we went home.

Local wiring has to be seen to be believed. The federal authority puts a transformer beside a village, and everybody strings wires to it. Overhead is a crazy network of conductors, tied to trees by string, propped up by clothespoles, wound around timbers. Cables are patched together out of whatever lengths and sizes of wire can be found. Splices are made by manually twisting the wires together, and they are often left bare. Switch boxes lie on the ground or dangle from rafters by the wires that energize them. Ground wires don't exist. 120-volt wires get confused with 220-volt wires, refrigerators burn up, radios pop, and lights explode. Cables run through puddles of water. No wonder there are power failures. Without good engineers, responsible electricians, and scrupulous administration of electrical codes, electricity as we know it cannot exist. The Electrical Age is a house built on on sand, and the grains of sand are people.

North American computing has just about reached the level of Mexican electricity. Hardware is remarkably reliable, considering the youth of most of the industry, and, for certain kinds of problems, the new software is marvelous. We begin to see sensible word processors, and the calculating spreadsheets have immensely simplified financial planning. There are adequate systems for running farms, drugstores, and churches. But beyond these happy developments is a vast troubled sea of incompatibilities. Software made for one computer won't run on another. Apple, Radio Shack, and Cromemco are three different worlds, and with its PC, IBM creates still another.

Worst of all is the incompatiblity between user and system. A man buys a computer because his friend liked his and then finds out that the best software for doing his particular job is made for a different type of computer. If it does work, he finds that it won't do the main thing he hoped it would, or not without enormous difficulty. When he seeks help from his suppliers, he finds they are more ignorant than he. When he consults his instructions, known as **documentation**, the incompatibilities multiply again. As Nick used to say, "They expect that you already know what you are trying to find out." When to this chaos we add the misspellings, needless jargon, bad grammar, tortured sentences, and incoherent fragments in which this documentation is customarily written, the incompatibilities multiply again. For these reasons, plugging a computer into a given problem is many times harder than plugging in a household appliance—even if you already know something about computers. I offer the previous chapters as testimony.

Most of my troubles with my computer arose from inadequate software, bad service, and bad documentation. I think I may complain of Microsoft BASIC's crippling string functions, even though I suppose there are many "good reasons" for them, but couldn't its designers, in the face of a universally acknowledged information explosion, have accommodated the vast amount of text crying out for computer management? Couldn't Centronics have taken steps to assure that the vast numbers of CP/M systems already in existence could use the paramount feature of their 737 printers? Couldn't the designers of CP/M and CDOS just as easily have written operating systems and documentation that catered to the normal expectations of intelligent speakers of English? And couldn't Lifeboat Associates have rescued a drowning customer?

The technology is good enough, but there has been a failure of its human interface. Technology appears to contemplate only itself. The problem is endemic, but the manifest chaos in the computer industry illustrates it especially well. And ironically, that industry is occupied in the most human activity of all, the transfer, analysis, and transformation of information.

As I swing in my hammock and watch the waves roll into the lagoon, I think of Tracy Kidder. In his best-selling romance of computing, *Soul of a New Machine*, not far from the end, Tracy Kidder wrote that he was

> struck by how unnoticeable the computer revolution was. You leave a bazaar like the National Computer Conference expecting to find that your perceptions of the world outside will have been altered, but there was nothing commensurate in sight, no cyborgs, half machine, half protoplasm, tripping down the street; no armies of unemployed, carrying placards denouncing the computer; no TV cameras watching us. . . . Computers were everywhere, of course—in the cafe's beeping cash registers and the microwave oven and the juke box, in the traffic lights, under the honking cars snarled out there on the street (despite those traffic lights), in the airplanes overhead—but the visible differences seemed insignificant.

Marshall McLuhan, author of *Understanding Media*, would have said, if he had come upon this passage, "Exactly. 'That is the voice of the current somnambulism.'" McLuhan could understand media of information transfer because he approached them from a perspective that no one before him could imagine and that is still difficult to imagine. What we normally see in a given medium is that it makes easier a few things that were once hard or impossible to do. But McLuhan makes us look at "media as extensions of man." They extend our powers of speech, hearing, vision, and muscles. They extend our outreach and by doing so catapult us into a whole new world. So, instead of focusing on their convenience, which is all the ordinary person notices, McLuhan asks us to look at the precise way in which they extend our powers. Knowing this, we can see how this extension will change the limits of human life, the human condition.

Each new medium transforms the conditions of life. What the flashlight happens to single out is not the main point. The main point is that *we can see in the dark*; the electric light has turned night into day. The important thing about railroads was not that we could get oranges from Florida but that they reorganized the country, giving rise to new centers like Chicago, and opened the West. The important thing about the printing press was not that books could be duplicated faster but that information could be widely disseminated. A massive organization like the United States would have been impossible without an efficient means of disseminating its laws and policies; we would have become a loose fabric of warring duchies and city-states in several vaguely defined nations, as was the case in the Middle Ages. The important thing about the telephone is not that I can talk to my brother in India but that my own voice can be heard in India and I can hear what India says with my own ears.

The total effect of electricity is that information of all sorts moves instantaneously and shrinks the whole world to the size of a primitive village. When a man's unassisted voice was the sole means of communication, no community could extend beyond earshot. With electricity, we become a "global village." For an example of this effect, think how intimately we became involved with the Iranian people during the hostage crisis. Because of television, we *knew* Khomeni, Bani Sadr, and the rest. They were not just "live" but living in our living rooms. Without TV, most of us would have passed up the endless, stale dispatches in the newspapers and contented ourselves with the headlines.

Because we don't perceive that media alter reality in this way, we are numb to their effects, like people walking in their sleep. We remain in a daze until the effects are so obvious that we take them for granted. But McLuhan was not dazed, even as early as 1964—only 15 years after Echert and Mauchly produced UNIVAC, the first commercial computer, and 15 years before Tracy Kidder watched the people of New York walking in their sleep as if nothing were going on at the National Computer Conference. In *Understanding Media*, McLuhan had little to say about computing per se. But his pronouncements on the Electrical Age in general may be substantiated by reference to the medium of computing alone. In what follows I attempt to do so.

Nothing matters any more but information. Iterative manual work disappears because that is what computers do best. Electricity is like light, which turns whatever it falls on into information, to use as we wish. Electricity is similarly indiscriminate with regard to the information it transmits—by satellite, telephone, TV, tape recorder, thermostat, headlight, slide projector, or computer. Because production is automated, information by which to instruct machines and aim products at the market is all that counts. If given the right *information*, the computer can memorize, organize, analyze, manufacture, keep accounts, make decisions, do research, even teach. At the elementary level the computer automates drill in arithmetic, reading, and writing. Learning becomes a game, as it always could be when effectively managed. There is no barrier to a ghetto child's learning the three R's. The teacher, free from busywork, concentrates on perfecting the information system. The pupils get more individual attention from the computer than they could ever get from a teacher in a class of forty. The focus shifts from managing the classroom to moving the information. Similarly, when editing and typing are automated by a word processor, the writer can concentrate entirely on the information he wishes to transfer. Information is all that counts.

Knowledge becomes "a single unified field," a "mosaic." Already, the private citizen can hook into hundreds of on-line data bases. These services will obviously expand forever in depth and breadth. The day will come when my computer will be able to tell me almost instantly who said "What's in a name?"; the cosine of a 16 degree angle; how many home runs Babe Ruth hit in 1927; what's on in London; what was on in London 200 years ago; the next, cheapest, fastest plane to Zürich; the best vintage of the best wine for capon at what price; today's hog prices; the history of a piece of legislation; the formula for benzine; the date of Mars' next opposition; front, rear, and sideways elevations of the Acropolis; the number of times "ywis" appears in Chaucer; how to use the binomial theorem. In a reference work, our fingers do the walking; now the computer does the walking. The field of knowledge instantly available to one man is potentiallly enormous. Each according to his ability, we can become fairly good specialists in any field, but as information-gathering gets easier and easier, we are more likely to become generalists like Leonardo and Benjamin Franklin.

"Jobs . . . disappear." It is not just that computer-controlled machines take over the work of machinists, accountants, draftsmen, engineers, actuaries, auto workers, technicians, and typists. The very concept of "job" disappears. Instead of telling a typist to send letter B to Mr. X, the boss sends it himself to Mr. X by electronic mail. His computer becomes his secretary, and his secretary becomes his research assistant. No two ex-typists do the same work. Each one becomes an entrepreneur. The assistant works at home, sending his or her work to the boss by electronic mail. The boss works at home. The office itself disappears. Everyone has to know more about the business because everyone is managing part of it. Even the programmer's job disappears, because programming languages are so simple that nearly everyone in the business knows how to program. (And they make better programs, because they know exactly what they want them to do.) The minuscule tasks for day-laborers, in and out of the office, disappear. Technological unemployment? The work available in the information business is limitless. Increase in unemployables? As the cost of good teaching goes down, the pupil's opportunity to learn approaches the limits of his innate capacity and depends less and less on his parents' position. The computer gives knowledge to the people.

"Automation ... ends subjects in the world of learning." This effect follows logically from the disappearance of jobs. Job training no longer works because businesses no longer provide clearly defined slots into which they can plug any chemist, typist, mechanic, data processor, or other pretrained specialist. Since the information on which a business runs flows effortlessly to and from all hands (unless classified), each member, thus informed, may carve out his own niche according to the fullness of his grasp and his general abilities. If the business depends on, let's say, chemistry, biology, electronics, behavioral sciences, and economics, each employee's success depends on knowing more about these things. Specialization fails. It is generally recognized that computer systems designed by programming specialists in a Data-Processing environment have almost universally failed to serve the true needs of managers. The reason, also universally recognized, is that Data Processors haven't understood business and managers haven't understood computers. Managers, moreover, will have to understand the ever-enlarging real world made possible by instant information flow; they will more than ever need a general education. Since communication will have ever and ever higher priority, they will need to study languages and literatures. Since understanding systems will be the paramount skill, they will need to study politics, economics, systematic philosophy, and history. The boundaries between subjects will break down as learning focuses more and more on the system of the whole. McLuhan says, "Automation makes liberal education mandatory."

"Starting with the effect" is the new approach in planning. Because computers can automate any process that a machine can perform and, moreover, enable a given machine to produce a wide variety of products, the character of the product is no longer dictated by the machine. As we move toward (but perhaps not to) a state of affairs in which any business can make almost anything, management is free to produce what the customers want instead of selling them what its machine happens to make, and to adjust easily to changing demand. In the computing industry there has been much talk recently of "top-down design," which means starting with the user's needs and tailoring hardware and software to these. The microcomputer industry, it is plain, has reached such a fluid state that one hardly has time to think of something a user might need before it appears on the market.

"The social patterns ... latent in automation are those of self-employment and artistic autonomy." All observers agree that a principal fault of mass production is that, because each worker contributes such a tiny part of the final product, he can't say, "I created this," and take pride in its beauty, perfection, and value. All the credit belongs to the corporation. In the days when all commodities were the products of individual craftsmen, this wasn't so. The computer restores the pre-industrial state of man, all of us artists and artisans with an unbelievably versatile tool with which we can create almost anything we can imagine. Instead of being a minuscule part of an assembly line, we own an assembly line. The opportunities for self-employment are everywhere we look. Everyone may have work that is worthy of him.

When I contemplate the present state of computing, lost in a tulgy wood and desperately galumphing hither and yon, McLuhan's brave new Electrical Age seems far distant, perhaps even a mirage. I cannot imagine how we are to get from here to there. As I swing in my hammock watching the waves, light years away from Silicon Valley, my thoughts fix on IBM.

IBM, on whose 360 I labored eight long years at night and on weekends. IBM, to read whose documentation and operate whose computers required a degree in computer science. IBM, whose marketing psychology was as brilliant as its technology was stupid. IBM, who until forced to admit otherwise, believed that Data Processing was all there was. IBM could not see where computers were going. It was numb.

What is **Data Processing**? It is a way of using a computer which assumes that computers are for computation, that the world consists of numbers. Data Processing tolerates lists—of personnel, parts, customers, answers to questionnaires—but only in order to compute salaries, inventories, bills, and preferences. It views the computer as a **mainframe**, a great factory whose input is lists and numbers and whose output is computations of these numbers and updated lists. Its method is batch processing—large batches of raw data in and large batches of updates out. Its idea of efficiency is larger batches faster. It rates computer systems by their "power," and it measures power by the number of input and output parameters you can change. Since power leads to complexity, it welcomes complexity as a sign of power. It generates a large dictionary of technical terms by which to describe this complexity and then reifies the terms, as if they were natural phenomena, like cows and rocks. Exalted by esoteric knowledge, its practitioners regard ordinary people as irritating encumbrances and "users" as idiots to be indoctrinated, trained, and locked out of the computer room. It believes that the way we do it is the way it is to be done, and that what we do is all there is to do.

In 1970, when I had 21,000,000 characters of data on the 18th-century London stage to load into an IBM 360, IBM offered me the keypunch. To correct keypunching errors, you had to find the card (one in tens of thousands) containing the error and repunch it. Or you could, as I did, punch your corrections on another set of cards and let the computer do the fixing. But because you couldn't watch what the computer was doing, like as not you put the right correction in the wrong place or the wrong correction in the right place, making the text worse than it was before.

For text-editing, IBM also offered the Magnetic Tape Selectric Typewriter (MT/ST), one of those tape recorders on which you edit as it plays text through a typewriter (described in "Cetology"). But it required the keyboarding dexterity of an organist, and when I tried it, my text got steadily worse. There were so many buttons to keep track of, and I couldn't see what was going onto the output tape until the damage was done. Even so, it was an improvement on punch cards.

But even if I could have mastered the MT/ST, I couldn't have used it for entering my 21,000,000 characters, because IBM had made sure that MT/ST tapes were incompatible with computers, its own or anyone else's. The reason was that the company had made such a large investment in key punches that it couldn't afford to let people enter data from MT/STs. I got around IBM that time by having my 8,026 pages typed onto paper and then reading them onto computer tape wth an optical scanner. IBM, naturally, did not make an optical scanner, again to protect its keypunch.

What I needed, of course, was a modern word processor. But IBM could not imagine such a machine, although the technology was readily available and upstarts like CPT, Lanier, Lexitron, Redactron, and others had begun to take advantage of it. Since their machines were prohibitively expensive and hard to use anyhow, I got around IBM by transferring all my optically scanned text into Lawrence's PDP-11 time-sharing computer and editing it on the Beehive screen with Reid Watts's SITAR. Nearly a decade passed before IBM, pressed into action by the frightening success of true word processors, brought out its Displaywriter.

Along with the glorified MT/STs came the micro revolution, which gave computing power to the people. Before microcomputers, it had become practically impossible for executives, especially junior executives, to get computing service from mainframes because of the way you had to use them. First, you had to write your program or find someone to write it for you; then you had to punch out six to twenty cards of incomprehensible gobbledygook whose function was to describe the job you wanted the computer to do. You then put these cards in the computer center's job queue. When your cards finally got processed, a week to ten days later, like as not there was a comma missing somewhere in the gobbledygook, causing your job to abort. So you corrected the cards, resubmitted the job, and waited another week to ten days, hoping against hope that there wasn't another error in them. IBM did not bring out a personal computer until a frighteningly large part of its clientele started buying easy-to-use personal computers from upstarts to get around the log jam at the computer center. Then, after nearly a decade of personal computing had passed, recognizing that microcomputers were a severe threat to its mainframe business, IBM thrust its hastily assembled PC on the market.

This record shows that IBM has consistently blocked progress, while all true innovation came from upstarts. IBM may have thought it was good business to wait and see, but the fact is that if it had been first with word processors and personal computers, it would have been spared the enormous expense of a rearguard action. Its inability to understand the significance of cheap chips led to a corporate failure tantamount to the defeat of the Spanish Armada by a swarm of tiny English ships, granted that the company has scraped through by the skin of its teeth.

The cause was indeed the failure of IBM's human interface, both in its self-defeating protectionism and its inability to imagine the real world. Why couldn't the company perceive that processing words is the primary human activity, that filing cabinets and libraries contain hundreds of times more words than numbers, that even the numbers are useless without words to give them meaning, that the numbers themselves are words, too. As the micro rebellion has proved, the real need was always Word Processing, for Word Processing is certainly either the first or second reason why a person buys a microcomputer today. If, twenty years ago, convenient word processors had been developed, the Word-Processing tail would now be wagging the Data-Processing dog. But the mainframe industry, led by IBM, could not imagine two obvious truths: 1) that insertion and deletion of text by computer would save astronomical amounts of woman-

and man-hours; and 2) that the market for Word Processing was there, whether the market knew it or not.

Now, IBM threatens to take over the personal computer market. It seems quite obvious that the ideal matrix for the realization of McLuhan's brave new world is a free market in which the unseen hand of competition selects the best products, bringing the greatest benefit to the greatest number of people. But by bringing out a computer with a unique bus, CPU chip, and operating system, IBM made a bid to force its own standards on the whole industry. It was like bringing out a hi-fi system that played only 22 rpm records—suicidal for anyone but IBM, who sold millions of these idiosyncratic machines despite the fact that hardly any existing software would play on them.

Because the PC was a helter-skelter emergency product to get IBM's foot in the door, the bus had open slots, and the door was open for other people's hardware. Everyone got into the action, and everyone made money. The excitement was terrific. *Time*'s front cover gleefully cried out, "Big is bountiful." But it is a one-two punch, and we haven't seen the second punch.

IBM always wants to sell everything that goes into, onto, or through its computers. So ultimately, of course, it will start slamming the doors. It will bring out high- and low-end computers that encroach on the PC's market. It will bring out its own line of hardware and software for the PC. And the new machines will of course go to market with IBM's own line of accessories. By originally opening up a free market for PC accessories, whether accidentally or on purpose, IBM succeeded in establishing the PC bus, chip, and operating system as standards for a large part of the industry. But when it preempts all the slots and software opportunities of its new machines, it will slam the door on the upstarts. For who will buy a gadget from Gee-Whizz Microstuff of Little Rock when he can get one from Big Brother of Armonk? We may at last have a universal standard, but it will belong entirely to IBM.[1]

---

[1] May 1984: I wrote the previous paragraph in the fall of 1983. By the time this book went to press, most of these predictions had come true.

We cannot afford to trust IBM with the responsibility for innovation; innovation is expensive, and a company which can sell anything doesn't need it. What are we to do about this Jabberwock, this killer corporation, whiffling through our tulgy wood, and burbling as it comes? Why have so many hardware and software houses (including such illustrious forefathers of our microcountry as Microsoft and Digital Research) staked their fortunes on this wolf in Charlie Chaplin's clothing? I lay it to technology's inability to imagine the real world. We see this lack of vision both in IBM's inability to innovate on its own and in the microcomputer industry's "me-too" mode of competition with the awakened giant.

As I swing in my hammock and watch a pelican glide along the updraft from a wave, I think of Thomas Kuhn's ghostly "paradigms," with which I have so often struggled in my attempts to convey his *Structure of Scientific Revolutions* to my students in Lawrence's Freshman Studies course. Despite its difficult prose style, the book has kept its place in the course year after year because it raises unanswerable questions about the scientific method, for so many centuries revered as the sure path to ultimate truth about the nature of things.

Before Kuhn, one customarily attributed steady progress to science by virtue of **the scientific method**, which works something like this: a scientist proposes an explanation of a natural phenomenon, called a "hypothesis"; he proves his hypothesis by inventing an experiment so constructed that if his hypothesis is true, a predicted result occurs; if the predicted result does not occur, the hypothesis is false; if the predicted result *does* occur, other scientists confirm the hypothesis by applying it to a wider and wider set of phenomena; eventually, a scientist applies it to a phenomenon that should give the result predicted by the hypothesis but doesn't, and the hypothesis is rejected; then another scientist comes up with a hypothesis that explains not only the recalcitrant phenomenon but also all previous experimental evidence, and the cycle begins again. By discarding inadequate hypotheses and adopting more comprehensive ones, science necessarily and inevitably moves closer and closer to ultimate truth.

According to Kuhn, this familiar view of science is wrong. By close analysis of "crises" in science—those moments in history when a scientific discipline faces irreconcilable "anomalies" (negative results) in its **paradigm** (super-hypothesis, underlying assumption, all-embracing theory, mind-set, worldview, frame of reference)—Kuhn demonstrates that, instead of throwing out a paradigm as a disproved hypothesis and looking about for a better one, as the "scientific method" predicts, scientists habitually see anomalies as failed experiments and argue mightily against any alteration of the paradigm. And when a Ptolemy is finally discarded in favor of a Copernicus, we do not have a more comprehensive theory of the solar system but an entirely *different* one. Ptolemy's earth-centered hypothesis isn't negated by Copernicus' sun-centered one; it can still predict the positions of the planets. Similarly, Einstein's physics does not add a dimension to Newton's: neither theory can be true if the other is. But still we use Newtonian physics for Newton's problems, and it works, though it can't do anything with Einstein's problems, which do not go away. Instead of ever-increasing certainty about the nature of things, we have discontinuous pockets of success. So much for the notion of steady progress.

To explain our illusion of steady progress, Kuhn defines a field of activity called **normal science**, in which scientists focus on the extrapolation of a given paradigm. Within its bounds, successes multiply, but at some cost. For the normal scientist works as a member of an isolated community, responsible only to the other scientists in his field, who in turn are the only judges of the value of his work. He has no *professional* interest in anything or anybody outside this closed circle. He starts and finishes with his peers' assumptions about the real world, even when his results call their view of it in question. When anomalies crop up, they are most often recognized by young scientists who have not been conditioned by the ruling paradigm.

Kuhn's paradigms help me to understand the recent history of computing. Data Processing and Word Processing are competing paradigms. Mainframe Computing and Personal Computing are another mutually exclusive pair. Data Processing sees Word Processing as an uncomfortable anomaly, and Mainframe Computing cannot abide Personal Computing. But the paradigms are shifting, and normal science is being redefined. The "integrated" or all-purpose software we hear so much about these days (Lotus 1-2-3, Apple's Lisa) is based on a word processor. IBM calls its microcomputers "entry-level machines," in the fond hope that their users will eventually upgrade to mainframes, but the farmer's Apple is all he will ever need. The buyer of an automatic washer does not upgrade to a steam laundry.

But here I am really dealing with technology, not science, and perhaps Kuhn doesn't apply. Technology, let's call it engineering, is the human interface of science, and it ought to be less self-contemplative. While science rightfully dedicates itself to following the truth wherever it may lead, engineering is ostensibly dedicated to serving human needs. But normal computer engineering in our country (I include software engineering) appears to have been just as blindly engaged in extrapolating paradigms as normal science is, as if technology were an end in itself. The abnormal engineering of arrant schoolboys has produced all true innovation. But even under the new paradigm, the human interface is crude. To what do we attribute this deficiency? As I watch the waves endlessly breaking, I think of Eichner's essay.

In January, 1982, Hans Eichner of Toronto University published an article called "The Rise of Modern Science and the Genesis of Romanticism" in *Publications of the Modern Language Association*, the principal journal of my profession. I am not surprised that it won a prize as that journal's best essay of the year, because Eichner succeeded in climbing one of the impossible Everests of literary scholarship: he defined the essential nature of Romanticism. In doing so, perhaps he revealed the source of our dilemma.

In order to define Romanticism, Eichner, like Kuhn, focuses on history. He finds that the most important development of the century preceding Romanticism, which emerged around 1800, is science. This fact is undeniable, for who has had more effect on the world since Christ and Mohammed than Isaac Newton?

Eichner then looks at the main premises of the philosophy of science that the Romantics confronted and lists their unpalatable consequences: Premise 1: The world is an immense self-sufficient machine. Consequence: There is no God, no one in charge, no divine justice, no point to existence. Premise 2: Everything that happens is the result of the mechanical interaction of bodies of dead matter. Consequence: No better world is possible than the one we live in. Premise 3: Nature is not an organic purposeful being as we think ourselves to be, but a purposeless machine. Consequence: We are aliens on this earth. Premise 4: The human body is a machine, and our thoughts are a product of this machine. Consequence: Our thoughts are accidental and irrelevant. Premise 5: The laws of nature totally control the parts of matter that make up the human body. Consequence: There can be no freedom of the will.

This philosophy of science left human enterprise totally without hope. According to Eichner, the poets we call Romantic, being unable to refute these premises and their consequences, simply denied them. The defining principle of Romanticism, therefore, is the flat affirmation of human will and purpose in the face of science's irrefutable negation of them. I shall test Eichner's definition by applying it to English Romanticism:

1. There is no God: Shelley answers in a dialog of *Prometheus Unbound*,

> ASIA: Who made the living world?
> DEMOGORGON: God.
> ASIA: Who made all
>   That it contains? Thought, passion, reason, will,
>   Imagination?
> DEMOGORGON: God: Almighty God.

2. No better world is possible: Blake answers,

> The desire of Man being Infinite, the possession is Infinite & himself Infinite.

3. We are aliens on this earth: Wordsworth answers,

> I have felt
> A presence that disturbs me with the joy
> Of elevated thoughts; a sense sublime
> Of something far more deeply interfused,
> Whose dwelling is the light of setting suns,
> And the round ocean and the living air,
> And the blue sky, and in the mind of man.

4. Our thoughts are accidental and irrelevant: Keats, addressing a friend who questions "the authenticity of the Imagination," answers,

> I am certain of nothing but of the holiness of the Heart's affections and the truth of the Imagination. . . . What the Imagination seizes as Beauty must be truth.

5. There is no freedom of the will: Byron, as Manfred defying the forces of nature, answers,

> Scoff not at my will!
> The mind, the spirit, the Promethean spark,
> The lightning of my being, is as bright,
> Pervading and far darting as your own
> And shall not yield to yours, though cooped in clay.

Eichner goes on to show that if the scientific position is true, the Romantic one can't be and if the Romantic position is true, the scientific one can't be. There is no common ground. All attempts to make a philosophically rigorous bridge between the basic premises of scientific and human endeavour have failed. And *furthermore*, nothing has changed since 1800. Scientific method is necessarily founded on the same materialistic determinism. You can't *do* science if you assume anything else. And poetry still refuses to have any of science. When I say poetry, please understand me to mean all art, every field of work that attempts to give meaning to human experience, including history, journalism, and "soft" sciences like government, psychology, and anthropology, insofar as they are not behavioristic.

Now, if the schism between science and poetry is as absolute as Eichner maintains and if it is indeed still with us, then it is no wonder that computing's human interface leaves much to be desired. For certainly the schism has been institutionalized in our educational system: humanities, except at liberal arts colleges and such places as Cal Tech and MIT, are virtually excluded from scientific and engineering curricula. And students with a humanistic bent avoid science like the plague. Scientists, who customarily see the past as a collection of failed hypotheses, have no practical use for poetic subjects. They classify them as entertainment. As the computer whiz kid said to the talk show host when asked his opinion on education, "They should teach nothing but math and computing, and throw out all that other stuff. Who needs history?"

But what will he *do* with his computing skill, if he has no knowledge of the world? It is poetry that provides this knowledge and points the way to action. Consider the power of advertising. By dramatizing what we might like to be—efficient, hygienic, natural, sweet-smelling, blonde, masculine, with-it, and one up on our neighbors—the image-makers not only persuade us to buy their products but convert us to a nation passionately engaged in becoming efficient, hygienic, natural, sweet-smelling, blonde, masculine, with-it, and one up on our neighbors. If Charlie Chaplin, the least mechanically adept character in cinema history, can have fun with a PC, IBM would have us believe, then so can we. The author of this brilliant advertising campaign deserves a Nobel Prize in poetry—except for the fact that his dominant image is a patent lie. Advertisers are prostitute poets. True poets use the same methods, but they propose to make attractive what they believe to be the truth. We have just watched a whole generation receive inspiration and direction from Bob Dylan and rock music. When he sang, "The times, they are a-changin'," he was one very big reason why they were.

How do we know that a poet is telling the truth? Unlike the scientist, whose work is validated by his peers, or the advertiser, whose work is validated by the cash register, the poet seeks validation from everybody everywhere now and in time to come. If works live on, as Shakespeare's do, we say that they must contain some universal truth. "The poet," says Coleridge, "brings the whole soul of man into activity." The desire to move all humanity forever, not just a few peers or suckers, keeps the poet honest.

Our dilemma, it would seem, is that the only force in our society that can civilize the raw power of computing is poetry. Not poetry, certainly? But where else can we turn? As Coleridge said, "Art is the mediatress between and reconciler of nature and man," or, as we might say, creative output is the human interface of the environment. Computers are now deeply embedded in our environment. But ever since Wordsworth declared, "Our meddling intellect / Misshapes the beauteous forms of things, / We murder to dissect," poets have had very little use for technology except to condemn it. They have become a very poor interface. The Romantics, says Eichner, "Threw out the babe with the bath."

A few poets *do* watch science and technology—Thomas Pynchon, in *Gravity's Rainbow* and other works, and Robert Pirsig, in *Zen and the Art of Motorcycle Maintenance*. Pirsig puts his finger on the pulse of America and finds the same antipathetic symptoms that Eichner does. He feels that there is in our society a "mass movement" which says to technology in one voice, "Don't have it here, have it somewhere else." In an agony of doubt, Pirsig ranges the whole history of thought trying to find a rigorously philosophical bridge between his mechanical motorcycle and his cosmic imagination. He thinks he has it with Kant's distinction between noumena and phenomena. Eichner also recognizes Kant's heroic attempt but rejects his reasoning, and Pirsig's experience confirms Eichner's analysis.

My computer is Pirsig's motorcycle. I do not agonize over its immense distance from me. I am content to say that it is a machine and I am not. Its intelligence is eternally artificial, and mine is eternally not. It is dead, and I am alive. Whatever life it has, I give it. It is a good logician, but it has no *imagination*. As I swing in my hammock and watch the white clouds cross the clear blue sky, I think of Shelley.

In his *Defence of Poetry*, Shelley wrote

> A man, to be greatly good, must imagine intensely and comprehensively; he must put himself in the place of another and of many others; the pains and pleasures of his species must become his own. . . . Poetry enlarges the circumference of the imagination by replenishing it with thoughts of ever new delight which have the power of attracting and assimilating to their own nature all other thoughts and which form new intervals and interstices whose void forever craves fresh food. Poetry strengthens [the imagination] in the same way that exercise strengthens a limb.

I think Shelley says three things here. The first is that we can't help anyone unless we know what he likes and what he is up against. The second is that without imagination, we cannot put ourselves in another person's place. And the third is that the study of poetry, by stimulating the imagination, increases its power to assimilate more and more experience. Once it gets started, you can't stop it. If Shelley is right, every parent should read fairy tales to every child, and every scientist, engineer, and programmer should study great works of the imagination in college if he or she means to leave the world better than he or she found it.

And if Shelley is right, poets (I still mean nonscientists of all persuasions) should be well qualified to interface the computer industry with the world. The industry is ready, for "friendliness" is its favorite buzzword. Here, at last, is well-paid work for starving poets: let them design friendly systems, develop friendly educational software, and write friendly documentation. The industry has already started hiring poets, and, as Shelley would predict, they catch on fast. It is high time for poets to stop wishing that technology would go away and instead get into it. The future happiness of humanity depends on them, for they are, as Shelley also said, "The unacknowledged legislators of the world." If they don't shape our values, Madison Avenue will.

Friendliness is not jocularity and stick figures, as some documenters seem to believe; it is inherent clarity; it begins with clear design and ends with clear documentation. But beneath it all is a commitment to the user that puts his need before the merchant's profit. As I swing in my hammock and watch a schooner give to and take from the wind and the waves, I think of Ruben.

Ruben is a jack of all trades at Akumal. For some reason, he took it upon himself to make our welfare a principal con-

Ruben (right) and Carlos, his apprentice

cern of his. Knowing we were running low on butane, he went out of his way to drive several miles and tell us that the butane truck was at the hotel. Knowing that we were having trouble with our pump, he made it a point to drop in and see how we were doing. When we needed 100 feet of electrical cable to deliver more power to the pump, he drove off and brought back 200 feet of his own cable. He had an eight-hour job, but he would rush over before or after work to do plumbing or electrical work. We always had to force him to take money. He made a terrible face, shook his head furiously, and said "No, no, no!"

Santos and Silvia were the same. When it came time for their long overdue vacation, which was their absolute right, and they were unable to find any substitute help, they came to us and said, "We're not going." They hadn't been home for three months, and we knew how much they longed for the warmth of their own village. We had to force them to go.

Most Americans at Akumal had the opposite experience with Mexicans. The natives never did what they said they would, they did it carelessly, they did less than they were paid for. Why did we have a different experience? I think we owed it to Dear Boo's daughter Kay, from Glendale, Ohio, where the help were members of the family. First of all, Kay had to communicate. She worked daily on her Spanish, and when she couldn't find the word, she acted out the idea. She said "please" and "thank you" and "how are you" and "how nice." On special occasions, she gave presents. Once, when we were about to leave Mexico after a three-month visit, she gave a bottle of whisky to Jorge and his brother José Luis, contractors, who had rushed over several times when there was no electricity to fill our roof tank by means of their gasoline-fueled pump. On receipt of the gift, Jorge said, "You are different." Puzzled, I said, "Yes, we're poorer than the others." "No," he said, "You're richer." That is without doubt the nicest thing that anyone ever said to us. But we only did what Dear Boo would have done, and it is she who really deserves the credit.

Swinging in my hammock and watching the waves become horses with white manes, I think of William Faulkner's letter to Warren Beck. Warren Beck of Lawrence University was one of the first to appreciate Faulkner's novels. After reading some essays that Professor Beck had written, Faulkner thanked him and wrote:

> I have been writing all the time about honor, truth, pity, con-sideration, the capacity to endure well grief and misfortune and injustice and then endure again, in terms of individuals who ob-served and adhered to them not merely for reward but for vir-tue's own sake, not even merely because they are admirable in themselves, but in order to live with oneself and die peacefully when the time comes. I don't mean that the devil will snatch every liar and rogue shrieking from his deathbed. I think liars and rogues and hypocrites die peacefully every day in the odor of what they call sanctity. I'm not talking about them, I'm not writ-ing for them. But I believe there are some, not necessarily many, who do and will continue to read Faulkner and say, "Yes. It's all right. I'd rather be Ratliff than Flem Snopes. And I'd still rather be Ratliff without any Flem Snopes to measure by even."

Mexico runs on friendship. The United States runs on mon-ey, on contracts. For exactly this amount and quality of work, we pay exactly this amount of money, and that's the end of it. No wonder the gringos don't get along with the Mexicans. They operate on different paradigms.

Wherever the old world hangs on, wherever the idea of a gentleman persists, as it does in Mexico and in Faulkner's South, you see the difference. A gentleman (or gentlewoman, of course) thinks money is dirty and lives in constant fear that it will soil his honor. This attitude astonished Hemingway when he confronted Europe, and he epitomized it in the Spanish bullfighter, the English Lady Brett, and the Italian count. But when our Calvinist forefathers broke away from England, they broke away from the idea of a gentleman. Most of them belonged to that "nation of shopkeepers" of which Napoleon complained. Our revolution, with its emphasis on rights instead of obligations, split us off even more. And the scientific frame of mind, which automatically switches off the past, is equally hostile to medieval courtesies. Thus we have been Snopified. A Snopes fixes his mind on what belongs to him by right, on what you owe him, and on what he can get out of you without being taken to court. IBM is a Snopes. Ratliffs, who concern themselves with what belongs to you, with what they owe you, and with what is just and fair regardless of the law, are nearly extinct.

The microcomputer community has given me friendly service, with a few notable exceptions. The friendliness of the service seems to depend on the youth of the business. When I was getting ready to take the Z-2D to Mexico, I was bowled over by the friendliness of SemiDisk Corporation. I was talking to a pleasant fellow on the phone, telling him that I couldn't get the SemiDisk to work with a battery backup, and almost before I could finish, he said, "You must have a bad board. What's your address? I'll send you a new one right away." I asked him if he were Richard, because I'd talked to someone there named Richard before. "Oh, you mean the other Richard," he said. "He's the one who takes care of the money. I'm the one who gives it all away." The new board came the next day. He said I could send the old board back when I got around to it. It was worth $2,000.

Even top-100 computer companies sometimes listen. When I wrote a letter to the president of Cromemco complaining that one version of CDOS wasn't altogether compatible with CP/M, he wrote back sympathizing and told me that the next version would take care of that. A few weeks later, I received a free copy of the next version. Lamont Crabtree of Beehive's Factory Service is the finest gentleman I have known in this business. Besides patiently helping me debug my *London Stage* Beehive on the telephone, he would overlook company rules and send me a new board without having my old one in hand. In one emergency, he told me to call him at home Saturday if I didn't have a replacement Friday. I called him, he went over to the factory, found it lying on a table in the shipping room, and sent it himself.

In its infancy, before the Snopeses got into it, the whole microcomputer industry was like that. It was part of the hippy rebellion against the corporate structure. Those computer enthusiasts were a band of brothers allied against the mumbo-jumbo of Data Processing, they were against all that "sign here, do exactly this or else" baloney, and they gave their programs, knowledge, and services to each other. Their magazine was called *The People's Computer Company* (now holding on as *Dr. Dobbs' Journal*). Some day, if, as McLuhan says, we all become members of the same village, that kind of friendliness will come again.

As I swing in my hammock and watch the turquoise sea turn pink from the sunset's reflected light, I think of Dear Boo. Her guiding principle was encapsulated in that tiny bit of verse:

> Politeness is to do or say
> The kindest thing in the kindest way.

Her commitment was the same as Shelley's and Faulkner's. Indeed, she was a daughter of the Middle Ages, who agreed with Chaucer when he said, "He nys nat gentil, be he duc or erl," unless he "doeth gentil dedis." So, too, friendliness is not those jocular manuals full of stick figures; it is a commitment to the user's welfare. It is not Charlie Chaplin making believe that a PC is a barrel of fun; it is Lamont Crabtree going the extra mile. As I walk among the ruins of Chichén Itzá, I think again of Data Processing.

This great pyramid, these temples, these sculptures and inscriptions came into being in order that the gods might see fit to grant crops, children, and victory. What a stupid way to raise crops, get children, and win wars! But for six centuries the paradigm succeeded, until, when it could not adjust to anomalies— perhaps overpopulation and soil exhaustion—its gods failed and a whole civilization died. Data Processing was such a religion. Its god was IBM, its pyramid was The Corporation, its temples were computer rooms, its sculptures were machines, and its inscriptions were manuals. It, too, had a priesthood that wrote and interpreted the inscriptions, required human sacrifice as a condition of fulfillment, and promised profit to those who observed its dogmas. Now it, too, is in ruins.

> And what rough beast, its hour come round at last,
> Slouches towards Bethlehem to be born?
>
> —W. B. Yeats

INDEX OF BOLDFACED
COMPUTER TERMS

address, 25
argument, 45
assembly language, 25, 132
batch processing, 42
baud rate, 169
benchmark, 97
bit, 25, 33
block, 113
block send, 33
bootstrap loader, 76
buffer 138
bus, 20
byte, 25, 33
central processing unit, 23
compiler, 30
control characters, 35
CPU, Central Processing Unit, 23
CRT, Cathode Ray Tube, 47
cursor 34
cylinder 79
documentation, 221
document-oriented, 48
dot-matrix, 36
double-density, 184, 206
dumb terminal, 33
extension, 76
formatter, 50
front end, 108
glitch, 31
hexadecimal, 80
high-level language, 25
initialize, 78

instruction set, 26
intelligent terminal, 33
interactive computing, 42
interpreter, 30, 116
I/O bound, 190
kilobyte, 33
machine code, 25
mainframe, 228
mnemonics, 26
motherboard, 20
OEM, 34
off-line, 33
operating system, 21
page-oriented, 48
pattern, 107
pointers, 113
proportional spacing, 38
record I/O, 113
ROM, 76
S-100, 20
slot, 20
string functions, 28, 137
subroutine, 138
system call, 131, 208
time-sharing, 42
track, 79
transparent, 185
upward compatible, 23, 32
VDT, Video Display Terminal, 47
virtual array, 115
wraparound, 34
Z80, 22